STATS, RECORDS & ROCK 'N' ROLL

THIS IS A CARLTON BOOK

Published by Carlton Books Ltd
20 Mortimer Street
London W1T 3JW

Text © 2017 Carlton Books Ltd
Design © 2017 Carlton Books Ltd

ISBN 978-1-78097-930-4

A CIP catalogue for this book is available from the British Library

Printed in Dubai

10 9 8 7 6 5 4 3 2 1

STATS, RECORDS & ROCK 'N' ROLL

FINE-TUNED INFOGRAPHICS TO ROCK YOUR WORLD

DANIEL TATARSKY & IAN PREECE

ILLUSRATED BY
ROBIN RICHARDS

CARLTON
BOOKS

INTRODUCTION

What is it about music that makes it so special? You can go twenty years without having listened to a song but the moment it comes on the radio, turntable, iTunes shuffle, or however else you consume music, the lyrics appear, as if by magic, in your head. You sing along, the words lining up in your mind as the notes enter your ears. Whether you're an expert musician or the sort of person who should only sing in the shower, music is a part of our lives.

The nature of music means that it is very much driven by the sense of hearing. So the idea of this book, at first, may seem a little incongruous. You will quickly see, though, that it is a feast for the visual sense. There's also an amazing amount of information to get your brain cells active and excited – so much so that even without hearing any music when you flick through the pages you will be transported to some of your favourite sounds, and hopefully be heading straight out to the nearest record shop, or hunting down some long-lost LP at home.

The book travels through the centuries – from the very earliest music created by hitting stones with bones, to the latest developments in musical creation and delivery like the mp3. Eighty fact-filled spreads bring you all the way to the social-media era, where an artist's number of followers and virtual friends is often more important than the actual number of records of they sell. Talking of records, now that vinyl has come back into fashion, you'll also find absorbing details of the various media upon which music has been delivered to our ears, as well as the diverse number of broadcast systems, stations and players.

It's a journey through music's history in all of its forms, but there's also the description of a literal, interplanetary musical journey as we track the millions of miles covered by the two *Voyager* spacecraft with their vital cargo, which included a golden phonograph embedded with the "sounds of the earth". From children chattering, messages from politicians, images of earth and, of course, music.

Martians, Venutians and maybe even Klingons will be able to boogie down to the sounds of Chuck Berry's "Johnny B. Goode" or relax under their moons to some Bach.

The aim of that record was to show any being in the universe all that was great and beautiful about our planet. This book does that too, but also shows some of the darker sides of the music industry: from the bad behaviour of rock stars and the damage they do to hotels, to the sad history of failed rock and roll marriages, and the pitiful royalties paid out by streaming services like Spotify. The costs of all these are calculated and examined.

As in all aspects of life, there are winners and losers in the music world and we cover many of them within these pages. Amongst the winners are the Oscar-celebrated composers and the wonderfully varied one-hit wonders. At the other end of the scale you'll find those destined to be the bridesmaids. The details of classic number 2s will have you thumping your turntable in astounded disgust. Is it really possible that Joe Dolce's "Shaddup Your Face" stopped Ultravox's towering "Vienna" from reaching top spot? Sorry to say, the answer is yes. Can you remember which TV duo put their own wall up to stop Oasis' "Wonderwall" from hitting number 1? You'll cry when you find out. There are some amongst these, though, that will start a pub debate to last the ages: "Golden Brown" or "A Town Called Malice"? You decide.

The information is presented in a variety of forms. There are the obligatory charts; after all what is music without a chart? You'll also find maps: maps of the geographical kind, but also maps of the mind and sound maps of various musical hot-spots. There are graphs, flow charts, pie charts, and even some which could be described as works of (ch)art. What is for sure is that every page is packed with detail and illustrated with clarity and imagination and cutting-edge design. So sit back, insert your favourite disc, or put the needle on the record, and dive in.

Daniel Tatarsky and Ian Preece, June 2017

CONTENTS

NICE SONG, SHAME ABOUT THE FILM
16-17

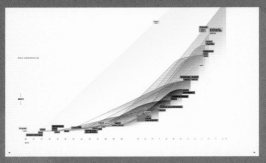

HITTING THE HIGH NOTES
18-19

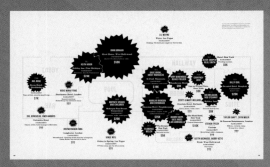

BAD-BEHAVIOUR
20-21

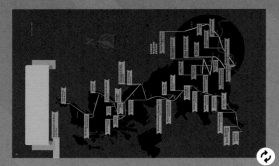

FROM JOHN O'GROATS TO LAND'S END
22-23

HOW THE REVENUE FROM MUSIC SALES IS DIVIDED UP
24-25

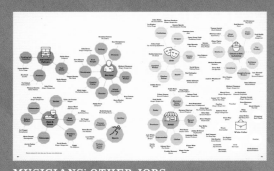

MUSICIANS' OTHER JOBS
26-27

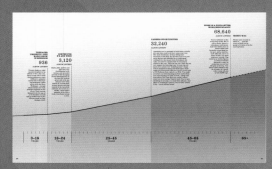

ALBUMS LISTENED TO IN A LIFETIME
28-29

IT'S A GOOD NUMBER
30-31

KEY

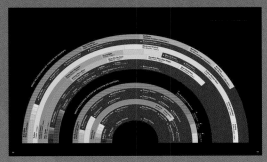 = ROTATE PAGE

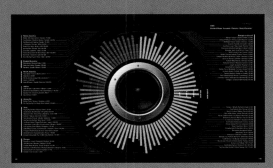

PARTY TIME AROUND THE WORLD
32-33

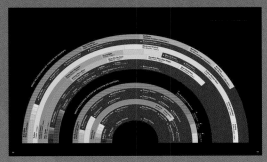

SING ME A RAINBOW
34-35

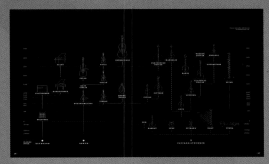

EVOLUTION OF STRING INSTRUMENTS
36-37

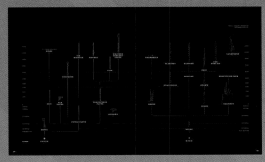

EVOLUTION OF WOODWIND INSTRUMENTS
38-39

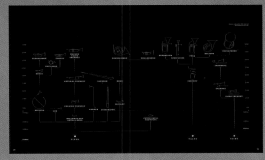

EVOLUTION OF BRASS INSTRUMENTS
40-41

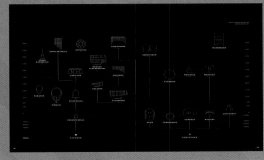

EVOLUTION OF PERCUSSION INSTRUMENTS
42-43

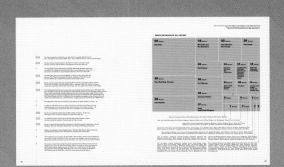

JOHN PEEL'S FESTIVE 50
44-45

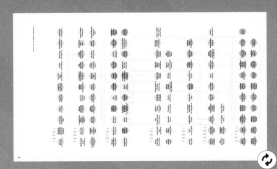

WHAT'S IN A NAME?
46-47

COOL INDEPENDENT RECORD LABELS
48-49

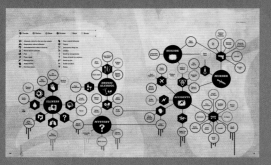

WHAT'S UP WITH THE 27 CLUB?
50-51

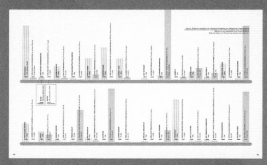

LITERARY BAND NAMES
52-53

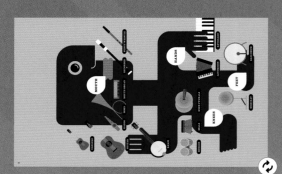

ONE MAN BAND
54-55

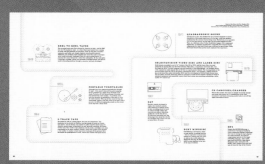

IT WASN'T ALL IN THE DELIVERY:
9 FAILED MUSIC FORMATS
56-57

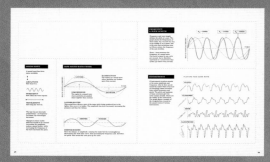

WE ARE WAVING
58-59

FOR QUEEN AND COUNTRY
60-61

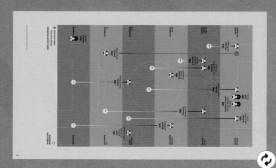

WORLD CUP SONGS
62-63

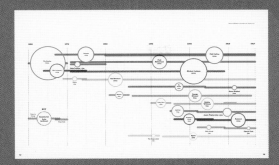

GOING IT ALONE
64-65

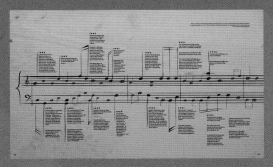

THE ROOTS OF THE "NEW CLASSICAL"
66-67

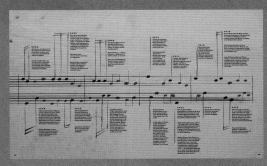

THE ROOTS OF THE "NEW CLASSICAL"
CONTINUED...
68-69

THE ART OF MUSIC
70-71

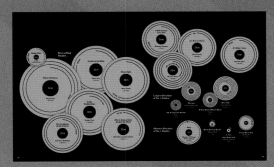

SEVEN INCHES OF GOLD
72-73

GET YOUR GROOVE ON
74-75

POP OF THE POPS
76-77

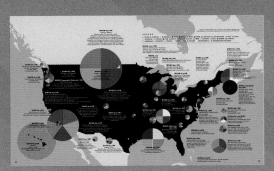

INTERESTING RADIO STATIONS
ACROSS AMERICA
78-79

JANUARY TO DECEMBER
80-81

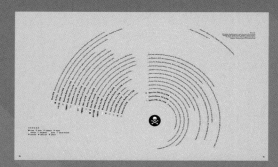

THE PIRATE RADIO STATIONS OF 1980S AND 1990S LONDON
82-83

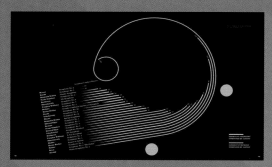

DAH DAH DAH DAAAAAAAAH!
84-85

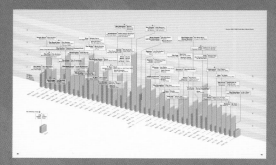

CLASSIC NUMBER 2S
86-87

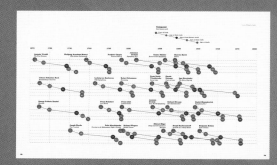

EARLY STARTERS, LATE FINISHERS
88-89

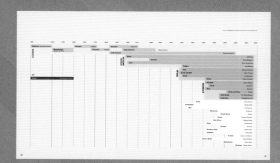

FROM MEDIEVAL TO MASHUP
90-91

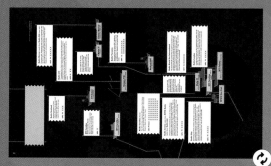

1960S PIRATE RADIO SHIPS
92-93

COUNTRY MUSICIANS NOT ENTIRELY FROM THE COUNTRY
94-95

STUDIO KINDA CLOUDY. THE RECORDING
STUDIOS OF KINGSTON, JAMAICA. MID-1970S
96-97

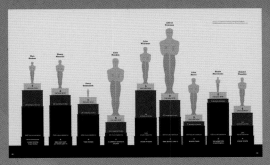

A SOUND TRACK
98-99

LOST LONDON MUSIC VENUES
100-101

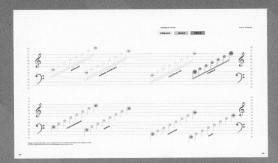

DO RAY ME ME ME ME
102-103

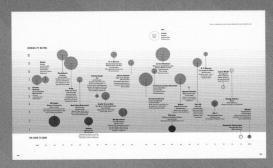

THE "CURSE" OF THE MERCURY PRIZE
104-105

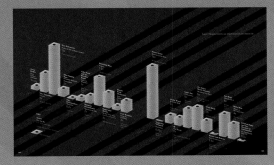

ONE HIT WONDERS
106-107

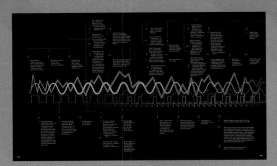

DAWN OF THE SYNTHESIZER
108-109

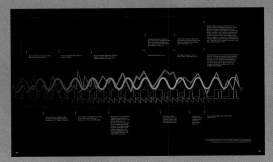

REBIRTH OF THE SYNTHESIZER/
SYNTH IS COOL AGAIN
110-111

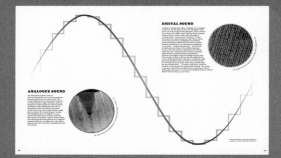

COMPARING SOUND WAVES
112-113

GRIME MAP OF LONDON
114-115

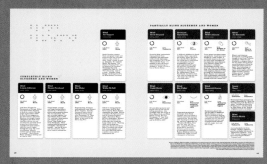

BLIND BLUESMEN AND WOMEN
116-117

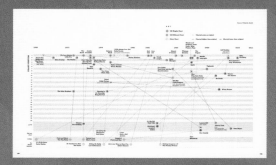

COVERED IN GLORY
118-119

HOTELS IN SONGS
120-121

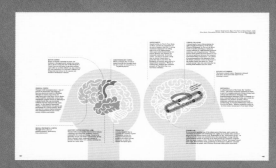

MUSIC FLOODS THE BRAIN
122-123

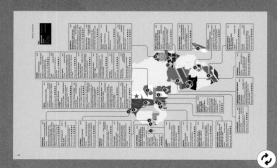

SOUND MAP OF AFRICA
124-125

SOUND MAP OF GERMANY
126-127

TWENTY-FOUR HOURS FROM TULSA
128-129

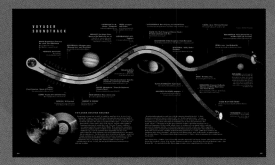

VOYAGER SOUNDTRACK
130-131

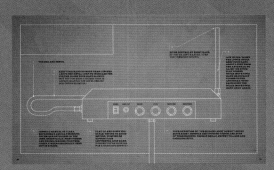

IT'S A LONG WAY TO PERRY COMO
132-133

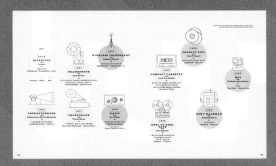

IT'S ALL IN THE DELIVERY
134-135

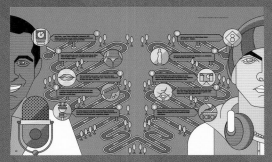

HOW TO PLAY THE THEREMIN
136-137

TO DIE FOR
138-138

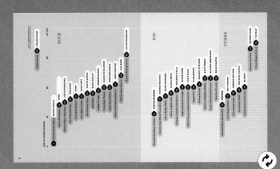

WHAT'S IN A NAME
140-141

SUMMER OF LOVE SONGS
142-143

ANTI-WAR SONGS
144-145

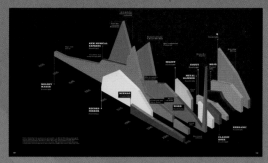

UK MUSIC PRESS
146-147

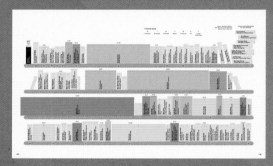

HARDCORE MUSIC FAN'S BOOKSHELF (PT.1)
148-149

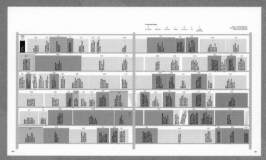

HARDCORE MUSIC FAN'S BOOKSHELF (PT.2)
150-151

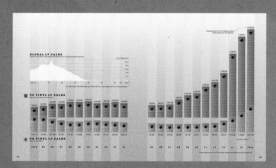

VINYL RENAISSANCE
152-153

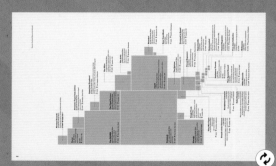

MUSIC WEBSITES
154-155

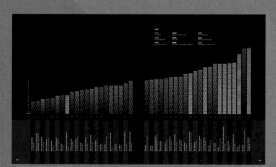

SPEED UP YOUR HOUSE PARTY
156-157

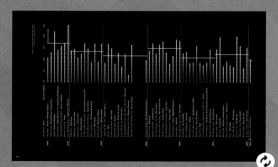

BEATING NUMBER ONE
158-159

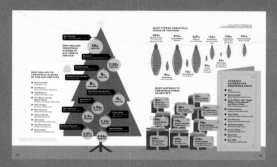

IT'S CHRISTMAS
160-161

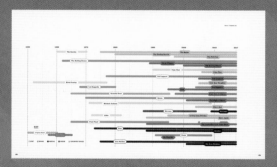

THE HIGHEST FORM OF FLATTERY
162-163

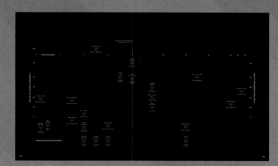

TAPE SPLICING AND LOOPING
164-165

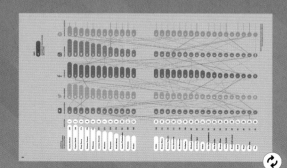

GHOSTLY MAP OF LONDON'S RECORD SHOPS
166-167

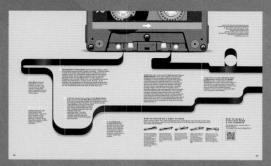

MONEY CAN'T BUY ME LOVE
168-169

IT'S A SOCIAL THING
170-171

THE MOST SUCCESSFUL LABELS IN HIP HOP
172-173

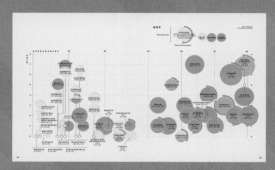

VISIONARY EUROPE
174-175

ACKNOWLEDGEMENTS &
CREDITS 176

NICE SONG, SHAME ABOUT THE FILM

Many years later we can all hum the Oscar-winning song from Arthur but can you remember the plot? Really? When an animated film's song gets the little golden statue, the rule is that the film will always do well at the box office. This is not always the case for dramas! The nine animated films to pick up the Oscar for best song have all been in the top 20 in that year's box office winners. Of the 17 most recent dramas to do so, nearly half have finished the year outside the top 20, and over a third have come outside the top 50.

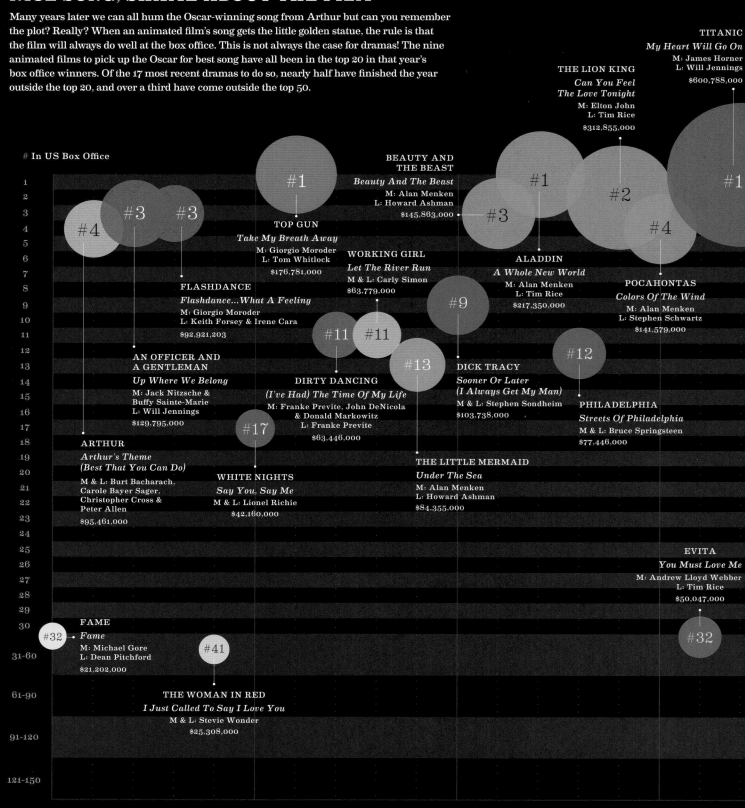

TITANIC
My Heart Will Go On
M: James Horner
L: Will Jennings
$600,788,000

THE LION KING
Can You Feel The Love Tonight
M: Elton John
L: Tim Rice
$312,855,000

BEAUTY AND THE BEAST
Beauty And The Beast
M: Alan Menken
L: Howard Ashman
$145,863,000

TOP GUN
Take My Breath Away
M: Giorgio Moroder
L: Tom Whitlock
$176,781,000

WORKING GIRL
Let The River Run
M & L: Carly Simon
$63,779,000

ALADDIN
A Whole New World
M: Alan Menken
L: Tim Rice
$217,350,000

POCAHONTAS
Colors Of The Wind
M: Alan Menken
L: Stephen Schwartz
$141,579,000

FLASHDANCE
Flashdance...What A Feeling
M: Giorgio Moroder
L: Keith Forsey & Irene Cara
$92,921,203

AN OFFICER AND A GENTLEMAN
Up Where We Belong
M: Jack Nitzsche & Buffy Sainte-Marie
L: Will Jennings
$129,795,000

DIRTY DANCING
(I've Had) The Time Of My Life
M: Franke Previte, John DeNicola & Donald Markowitz
L: Franke Previte
$63,446,000

DICK TRACY
Sooner Or Later (I Always Get My Man)
M & L: Stephen Sondheim
$103,738,000

PHILADELPHIA
Streets Of Philadelphia
M & L: Bruce Springsteen
$77,446,000

ARTHUR
Arthur's Theme (Best That You Can Do)
M & L: Burt Bacharach, Carole Bayer Sager, Christopher Cross & Peter Allen
$95,461,000

WHITE NIGHTS
Say You, Say Me
M & L: Lionel Richie
$42,160,000

THE LITTLE MERMAID
Under The Sea
M: Alan Menken
L: Howard Ashman
$84,355,000

EVITA
You Must Love Me
M: Andrew Lloyd Webber
L: Tim Rice
$50,047,000

FAME
Fame
M: Michael Gore
L: Dean Pitchford
$21,202,000

THE WOMAN IN RED
I Just Called To Say I Love You
M & L: Stevie Wonder
$25,308,000

In US Box Office

1 2 3 4 5 6 7 8 9 10 11 12 13 14 15 16 17 18 19 20 21 22 23 24 25 26 27 28 29 30 31-60 61-90 91-120 121-150

1980   1985   1990   1995

KEY

FILM GENRE

FILM TITLE   THRILLER   DRAMA   ANIMATION   COMEDY   DOCUMENTARY   ACTION   MUSICAL

Song
Music & Lyrics
Box-office Taking

FROZEN
Let It Go
M & L: Kristen Anderson-Lopez
& Robert Lopez
$400,738,009

MONSTERS INC.
If I Didn't Have You
M & L: Randy Newman
$255,873,000

In US Box Office

#1

TOY STORY 3
We Belong Together
M & L: Randy Newman
$415,004,000

#1

#4

#3

#4

#6

TARZAN
You'll Be In My Heart
M & L: Phil Collins
$171,091,000

THE LORD OF THE RINGS
*Into The West from The Lord of the
Rings: The Return of the King*
M & L: Fran Walsh, Howard Shore
& Annie Lennox
$377,027,000

SLUMDOG MILLIONAIRE
Jai Ho
M: A.R. Rahman
L: Gulzar
$141,319,000

SKYFALL
Skyfall
M & L: Adele Adkins
& Paul Epworth
$304,360,000

#10

#16

THE PRINCE OF EGYPT
When You Believe
M & L: Stephen Schwartz
$101,413,000

#16

SPECTRE
Writing's On The Wall
M & L: Jimmy Napes & Sam Smith
$200,074,000

8 MILE
Lose Yourself
M: Eminem, Jeff Bass & Luis Resto
L: Eminem
$116,750,000

#23

THE MUPPETS
Man Or Muppet
M & L: Bret McKenzie
$88,631,000

HUSTLE & FLOW
*It's Hard Out Here For A Pimp
from Hustle & Flow*
M & L: Jordan Houston, Cedric Coleman
& Paul Beauregard
$22,202,000

CRAZY HEART
The Weary Kind
M & L: Ryan Bingham
& T Bone Burnett
$39,464,000

SELMA
Glory
M & L: John Stephens
& Lonnie Lynn
$52,076,000

#34

WONDER BOYS
Things Have Changed
M & L: Bob Dylan
$19,393,000

**THE MOTORCYCLE
DIARIES**
*Al Otro Lado Del Río from
The Motorcycle Diaries*
M & L: Jorge Drexler
$16,781,000

**AN INCONVENIENT
TRUTH**
*I Need To Wake Up from
An Inconvenient Truth*
M & L: Melissa Etheridge
$24,146,000

#61

#75

#99

#117

#110

#106

ONCE
Falling Slowly
M & L: Glen Hansard
& Marketa Irglova
$9,439,000

#150

1
2
3
4
5
6
7

13
14
15
16
17
18
19
20
21
22
23
24
25
26
27
28
29
30

31-60

61-90

91-120

121-150

2000   2005   2010   2015

HITTING THE HIGH NOTES

Notes in music correlate with a specific frequency, which is measured in hertz. Hertz is cycles per second, so something that is 1 hertz repeats once every second. Sound is carried on waves of air pressure and, the higher the hertz, the higher the pitch (or note). Generally, we can hear notes between 20 and 20,000 hertz (20 kHz). Dogs, on the other hand, can hear above 45 kHz, and cats above 65 kHz.

Different hertz equate to different notes, although there is some controversy around this. The note "A above middle C", or A4, is generally used as the starting point, or baseline, for tuning instruments. But the definition of it, in terms of hertz, is not universally agreed. Some people set it at 440 Hz others at 441, 442 or even 443. The important thing is that everyone playing in the same orchestra, or band, agrees. From there, they can tune their instruments across the scales and with each other.

The typical piano of 88 keys covers 8 octaves, with the lowest note being A0 (with a frequency of 27.5 Hz). Every full octave doubles the frequency, so A1 is 55 Hz, A2 is 110 Hz and so on. The highest note on a piano is C8, 4186.01 Hz.

Source: orchestralibrary.com

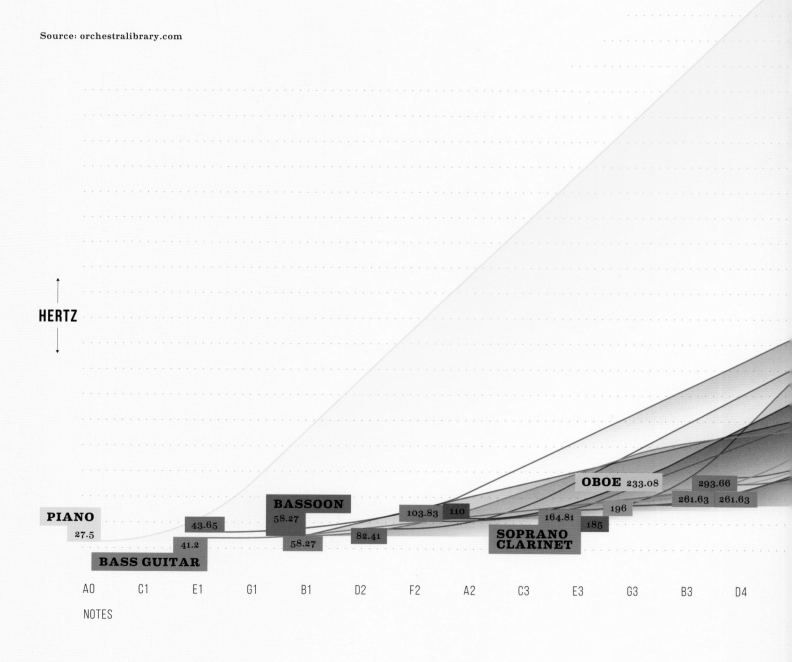

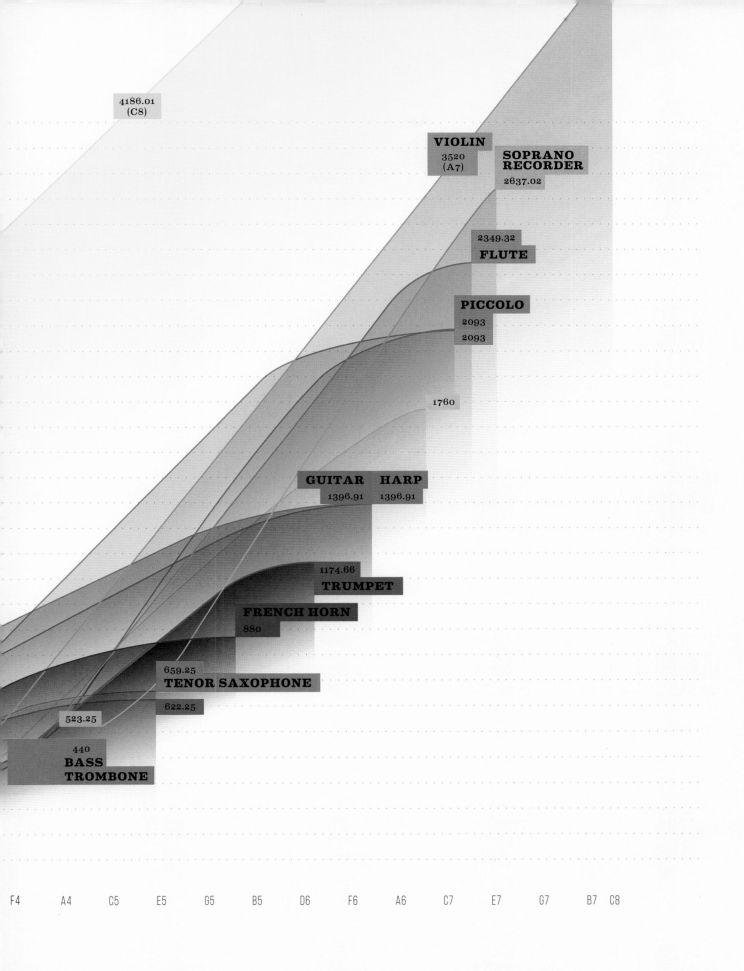

4186.01
(C8)

VIOLIN
3520
(A7)

SOPRANO
RECORDER
2637.02

2349.32
FLUTE

PICCOLO
2093
2093

1760

GUITAR   HARP
1396.91   1396.91

1174.66
TRUMPET

FRENCH HORN
880

659.25
TENOR SAXOPHONE
622.25

523.25

440
BASS
TROMBONE

F4   A4   C5   E5   G5   B5   D6   F6   A6   C7   E7   G7   B7 C8

BAD BEHAVIOUR

There's something about being a rock star that demands bad behaviour. It's almost inevitable with hours of boredom on the road, followed by the adrenalin high of a show, that young men and women, mixed with alcohol and drugs, will lead to mayhem.

LOBBY

POOL

BAR

JOHN BONHAM

Hyatt House, West Hollywood
DAMAGED!!!
Harley Davidson hallway rides.

$50K

1967
KEITH MOON

Holiday Inn, Flint Michigan
DAMAGED!!!
Furniture, Lincoln Continental.

$24K

2006
AXL ROSE

**Berns Hotel,
Stockholm**

DAMAGED!!!
Vase, mirror, security guard's leg.

$7K

2011
NICKI MINAJ FANS

Dorchester Hotel, London
DAMAGED!!!
General mayhem.
Nicki Minaj was invited to leave.

???

1994
SID, BONEHEAD, OWEN MORRIS

Columbia Hotel
DAMAGED!!!
Chairs, tables, hotel manager's Mercedes.

???

2012
JUSTIN BIEBER FANS

Langhams, London
DAMAGED!!!
Switchboard - blocking all the lines by calling him.
Justin Bieber was invited to leave.

???

2009
BRITNEY SPEARS
AND CHILDREN

**Mohegan Sun Resort,
Connecticut**
DAMAGED!!!
Curtains, walls, soiled pool.

$20K

2012
VINCE NEIL

Palms in Spring, Las Vegas
DAMAGED!!!
??? But it was epic by all accounts.

???

Sources: oasis-recordinginfo.co.uk, timeout.com, MTV,
dailymail.co.uk, craveonline.co.uk, theguardian.com,
Rock World magazine, budgettravel.com, pagesix.com,
NY Post, Gothamist, travelandleisure.com

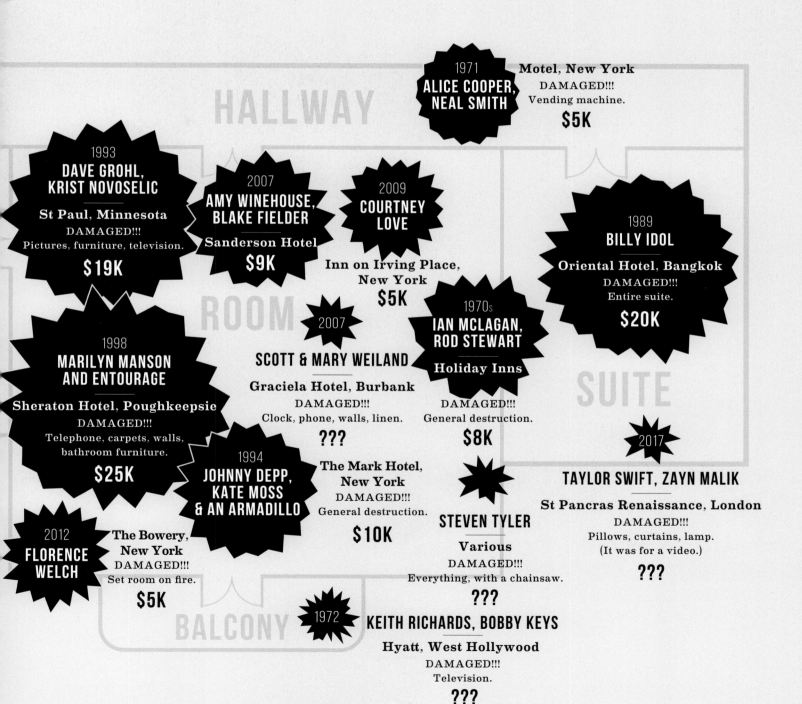

2010

LIL WAYNE

Wynn, Las Vegas
DAMAGED!!!
Nothing. The hotel pre-emptively barred him.

HALLWAY

1971
ALICE COOPER, NEAL SMITH
Motel, New York
DAMAGED!!!
Vending machine.
$5K

1993
DAVE GROHL, KRIST NOVOSELIC
St Paul, Minnesota
DAMAGED!!!
Pictures, furniture, television.
$19K

2007
AMY WINEHOUSE, BLAKE FIELDER
Sanderson Hotel
$9K

2009
COURTNEY LOVE
Inn on Irving Place, New York
$5K

1989
BILLY IDOL
Oriental Hotel, Bangkok
DAMAGED!!!
Entire suite.
$20K

ROOM

2007
SCOTT & MARY WEILAND
Graciela Hotel, Burbank
DAMAGED!!!
Clock, phone, walls, linen.
???

1970s
IAN MCLAGAN, ROD STEWART
Holiday Inns
DAMAGED!!!
General destruction.
$8K

1998
MARILYN MANSON AND ENTOURAGE
Sheraton Hotel, Poughkeepsie
DAMAGED!!!
Telephone, carpets, walls,
bathroom furniture.
$25K

SUITE

2017
TAYLOR SWIFT, ZAYN MALIK
St Pancras Renaissance, London
DAMAGED!!!
Pillows, curtains, lamp.
(It was for a video.)
???

1994
JOHNNY DEPP, KATE MOSS & AN ARMADILLO
The Mark Hotel, New York
DAMAGED!!!
General destruction.
$10K

2012
FLORENCE WELCH
The Bowery, New York
DAMAGED!!!
Set room on fire.
$5K

STEVEN TYLER
Various
DAMAGED!!!
Everything, with a chainsaw.
???

BALCONY

1972
KEITH RICHARDS, BOBBY KEYS
Hyatt, West Hollywood
DAMAGED!!!
Television.
???

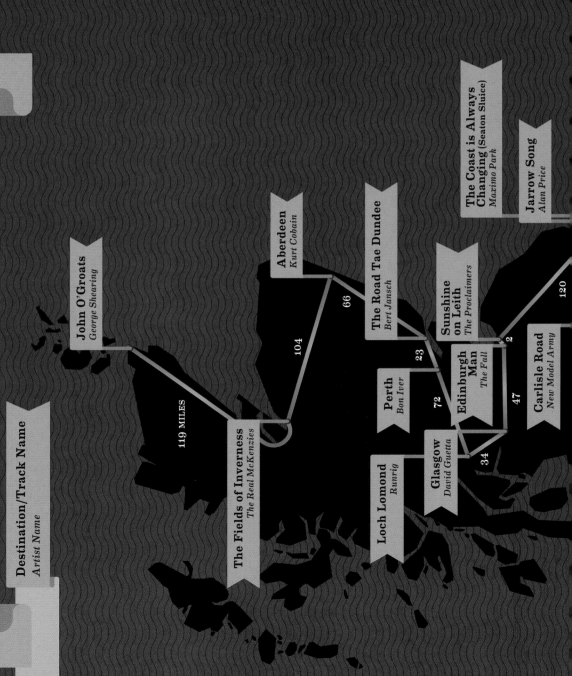

FROM JOHN O'GROATS TO LAND'S END

One of the main places we listen to music is in the car; on the radio, the CD player or, more likely now, via our phone. The UK is such a small place that there's very little history of road trip movies, but if there was then they'd need appropriate tunes. Here's an attempt at the longest journey possible, with an aptly named track for each destination, all the way from John O'Groats to Land's End. And there's a bonus trip around London too.

Destination/Track Name
Artist Name

John O'Groats
George Shearing

The Fields of Inverness
The Real McKenzies

Aberdeen
Kurt Cobain

The Road Tae Dundee
Bert Jansch

Sunshine on Leith
The Proclaimers

The Coast is Always Changing (Seaton Sluice)
Maximo Park

Jarrow Song
Alan Price

Perth
Bon Iver

Edinburgh Man
The Fall

Loch Lomond
Runrig

Glasgow
David Guetta

Carlisle Road
New Model Army

119 MILES

104

66

23

72

2

34

47

120

Sources: Spotify, Google

N

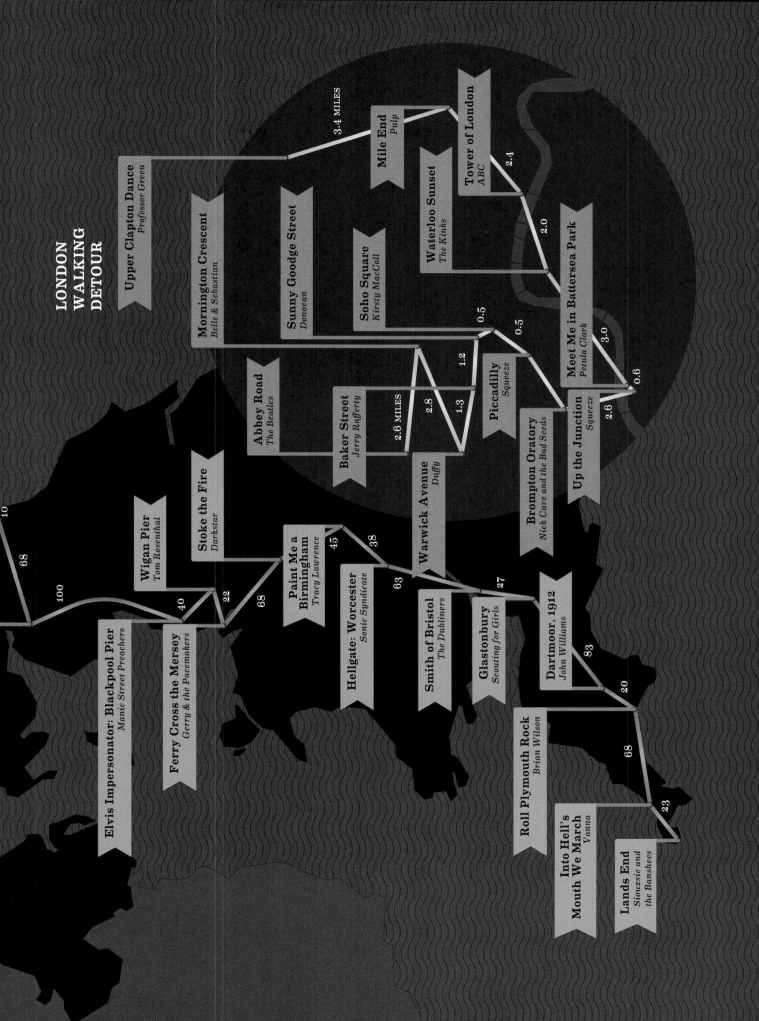

LONDON WALKING DETOUR

Upper Clapton Dance *Professor Green*

Mornington Crescent *Belle & Sebastian*

Sunny Goodge Street *Donovan*

Mile End *Pulp*

Soho Square *Kirsty MacColl*

Waterloo Sunset *The Kinks*

Tower of London *ABC*

Abbey Road *The Beatles*

Baker Street *Jerry Rafferty*

Meet Me in Battersea Park *Petula Clark*

Piccadilly *Squeeze*

Brompton Oratory *Nick Cave and the Bad Seeds*

Warwick Avenue *Duffy*

Up the Junction *Squeeze*

Elvis Impersonator: Blackpool Pier *Manic Street Preachers*

Wigan Pier *Tom Rosenthal*

Stoke the Fire *Darkstar*

Paint Me a Birmingham *Tracy Lawrence*

Ferry Cross the Mersey *Gerry & the Pacemakers*

Hellgate: Worcester *Sonic Syndicate*

Smith of Bristol *The Dubliners*

Glastonbury *Scouting for Girls*

Dartmoor, 1912 *John Williams*

Roll Plymouth Rock *Brian Wilson*

Into Hell's Mouth We March *Vanna*

Lands End *Siouxsie and the Banshees*

3.4 MILES

2.4

2.0

0.5

0.5

1.2

1.3

2.8

2.6 MILES

3.0

0.6

2.6

10

68

100

40

22

68

45

38

63

27

83

20

68

23

•23

HOW THE REVENUE
FROM MUSIC SALES
IS DIVIDED UP

ACROSS THE MUSIC INDUSTRY

Major record labels argue that they plough money
into recording, touring, marketing and PR.
Songwriters, on the other hand, point out that
record sales are just about the only way they can
make any money, whereas the big labels these
days often have a hand in the pie for profits
from everything (merchandising, publishing,
ticket sales), and that they don't even have to
manufacture anything for digital revenue (or
deliver CDs and vinyl to shops, etc.).

HOW UNITED KINGDOM DIVIDES REVENUE

10–13% RETAILER

8–15% BAND/ARTIST

30–40% RECORD LABEL

6% COPYRIGHT

10% MANUFACTURERS

17% VAT

8% DISTRIBUTORS

STEREO XL250123
RPM 33⅓

Sources: BBC, bandzoogle.com, theguardian.com, ibtimes.co.uk, pitchfork.com, musicbusinessworldwide.com

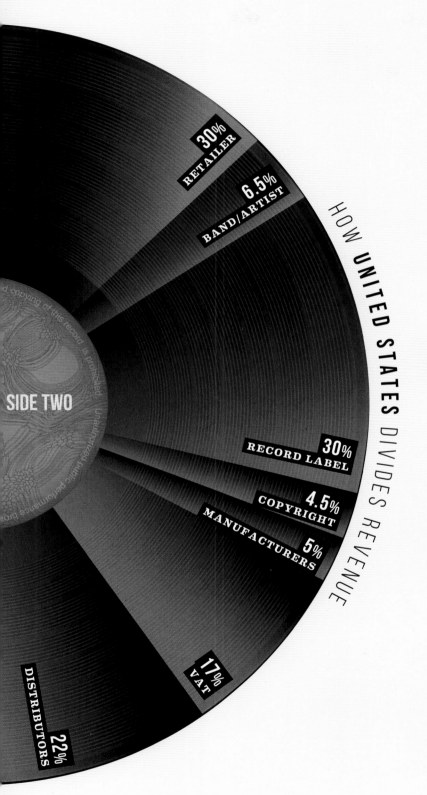

SIDE TWO

30% RETAILER

6.5% BAND/ARTIST

HOW **UNITED STATES** DIVIDES REVENUE

RECORD LABEL 30%

4.5% COPYRIGHT

MANUFACTURERS 5%

17% VAT

22% DISTRIBUTORS

DIGITAL MUSIC

Breakdown of Spotify & Pandora

73% LABEL   **16%** WRITER/ PUBLISHER   **11%** BAND/ ARTIST

21 CENTS   FOR   **7,800** PLAYS

'**Galaxie 500's "Tugboat"** was played 7,800 times on Pandora in the first quarter of 2012, for which its three songwriters were paid a collective total of 21 cents, or seven cents each,' wrote Damon Krukowski, of the band Galaxie 500, on Pitchfork in the early days of streaming, in 2012. And it wasn't as if Pandora or Spotify, at that point, were making a profit: their main aim was to grow their companies. 'In 2012 Pandora's executives sold $63 million dollars of personal stock in the company'. Actually making a buck on an old 7" single suddenly became very twentieth century.

0.004P PER STREAM

Taylor Swift and **Thom Yorke** went on to think the same, as Spotify revealed it was paying, typically, an average of 0.004p per stream, but maintaining it was handing over 70% of its revenue to labels – how much artists then receive from the label remains clouded in individual circumstance. In June 2016 Spotify revealed it had a 100 million paying subscribers, making them the world's most popular streaming service.

MUSICIANS' OTHER JOBS

With the exception of Rod Stewart's time as a grave digger, musicians' other jobs are rarely talked about. Who knew that Jamaican producer and reggae star Keith Hudson trained as a dentist, that Johnny Cash travelled the States as a home-appliance salesman, or that Art Pepper attempted to go straight while looking after stocks in a wholefood bakery?

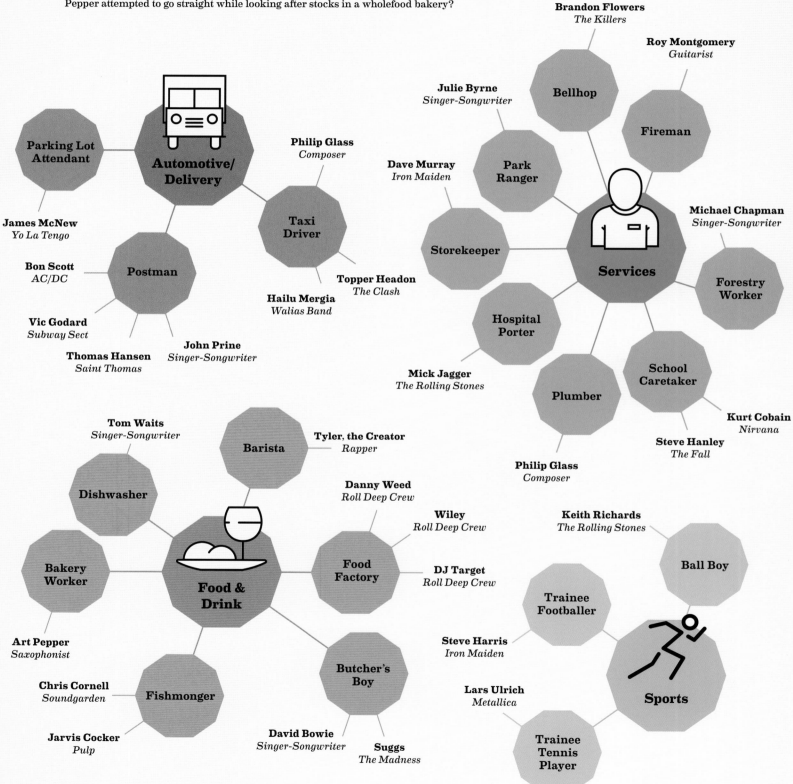

Automotive/Delivery

Parking Lot Attendant

James McNew
Yo La Tengo

Bon Scott
AC/DC

Postman

Vic Godard
Subway Sect

Thomas Hansen
Saint Thomas

John Prine
Singer-Songwriter

Philip Glass
Composer

Taxi Driver

Topper Headon
The Clash

Hailu Mergia
Walias Band

Services

Brandon Flowers
The Killers

Roy Montgomery
Guitarist

Bellhop

Julie Byrne
Singer-Songwriter

Fireman

Dave Murray
Iron Maiden

Park Ranger

Michael Chapman
Singer-Songwriter

Storekeeper

Forestry Worker

Hospital Porter

School Caretaker

Mick Jagger
The Rolling Stones

Plumber

Kurt Cobain
Nirvana

Steve Hanley
The Fall

Philip Glass
Composer

Food & Drink

Tom Waits
Singer-Songwriter

Barista

Tyler, the Creator
Rapper

Dishwasher

Danny Weed
Roll Deep Crew

Wiley
Roll Deep Crew

Bakery Worker

Food Factory

DJ Target
Roll Deep Crew

Art Pepper
Saxophonist

Chris Cornell
Soundgarden

Fishmonger

Butcher's Boy

Jarvis Cocker
Pulp

David Bowie
Singer-Songwriter

Suggs
The Madness

Sports

Keith Richards
The Rolling Stones

Ball Boy

Trainee Footballer

Steve Harris
Iron Maiden

Lars Ulrich
Metallica

Trainee Tennis Player

Sources: planetrock.com, nme.com, vh1.com, wxrt.cbslocal.com

Arts

Publishing
- Colin Meloy *The Decembrists*
- Ira Kaplan *Yo La Tengo*
- Myriam Gendron *Singer-Songwriter*
- Rennie Sparks *The Handsome Family*

Stripper
- Courtney Love *Hole*
- Cosey Fanni Tutti *Throbbing Gristle*

Cinema Usher
- Kele Okereke *Bloc Party*
- Pete Doherty *Libertines*

- Julian Cope *The Teardrop Explosives*
- Robbie Robertson *The Band*

Carnival Worker

Roadie
- David Byrne *Talking Heads*
- Noel Gallagher *Oasis*
- Bobby Gillespie *Primal Scream*

Playboy Bunny
- Debbie Harry *Blondie*

Construction/Industrial

Metal Worker
- Tommy Iommi *Black Sabbath*
- Will Carruther *Spacemen 3*
- Glenn Tipton *Judas Priest*

Grave Digger
- Joe Strummer *The Clash*
- Rod Stewart *Faces*

- Patti Smith *Singer-Songwriter*

Mechanic
- Ritchie Blackmore *Deep Purple*

Toy Factory

Bricklayer
- Michael Nesmith *Monkees*
- Terry Hall *The Specials*
- Eric Clapton *Cream*
- Andrew Weatherall *DJ*

Bulldozer Driver

Slaughterhouse Worker
- Lee "Scratch" Perry *Record Producer*
- Ozzy Osbourne *Black Sabbath*

Retail

Electrical Sales/Repairs
- Keith Moon *The Who*
- King Tubby *Record Producer*
- Prince Jammy *Record Producer*
- Johnny Cash *Singer-Songwriter*
- Patti Smith *Singer-Songwriter*

Books

Record Shops
- Paul Rutherford *Frankie Goes To Hollywood*
- Herman Chin Loy *Record Producer*
- Julian Cope *The Teardrop Explodes*
- Clive Chin *Record Producer*
- Stuart Staples *Tindersticks*
- Pete Wylie *Wah!*
- Abdou El Omari *Keyboardist*
- Augustus Pablo *Record Producer*

Furniture

Supermarket
- Jack White *The White Stripes*
- Calvin Harris *DJ*

Clothes
- Pete Burns *Dead or Alive*
- Johnny Marr *The Smiths*
- Freddie Mercury *Queen*
- Roger Taylor *Queen*
- Kanye West *Rapper*

White-Collar

Teacher
- Michael Chapman *Singer-Songwriter*
- Sheryl Crow *Singer-Songwriter*
- Art Garfunkel *Simon & Garfunkel*
- James "J.T." Taylor *Kool & The Gang*
- Damien Jurado *Singer-Songwriter*
- Gene Simmons *Kiss*
- Peaches *Singer-Songwriter*
- Mark E Smith *The Fall*
- Roberta Flack *Singer-Songwriter*
- Sting *The Police*
- Brian May *Queen*

Shipping/Rail Clerk
- Alan McGee *Biff Bang Pow!*

Music Journalist
- Neil Tennant *Pet Shop Boys*
- Bob Stanley *Saint Etienne*
- Ira Kaplan *Yo La Tengo*

Dentist

Civil Servant
- Ian Curtis *Joy Division*
- Morrissey *The Smiths*
- Keith Hudson *Record Producer*

ALBUMS LISTENED TO IN A LIFETIME

The first thing to say is: we know a few £50 women too. But it's the stereotype of the middle-aged man – born, for argument's sake, in the 1960s – perhaps on his way back to the office after a lunchtime pint, who nips into a branch of Fopp (or, before that, the Virgin megastore or Ray's Jazz) and then blows £50 on a handful of CDs and a copy of *Uncut* magazine, which endures. (This was, of course, in the days when record shops were plentiful – and middle-aged men could be found in significant numbers in offices.)

TEENAGER 'PRESENTS' OWN RADIO SHOW IN BEDROOM

936

ALBUM LISTENS

Twenty singles a night equates (roughly) to an album or two a day, say, three to four LPs a week during adolescent years (difficult to pinpoint exactly due to fluctuating hormones). 1980s arrive with the Sony Walkman – average album listens per week perhaps increases to five or six. Total records listened to by the age of 18 is therefore around 936 (a modest four to five LPs per week for four teenage years).

SORTED FOR E'S AND WHIZ

3,120

ALBUM LISTENS

Clubs, pubs, parties and gigs intervene (interspersed with intense and extended periods of life-changing record listening) but, by the time the student grant and early pay cheques have been blown on records (both student grants and jobs existed in the twentieth century), we're still at a steady, conservative estimate of six LPs a week, 312 album listens a year.

3–18
YEARS

18–24
YEARS

25–45
YEARS

CAREER OPPORTUNITIES

32,240

ALBUM LISTENS

Assuming you've managed to hold down a steady job, pay rises could even have come your way. The main beneficiary of those being your favourite record shop. By the time you're in your early thirties and nostalgic for a youth spent writing down the top 40 while listening to the radio, you start to compile lists of your top 75 albums of the year. Then the top 100. Then the top 135, topped, the following year, by your top 150 (and a few notable LPs 'bubbling under' those). You've stopped watching television (apart from music documentaries) and you travel to work with a CD Walkman then, latterly, an iPod. You might even have an understanding partner and/or kids. You start buying your kids records – cheap CDs from places like Fopp that you couldn't afford when you were young. Vinyl is back. You're now listening, on average, to at least four albums a day (more at weekends). Twenty years of four albums a day = 29,120 album listens.

WORK IS A FOUR-LETTER WORD/REDUNDANCY

68,640

ALBUM LISTENS

You're suddenly on the scrap heap of life. But, if you're lucky, there's a redundancy settlement. And what better place to head to than your favourite record shop (or, by now, online distributor)? After all, you're at home all day: you need some new records. You could be in double-figures in terms of albums listened to a day (at weekends you are) but life gets in the way. You listen to five albums a day on average, 35 a week, 1,820 a year, 36,400 across middle age.

WHEN I'M 64

Plenty more records to listen to . . . (just the worry of how you're going to fit them all in the nursing home).

45–65
YEARS

65+

IT'S A GOOD NUMBER

Songs are often referred to as numbers, as when a DJ might say, "This next number is one of my all time favourites." This may come from musical scores, particularly for musical theatre, where the songs would be numbered and the conductor or director might say, "Let's work on number 7." It could also come from the fact that all tracks have a unique catalogue number to identify them from each other. These songs take numbering to a new level.

1

TYGA
1 OF 1

AMERIE
1 THING

TINCHY STRYDER N-DUBZ
NUMBER 1

BEYONCE
1+1

STYLO G
MY NUMBER 1

2

SPICE GIRLS
2 BECOME 1

TINASHE SCHOOLBOY Q
2 ON

KEVIN GATES
2 PHONES

NINES, HUDSON EAST
LOVE 2 THE GAME

KOBE EMINEM
TALKIN' 2 MYSELF

KANYE WEST
BOUND 2

BLUR
SONG 2

DUA LIPA
ROOM FOR 2

KANYE WEST
PT. 2

RADIOHEAD $2 + 2 = 5$

THE NEIGHBOURHOOD
R.I.P. 2 MY YOUTH

ANN LEE
2 TIMES

COLEMAN HELL
2 HEADS

3

KANO GIGGS, WILEY
3 WHEELS UP

APHEX TWIN
#3

TERROR JR
3 STRIKES

EMINEM
3 A.M.

BRITNEY SPEARS 3

BTS (BANGTAN BOYS)
2! 3!

QUEENS OF THE STONE AGE
3'S & 7'S

CHERYL, WILL.I.AM
3 WORDS

NOAH AND THE WHALE
5 YEARS TIME

AMBER RUN
5 AM

J. COLE
4 YOUR EYEZ ONLY

MADONNA
4 MINUTES

KANYE WEST
FREESTYLE 4

NICKI MINAJ DRAKE

PRINCE
I WOULD DIE 4 U

MOMENT 4 LIFE

AVRIL LAVIGNE
4 REAL

TRAVIS SCOTT THE WEEKND
PRAY 4 LOVE

STEPS
5, 6, 7, 8

T-PAIN
WIZ KHALIFA
LILY ALLEN
5 O'CLOCK

DOLLY PARTON
9 TO 5

GABRIELLE
5 FINE FRØKNER

INSPIRAL CARPETS
SATURN 5

WILEY
6 IN THE MORNING

J BALVIN FARRUKO
6 AM

WRETCH 32
6 WORDS

LIL WAYNE CORY GUNZ
6 FOOT 7 FOOT

DRAKE
6 GOD

SNEAKER PIMPS
6 UNDER GROUND

TOM ROBINSON BAND
2-4-6-8 MOTORWAY

7

CATFISH AND THE BOTTLEMEN

BEYONCÉ
7/11

FALL OUT BOY
7 MINUTES IN HEAVEN

CATTLE & CANE
7 HOURS

NENEH CHERRY YOUSSOU N'DOUR
7 SECONDS

CRAIG DAVID
7 DAYS

HANKS WILLIAMS III
7 MONTHS 39 DAYS

LUKAS GRAHAM
7 YEARS

BON IVER
8 (CIRCLE)

N.W.A.
8 BALL

ELLIE GOULDING
FIGURE 8

DESTINY'S CHILD
8 DAYS OF CHRISTMAS

A TRIBE CALLED QUEST
8 MILLION STORIES

EMINEM
8 MILE

ED SHEERAN
GRADE 8

DRAKE
9

BIFFY CLYRO
9/15THS

50 CENT
9 SHOTS

JIMI HENDRIX
IF 6 WAS 9

DAMIEN RICE
9 CRIMES

WILLOW
9

JAMIROQUAI
CLOUD 9

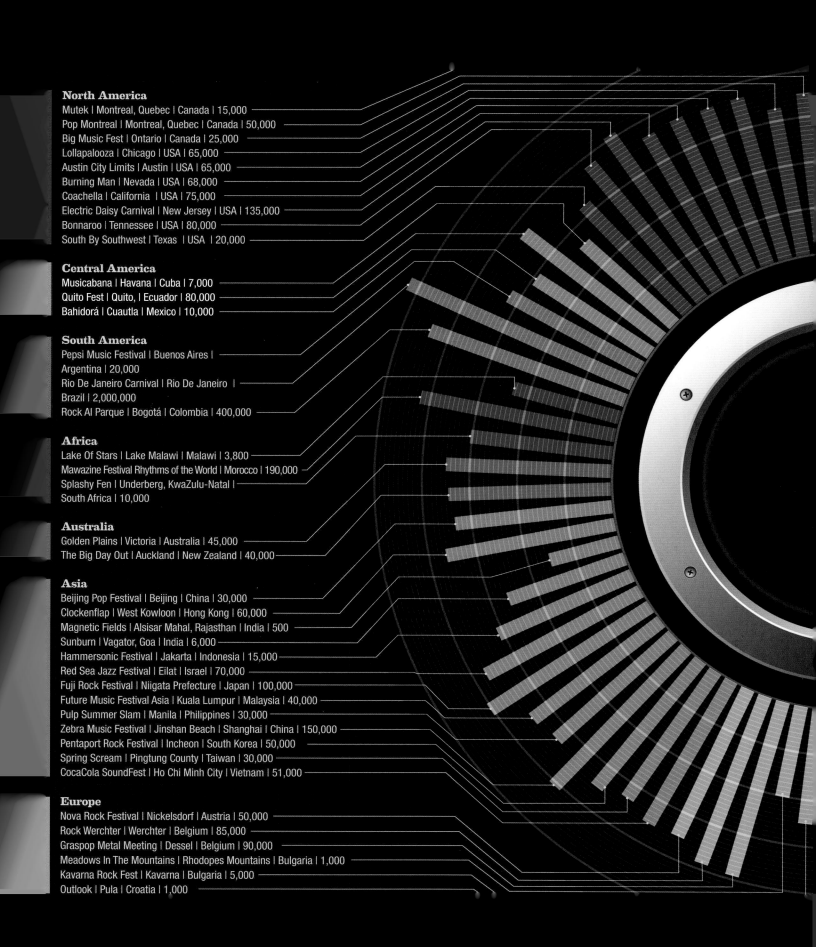

North America
Mutek | Montreal, Quebec | Canada | 15,000
Pop Montreal | Montreal, Quebec | Canada | 50,000
Big Music Fest | Ontario | Canada | 25,000
Lollapalooza | Chicago | USA | 65,000
Austin City Limits | Austin | USA | 65,000
Burning Man | Nevada | USA | 68,000
Coachella | California | USA | 75,000
Electric Daisy Carnival | New Jersey | USA | 135,000
Bonnaroo | Tennessee | USA | 80,000
South By Southwest | Texas | USA | 20,000

Central America
Musicabana | Havana | Cuba | 7,000
Quito Fest | Quito, | Ecuador | 80,000
Bahidorá | Cuautla | Mexico | 10,000

South America
Pepsi Music Festival | Buenos Aires |
Argentina | 20,000
Rio De Janeiro Carnival | Rio De Janeiro |
Brazil | 2,000,000
Rock Al Parque | Bogotá | Colombia | 400,000

Africa
Lake Of Stars | Lake Malawi | Malawi | 3,800
Mawazine Festival Rhythms of the World | Morocco | 190,000
Splashy Fen | Underberg, KwaZulu-Natal |
South Africa | 10,000

Australia
Golden Plains | Victoria | Australia | 45,000
The Big Day Out | Auckland | New Zealand | 40,000

Asia
Beijing Pop Festival | Beijing | China | 30,000
Clockenflap | West Kowloon | Hong Kong | 60,000
Magnetic Fields | Alsisar Mahal, Rajasthan | India | 500
Sunburn | Vagator, Goa | India | 6,000
Hammersonic Festival | Jakarta | Indonesia | 15,000
Red Sea Jazz Festival | Eilat | Israel | 70,000
Fuji Rock Festival | Niigata Prefecture | Japan | 100,000
Future Music Festival Asia | Kuala Lumpur | Malaysia | 40,000
Pulp Summer Slam | Manila | Philippines | 30,000
Zebra Music Festival | Jinshan Beach | Shanghai | China | 150,000
Pentaport Rock Festival | Incheon | South Korea | 50,000
Spring Scream | Pingtung County | Taiwan | 30,000
CocaCola SoundFest | Ho Chi Minh City | Vietnam | 51,000

Europe
Nova Rock Festival | Nickelsdorf | Austria | 50,000
Rock Werchter | Werchter | Belgium | 85,000
Graspop Metal Meeting | Dessel | Belgium | 90,000
Meadows In The Mountains | Rhodopes Mountains | Bulgaria | 1,000
Kavarna Rock Fest | Kavarna | Bulgaria | 5,000
Outlook | Pula | Croatia | 1,000

KEY:

Festival Name | Location | Country | Daily Capacity

Europe continued

INmusic Festival | Zagreb | Croatia | 25,000
Colours Of Ostrava | Ostrava | Czech Republic | 35,000
NorthSide Festival | Aarhus | Denmark | 15,000
Roskilde | Roskilde | Denmark | 130,000
Hard Rock Laager | Vana-Vigala | Estonia | 2,000
Provinssirock Festival | Seinäjoki | Finland | 28,000
Baleapop | Saint-Jean-De-Luz | France | 300
Rock En Seine | Paris | France | 30,000
Vieilles Charrues Festival | Carhaix | France | 55,000
Southside Festival | Neuhausen Ob Eck | Germany | 55,000
Hurricane Festival | Scheeßel | Germany | 75,000
Rock Am Ring | Mendig | Germany | 85,000
Rockwave Festival | Malakasa | Greece | 15,000
Sziget | Budapest | Hungary | 70,000
Secret Solstice | Reykjavik | Iceland | 12,000
Electric Picnic | Stradbally , Co. Laois | Ireland | 35,000
Heineken Jammin' Festival | Milan | Italy | 30,000
Positivus Festival | Salacgr va | Latvia | 30,000
Rock A Field Festival | Roeser | Luxembourg | 20,000
Lowlands Festival | Biddinghuizen | Netherlands | 55,000
Pinkpop | Landgraaf | Netherlands | 60,000

100
1,000
10,000
100,000
1,000,000

Belsonic | Belfast | Northern Ireland | 5,000
Øya Festival | Oslo | Norway | 60,000
Open'er Festival | Gdynia | Poland | 60,000
Rock In Rio Lisboa | Lisbon | Portugal | 80,000
Electric Castle Festival | Cluj-Napoca | Romania | 32,000
Afisha Picnic Festival | Moscow | Russia | 50,000
T In The Park | Perthshire | Scotland | 85,000
Exit Festival | Petrovaradin | Serbia | 35,000
Pohoda Festival | Trencin | Slovakia | 30,000
Sonar | Barcelona | Spain | 35,000
Primavera Sound | Barcelona | Spain | 30,000
Benicàssim International Festival |
Benicàssim | Spain | 50,000
Storsjöyran | Östersund | Sweden | 30,000
Montreux Jazz Festival | Montreux | Switzerland | 6,000
Zürich Openair | Glattbrugg | Switzerland | 40,000
Rock'n Coke | Hezarfen Airfield, Istanbul | Turkey | 30,000
Bestival | Isle Of Wight | UK | 79,000
Glastonbury Festival | Somerset | UK | 200,000
The Green Man Festival | Brecon Beacons | UK | 10,000

SING ME A RAINBOW

Most people know the mnemonic Richard Of York Gave Battle In Vain is a good way of remembering the colours in a rainbow. But what if there was a different way? It is possible to create a set-list of songs to trigger those multi-coloured memories. Below are the top five most played songs and followed artists for each colour on Spotify. Create your own playlist and, for the more ambitious, you could limit yourself to having a line-up of solely rainbow-coloured artists.

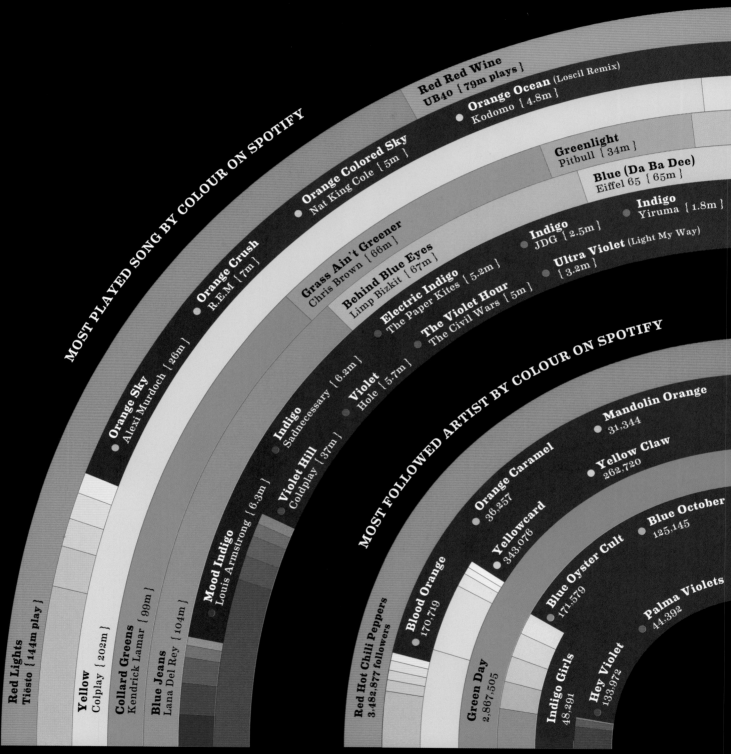

MOST PLAYED SONG BY COLOUR ON SPOTIFY

Red Red Wine
UB40 { 79m plays }

Orange Ocean (Loscil Remix)
Kodomo { 4.8m }

Orange Colored Sky
Nat King Cole { 5m }

Greenlight { 34m }
Pitbull

Blue (Da Ba Dee)
Eiffel 65 { 65m }

Indigo
Yiruma { 1.8m }

Grass Ain't Greener
Chris Brown { 66m }

Indigo
JDG { 2.5m }

Orange Crush
R.E.M { 7m }

Behind Blue Eyes
Limp Bizkit { 67m }

Electric Indigo
The Paper Kites { 5.2m }

Ultra Violet (Light My Way)
{ 3.2m }

The Violet Hour
The Civil Wars { 5m }

Orange Sky
Alexi Murdoch { 26m }

Indigo
Sadnecessary { 6.2m }

Violet
Hole { 5.7m }

Violet Hill
Coldplay { 37m }

Mood Indigo
Louis Armstrong { 6.3m }

Red Lights
Tiësto { 144m play }

Yellow
Colplay { 202m }

Collard Greens
Kendrick Lamar { 99m }

Blue Jeans
Lana Del Rey { 104m }

MOST FOLLOWED ARTIST BY COLOUR ON SPOTIFY

Mandolin Orange
31,344

Yellow Claw
262,720

Orange Caramel
36,257

Blue October
125,145

Yellowcard
343,076

Blue Oyster Cult
171,579

Blood Orange
170,749

Indigo Girls
48,291

Palma Violets
44,392

Hey Violet
133,972

Red Hot Chili Peppers
3,482,877 followers

Green Day
2,867,505

Source: Spotify (accurate as of 26/2/17. Min. 10,000 followers per artist)

Redbone
Childish Gambino { 67m plays }

Bruised Orange (Chain of Sorrow)
Justin Vernon { 3.8m }

Black and Yellow
Wiz Khalifa { 124m }

Red Eyes
The War on Drugs { 41m plays }

Blue in Green
Miles Davis { 31m }

Barefoot Blue Jean Night
Jake Owen { 55m }

Roses and Violets
Alexander Jean { 2.6m }

Green Eyes
Coldplay { 29m }

Blue Christmas
Elvis Presley { 50m }

Red Nose
Sage The Gemini { 38m plays }

Yellow Flicker Beat
Lorde { 55m }

Orange Goblin
31,302

Yellow Mellow
54,896

Agent Orange
26,307

The Red Jumpsuit Apparatus
249,233 followers

Yellow Ledbetter
Pearl Jam { 30m }

Yellowman
28,843

Al Green
326,070

The Moody Blues
122,619

CeeLo Green
214,726

Yellow Ostrich
27,604

Jonas Blue
121,873

Simply Red
238,163

Red
200,342

Tessa Violet
11,447

The Blues Brothers
109,969

Professor Green
159,218

Green Valley
77,201

August Red
190,821

Yellow
Robin Schulz { 24m }

•35

EVOLUTION OF STRING INSTRUMENTS

The lyre and the harp can lay claim to being the earliest string instrument. Both rely on the same simple construction, normally wooden, with strings of different lengths stretched across a frame. With subtle variations this basic design is still the same in all the string instruments we know today. The sound of a string instrument is created by the strings vibrating; the vibration is created in one of three ways, bowing, plucking or strumming, and striking.

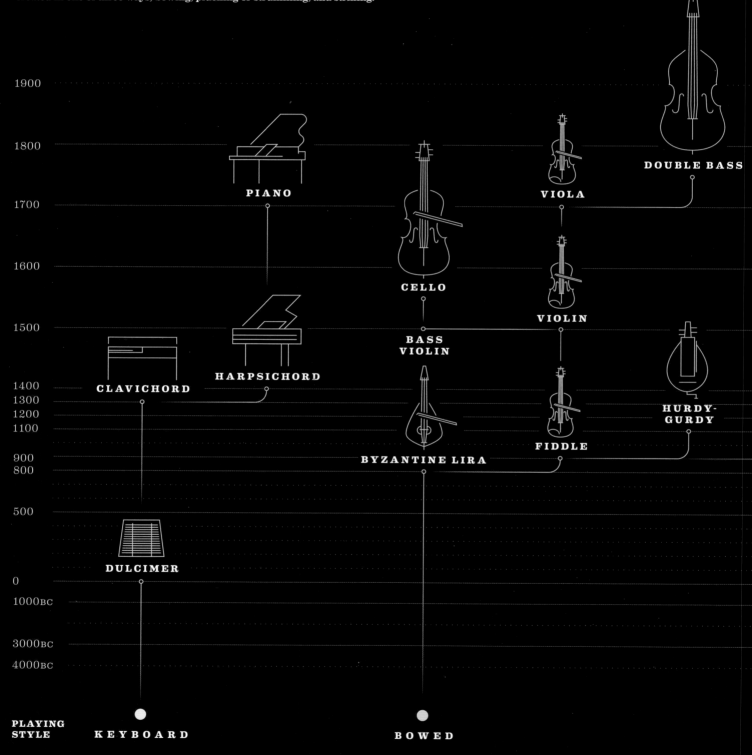

1900

1800

DOUBLE BASS

PIANO

VIOLA

1700

CELLO

1600

VIOLIN

1500

BASS
VIOLIN

CLAVICHORD

HARPSICHORD

HURDY-
GURDY

1400
1300
1200
1100

FIDDLE

900
800

BYZANTINE LIRA

500

DULCIMER

0

1000BC

3000BC
4000BC

PLAYING
STYLE   KEYBOARD   BOWED

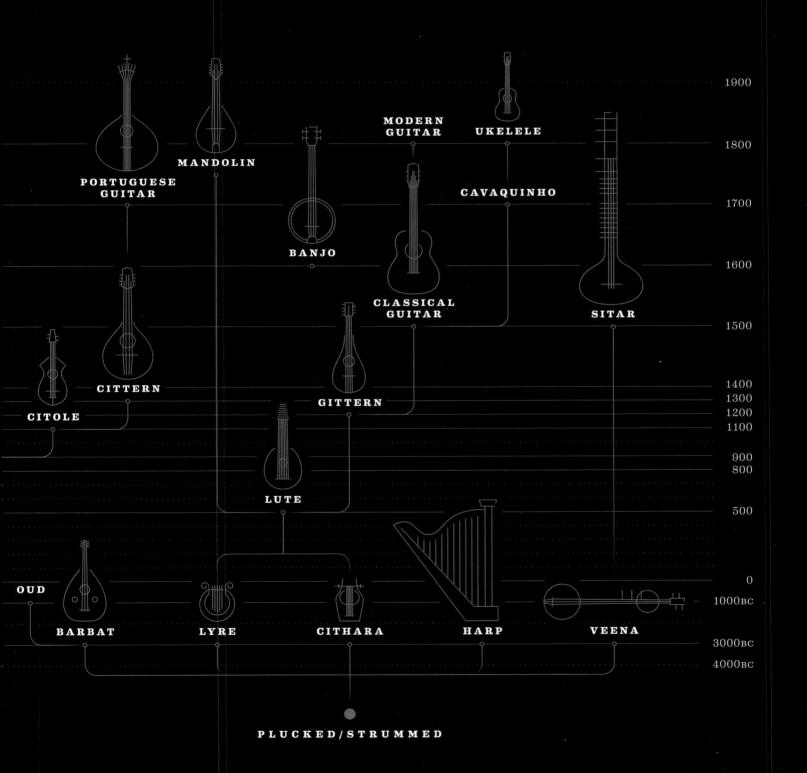

Sources: wikimedia, slideshare.net
Instruments not to scale.

1900

1800

MODERN
GUITAR   UKELELE

MANDOLIN

PORTUGUESE   CAVAQUINHO
GUITAR   1700

BANJO

1600

CLASSICAL
GUITAR   SITAR

1500

CITTERN

1400
1300
GITTERN   1200
1100

CITOLE

900
800

LUTE

500

0

OUD   1000BC

BARBAT   LYRE   CITHARA   HARP   VEENA

3000BC

4000BC

PLUCKED/STRUMMED

•37

EVOLUTION OF WOODWIND INSTRUMENTS

"You know how to whistle, don't you, Steve?" Lauren Bacall asked the question of Humphrey Bogart in *To Have and Have Not*. Mankind has been whistling since the dawn of time and the realisation that air flowing over an obstacle made a noise has led to a proliferation of musical instruments. In the time before a single instrument produced more than one note, a group of players would assemble and play their note in a pre-determined order to create melodies.

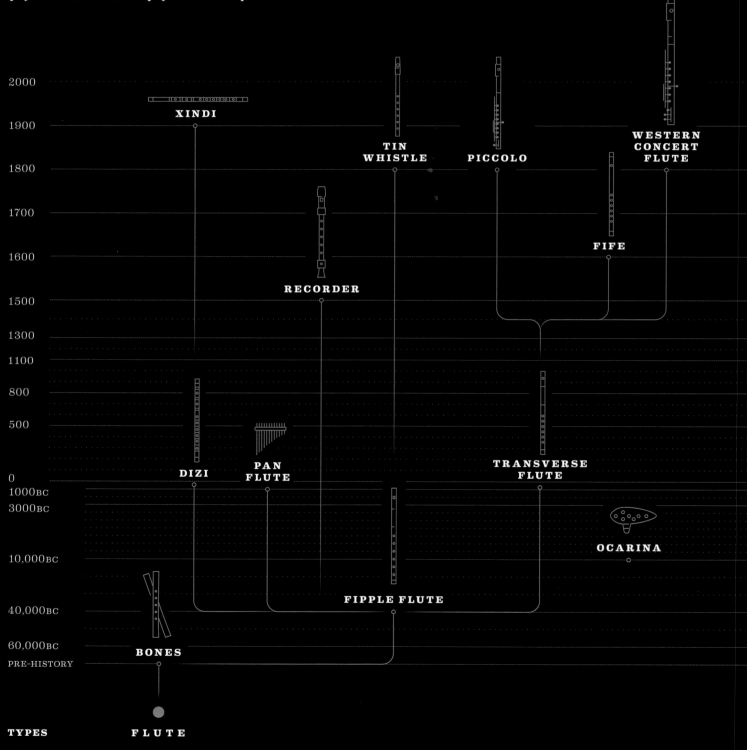

2000

XINDI

1900

TIN
WHISTLE   PICCOLO   WESTERN
CONCERT
FLUTE

1800

1700

FIFE

RECORDER

1600

1500

1300

1100

800

500

TRANSVERSE
DIZI   PAN   FLUTE
FLUTE

0

1000BC
3000BC

OCARINA

10,000BC

FIPPLE FLUTE

40,000BC

60,000BC

PRE-HISTORY

BONES

TYPES   FLUTE

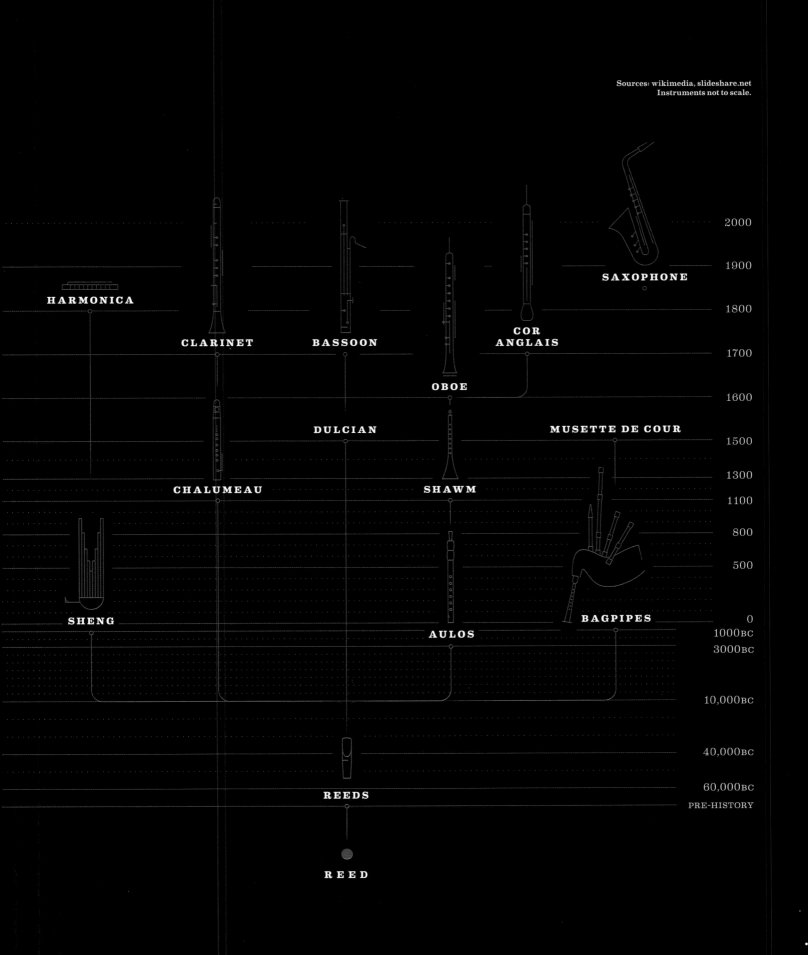

2000

1900

SAXOPHONE

HARMONICA

1800

CLARINET   BASSOON   COR
ANGLAIS

1700

OBOE

1600

DULCIAN   MUSETTE DE COUR

1500

CHALUMEAU   SHAWM

1300

1100

800

500

SHENG   BAGPIPES   0

AULOS   1000BC

3000BC

10,000BC

40,000BC

REEDS   60,000BC

PRE-HISTORY

REED

EVOLUTION OF BRASS INSTRUMENTS

Whilst most brass instruments are made of brass, it is disingeniously not a necessary requirement for them to be made of brass to be classed as part of the brass family. The element that links them is actually that the sound is produced by the player's vibrating lips. In effect, all brass instruments do is channel those vibrations to produce a variety of sounds.

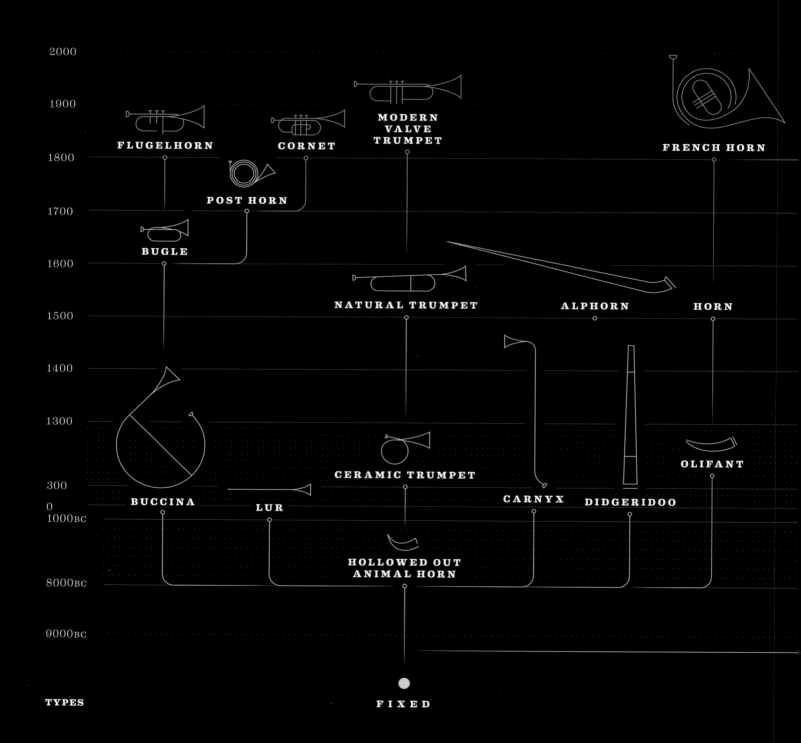

2000
1900
1800
1700
1600
1500
1400
1300
300
0
1000 BC
8000 BC
9000 BC

FLUGELHORN
CORNET
MODERN VALVE TRUMPET
FRENCH HORN
POST HORN
BUGLE
NATURAL TRUMPET
ALPHORN
HORN
BUCCINA
LUR
CERAMIC TRUMPET
CARNYX
DIDGERIDOO
OLIFANT
HOLLOWED OUT ANIMAL HORN

TYPES

FIXED

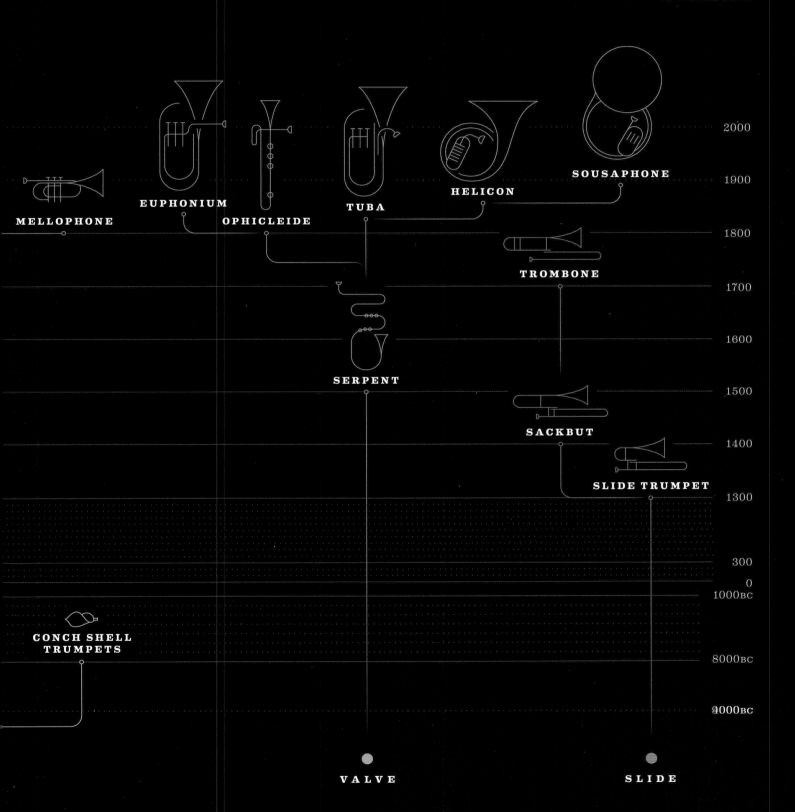

Sources: wikimedia, slideshare.net
Instruments not to scale.

2000

MELLOPHONE

EUPHONIUM

OPHICLEIDE

TUBA

HELICON

SOUSAPHONE

1900

1800

TROMBONE

1700

SERPENT

1600

1500

SACKBUT

1400

SLIDE TRUMPET

1300

300

0

1000BC

CONCH SHELL
TRUMPETS

8000BC

9000BC

VALVE

SLIDE

EVOLUTION OF PERCUSSION INSTRUMENTS

Percussion was probably the first *musical* sound made. Give a baby a stick and it will hit something with it. This makes a sound, and the sound is good, so the hitting continues.

Percussion instruments fall into two categories: pitched and unpitched. The latter has no defined note, whilst the former plays specific tuneable notes. Because of the difference, the unpitched percussions role is to maintain the rhythm whilst the pitched adds to the melody.

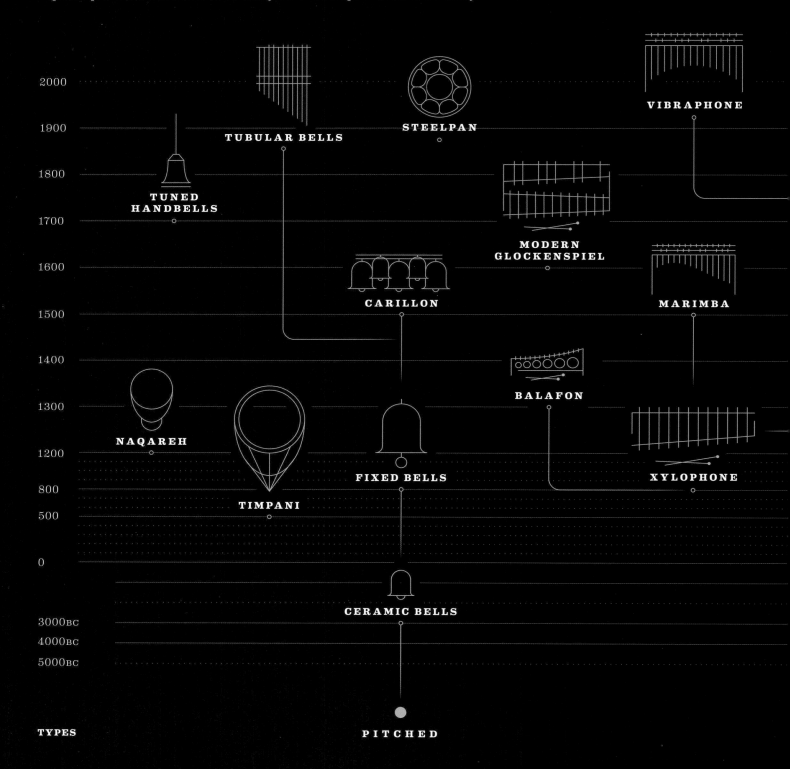

2000

1900   TUBULAR BELLS   STEELPAN   VIBRAPHONE

1800

TUNED
HANDBELLS

1700   MODERN
GLOCKENSPIEL

1600   CARILLON   MARIMBA

1500

1400   BALAFON

1300   NAQAREH

1200   FIXED BELLS   XYLOPHONE

800   TIMPANI

500

0

CERAMIC BELLS

3000BC

4000BC

5000BC

TYPES   PITCHED

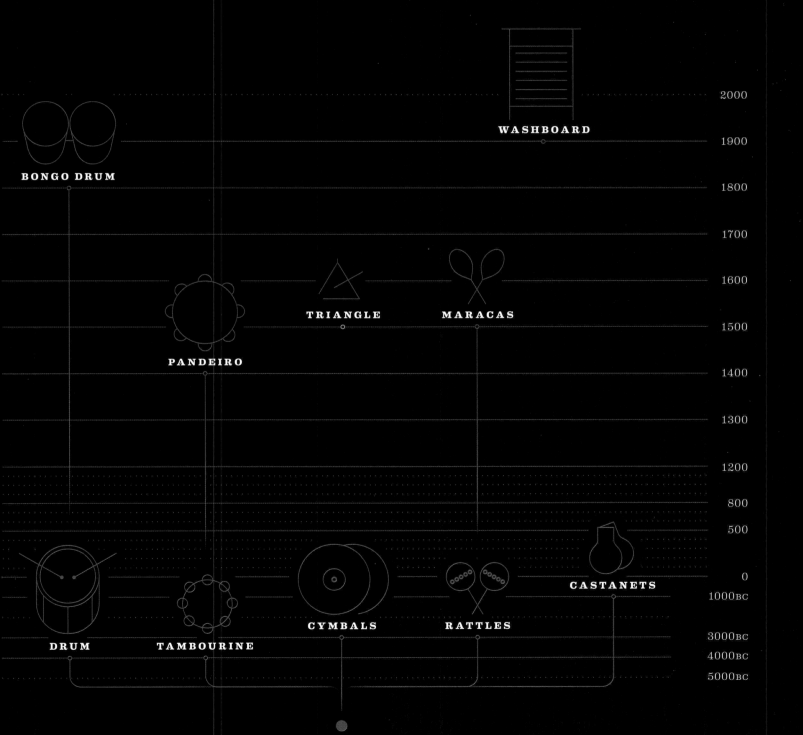

WASHBOARD

2000

BONGO DRUM

1900

1800

1700

TRIANGLE   MARACAS

1600

PANDEIRO

1500

1400

1300

1200

800

500

CASTANETS

0

CYMBALS   RATTLES

1000BC

DRUM   TAMBOURINE

3000BC

4000BC

5000BC

UNPITCHED

JOHN PEEL'S FESTIVE 50

John Peel was the legendary BBC Radio 1 DJ who presided over the night-time airwaves of Britain from 1967 until his death in 2004. He played everyone first: David Bowie, Marc Bolan, the Ramones, The Smiths, P.J. Harvey, Nirvana and The White Stripes to name just a few. His shows featured a considerable amount of reggae and African music, at a time when that went largely unheard (on national radio); he championed punk, techno, hip-hop, grindcore and happy hardcore, and kept his fellow DJs at arm's length. In 1976 he instituted an annual poll, the Festive 50. In the early years listeners voted for their all-time favourite tracks (hence the smattering of entries for the Beatles, Led Zeppelin and the Rolling Stones). From 1982, the Festive 50 reflected listeners' favourites of the year in question.

1977
The figures opposite exclude the year 1977, as Peel compiled that list himself
(No.1: The Motors, 'Dancing the Night Away'; No.2: Althea & Donna, 'Uptown Top Ranking').

1978
The Sex Pistols had four entries in the Top 20 in 1978, a year where punk
became mixed up with the likes of Led Zeppelin and Lynyrd Skynyrd.

'Teenage Kicks' by the Undertones, reputedly John Peel's favourite song, only
reached No.10 in 1978, but Peel had first aired it in only September of that year – a
year later it reached No.2, then remained a fixture in the Top 10 until 1982.

1979
The Fall's first entry was 'Rowche Rumble', at No.40 in 1979; their 88th, and
last, was 'The Theme from Sparta FC (part 2)', which was voted No.1 in the
last ever Festive 50, a couple of months after Peel's death in 2004.

1980
By the end of the 1970s Siouxsie and the Banshees were the most featured band, with 13
entries; the Sex Pistols were just behind with 9 – 'Anarchy in the UK' was No.1 for three
consecutive years from 1978 to 1980, No.2 in 1981, then No.1 again in the all-time poll of 1982.

1982
Peel reprimanded his listeners on more than one occasion for their conservative white indie taste.
One exception to that rule was Grandmaster Flash and the Furious 5's 'The Message', which reached
No.3 in 1982. Depressingly, though, despite the amount of hip-hop, reggae, ragga, Detroit techno,
jungle and African music Peel regularly played, the Festive 50s featured only a smattering of rap
from Public Enemy and Eric B & Rakim in the late eighties, no jungle or drum & bass in the mid-
nineties and only Dreadzone, a nineties fusion of reggae and beats towards the new Millennium.

Strangely New Order and Joy Division record exactly the same number of entries – 33.

In 1982, the poll split into two: an all-time Festive 50, and that year's Festive 50. Peel
invited listeners to vote for their all-time favourite tracks on one other occasion – the
turn of the Millennium. Both charts have been included in the calculations here.

1987
By the end of 1987 the Smiths led the Fall in terms of entries – by 36 to 33.
Who knows what would have happened if they hadn't split up.

1995
The Wedding Present, Pavement, Pulp, The Fall and the Inspiral Carpets
rule the roost in the early 90s, Pulp secured the Top 2 in 1995.

1996
By the second half of the nineties something of a Scottish invasion is underway, with the
Delgados, Belle and Sebastian, Mogwai and Arab Strap all featuring prominently.

Hefner, the Delgados, Gorky's Zygotic Mynci, Half Man Half Biscuit, Ballboy, Bearsuit
and Miss Black America were all stalwarts in the final years of the chart.

The timeframe was, of course, not favourable to 60s and early 70s acts, but the Festive 50
was a great leveller: the Sluts of Trust, a two-piece from Glasgow, match the Beatles, the
Beach Boys and Neil Young for entries; Bob Dylan was outgunned by the Inspiral Carpets.

For reasons of space (and sanity) the graphic opposite does not feature bands who only
registered one entry. So while Tim Buckley, Galaxie 500 and the Velvet Underground
did all make singular appearances in the Festive 50 – as did Harvey's Rabbit, Bang
Bang Machine and Freiwillige Selbstokontrolle – they were outdone by the likes of
Melt Banana and the Field Mice. John Peel would unquestionably approve.

Sources:David Cavanagh, *Good Night and Good Riddance, How Thirty-Five Years of John Peel Helped Shape Modern Life* (2015, Faber & Faber)
Ken Garner, *The Peel Sessions* (2007, BBC Books/Ebury).

MOST ENTRIES BY AN ARTIST

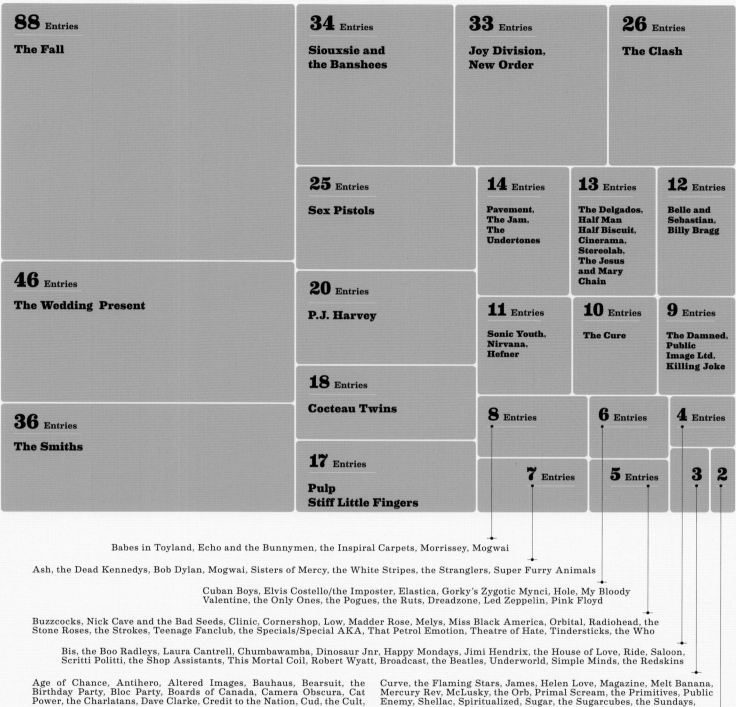

88 Entries

The Fall

46 Entries

The Wedding Present

36 Entries

The Smiths

34 Entries

Siouxsie and the Banshees

25 Entries

Sex Pistols

20 Entries

P.J. Harvey

18 Entries

Cocteau Twins

17 Entries

**Pulp
Stiff Little Fingers**

33 Entries

**Joy Division,
New Order**

14 Entries

**Pavement,
The Jam,
The Undertones**

11 Entries

**Sonic Youth,
Nirvana,
Hefner**

8 Entries

7 Entries

26 Entries

The Clash

13 Entries

**The Delgados,
Half Man
Half Biscuit,
Cinerama,
Stereolab,
The Jesus
and Mary
Chain**

10 Entries

The Cure

6 Entries

5 Entries

12 Entries

**Belle and
Sebastian,
Billy Bragg**

9 Entries

**The Damned,
Public
Image Ltd,
Killing Joke**

4 Entries

3

2

Babes in Toyland, Echo and the Bunnymen, the Inspiral Carpets, Morrissey, Mogwai

Ash, the Dead Kennedys, Bob Dylan, Mogwai, Sisters of Mercy, the White Stripes, the Stranglers, Super Furry Animals

Cuban Boys, Elvis Costello/the Imposter, Elastica, Gorky's Zygotic Mynci, Hole, My Bloody Valentine, the Only Ones, the Pogues, the Ruts, Dreadzone, Led Zeppelin, Pink Floyd

Buzzcocks, Nick Cave and the Bad Seeds, Clinic, Cornershop, Low, Madder Rose, Melys, Miss Black America, Orbital, Radiohead, the Stone Roses, the Strokes, Teenage Fanclub, the Specials/Special AKA, That Petrol Emotion, Theatre of Hate, Tindersticks, the Who

Bis, the Boo Radleys, Laura Cantrell, Chumbawamba, Dinosaur Jnr, Happy Mondays, Jimi Hendrix, the House of Love, Ride, Saloon, Scritti Politti, the Shop Assistants, This Mortal Coil, Robert Wyatt, Broadcast, the Beatles, Underworld, Simple Minds, the Redskins

Age of Chance, Antihero, Altered Images, Bauhaus, Bearsuit, the Birthday Party, Bloc Party, Boards of Canada, Camera Obscura, Cat Power, the Charlatans, Dave Clarke, Credit to the Nation, Cud, the Cult, Curve, the Flaming Stars, James, Helen Love, Magazine, Melt Banana, Mercury Rev, McLusky, the Orb, Primal Scream, the Primitives, Public Enemy, Shellac, Spiritualized, Sugar, the Sugarcubes, the Sundays,

AC Acoustics, Laurie Anderson, Aphex Twin, Arab Strap, Aztec Camera, Eric B & Rakim, Badly Drawn Boy, the Beach Boys, Big Black, Bonnie 'Prince' Billy, Birdland, Blancmange, the Bluetones, Blur, David Bowie, Jackson Browne, Captain Beefheart and the Magic Band, Dick Dale, Derek and the Dominoes, the Disposable Heroes of Hiphoprisy, the Doors, the Farmers Boys, the Flaming Lips, the Flatmates, French, Gang of Four, Kenickie, Lift to Experience, Little Feat, Lynyrd Skynyrd, the Magic Band, Mass, McCarthy, the Men they Couldn't Hang, Van Morrison, Mudhoney, Nina Nastasia, the Pale Saints, Plone, Prolapse, Quickchange, the Rolling Stones, Sebadoh, Sleeper, Smog, Solex, the Soup Dragons, Supergrass, Ten Benson, Transglobal Underground, the Very Things, the Woodentops, X-mal Deutschland, Yeah Yeah Yeahs, Neil Young, Zion Train, Trans Global Underground

WHAT'S IN A NAME?

It's well known that songs about Christmas come round every year, meaning an increase in sales. But what about songs with names in them? They were popular from the 1950s through to the 1980s, but since there's been a major drop-off. There've been no big hits with a name in the title this decade. Maybe it's because of the proliferation of new and varied names?

Sources: nme.com, Wikipedia, Rolling Stone

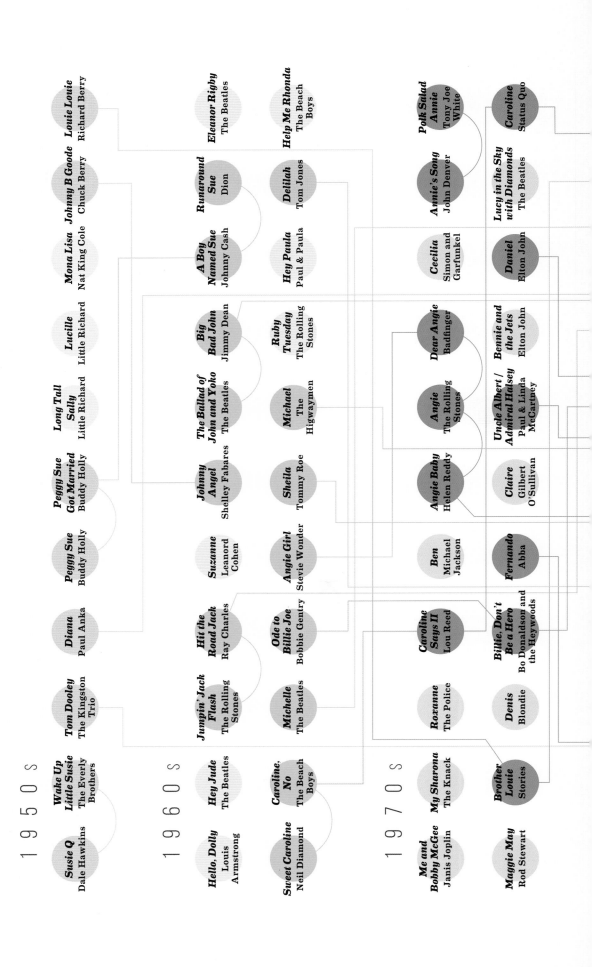

1950s

- **Susie Q** Dale Hawkins
- **Wake Up Little Susie** The Everly Brothers
- **Tom Dooley** The Kingston Trio
- **Diana** Paul Anka
- **Peggy Sue** Buddy Holly
- **Peggy Sue Got Married** Buddy Holly
- **Long Tall Sally** Little Richard
- **Lucille** Little Richard
- **Mona Lisa** Nat King Cole
- **Johnny B Goode** Chuck Berry
- **Louie Louie** Richard Berry

1960s

- **Hello, Dolly** Louis Armstrong
- **Hey Jude** The Beatles
- **Jumpin' Jack Flash** The Rolling Stones
- **Hit the Road Jack** Ray Charles
- **Suzanne** Leanord Cohen
- **Johnny Angel** Shelley Fabares
- **The Ballad of John and Yoko** The Beatles
- **Big Bad John** Jimmy Dean
- **A Boy Named Sue** Johnny Cash
- **Runaround Sue** Dion
- **Eleanor Rigby** The Beatles
- **Caroline, No** The Beach Boys
- **Michelle** The Beatles
- **Ode to Billie Joe** Bobbie Gentry
- **Angie Girl** Stevie Wonder
- **Sheila** Tommy Roe
- **Michael** The Higwaymen
- **Ruby Tuesday** The Rolling Stones
- **Hey Paula** Paul & Paula
- **Delilah** Tom Jones
- **Help Me Rhonda** The Beach Boys

1970s

- **Me and Bobby McGee** Janis Joplin
- **My Sharona** The Knack
- **Brother Louie** Stories
- **Maggie May** Rod Stewart
- **Sweet Caroline** Neil Diamond
- **Roxanne** The Police
- **Denis** Blondie
- **Caroline Says II** Lou Reed
- **Billie, Don't Be a Hero** Bo Donaldson and the Heywoods
- **Ben** Michael Jackson
- **Fernando** Abba
- **Angie Baby** Helen Reddy
- **Angie** The Rolling Stones
- **Dear Angie** Badfinger
- **Claire** Gilbert O'Sullivan
- **Uncle Albert / Admiral Halsey** Paul & Linda McCartney
- **Cecilia** Simon and Garfunkel
- **Annie's Song** John Denver
- **Polk Salad Annie** Tony Joe White
- **Bennie and the Jets** Elton John
- **Daniel** Elton John
- **Lucy in the Sky with Diamonds** The Beatles
- **Caroline** Status Quo

1 9 8 0 s

Jacob's Ladder — Huey Lewis and the News
Don't Cry for Louie — Vaya Con Dios
Dirty Diana — Michael Jackson
My Michelle — Guns N' Roses
Jack and Diane — John Mellencamp
Come on Eileen — Dexys Midnight Runners
Billie Jean — Michael Jackson
Mickey — Toni Basil
Robert de Niro's Waiting — Bananarama
Albert's Shuffle — Al Kooper and Mike Bloomfield
Oh Sheila — Ready for the World
Carrie — Cliff Richard
Arthur's Theme — Christopher Cross
Veronica — Elvis Costello
My Brother Sarah — The Fanatics
Amanda — Boston
Jessie's Girl — Rick Springfield
Tom's Diner — Suzanne Vega
Bettie Davis Eyes — Kim Carnes
Tom Sawyer — Rush

1 9 9 0 s

Personal Jesus — Depeche Mode
Oh Carolina — Shaggy
Jesus to a Child — George Michael
Cotton Eye Joe — Rednex
Dan Dare — Wedding Present
Barbie Girl — Aqua
It's a Shame About Ray — The Lemonheads
Buddy Holly — Weezer
Iris — Goo Goo Dolls
Jeremy — Pearl Jam

2 0 0 0 s

Billie Holiday — Warpaint
Albert Goes West — Nick Cave and the Bad Seeds
Caroline, Yes — Kaiser Chiefs
Stan — Eminem
Jesus Walks — Kanye West
Jesus, Etc. — Wilco
Hey There Delilah — All That We Needed
Maria Maria — Santana
Daniel — Bat for Lashes
Grace Kelly — Mika
Johnny Boy — Twenty One Pilots
Fernando Pando — The Virgins
Michael — Franz Ferdinand
Clint Eastwood — Gorillaz

2 0 1 0 s

Valerie — Mark Ronson
Jack — Breach
John Wayne — Lady Gaga
Peeping Tom — Jamie Berry
Sweet Annie — Zac Brown Band
Panic Like — Tom Riscas
Annie Wants a Baby — Red Hot Chili Peppers
I Love Penny Sue — Daniel May
Annie — Mac Demarco
Curly Sue — Takida
Fernando Chegue — Siglo XX
Fernando Bazua — Los Nuevos Illegales
Damn Daniel — Bombs Away
Mike Lowery — Shorty
Daniel in the Den — Bastille
Iron Mike — Skrapz
Caroline, Please Kill Me — Coma Cinema
Michael Jordan — Kendrick Lamar
Angie — Stereophonics
Louie's Lullaby — Harris Cole
Albert — Eddie Japan
Pack up the Louie — Caro Emerald

COOL INDEPENDENT RECORD LABELS

Everybody has something released by the legendary independent labels in their collection – be it from Rough Trade, 4AD, Mute or Domino in London, Warp in Sheffield, Constellation in Montreal, Merge in North Carolina or Stones Throw in Los Angeles. Here's over 100 of the coolest and, in some cases, perhaps lesser-known smaller, boutique independent record labels operating today. (Africa and Asia to follow in Volume 2.)

UNITED STATES

NNA Tapes
Burlington, USA

Further Records
Seattle, USA

Light in the Attic

Sublime Frequencies

Sahel Sounds
Portland, USA

Mississippi Records

Yellow Electric

Strange Attractors Audio House

Time Released Sound
Oakland, USA

Constellation Tatsu

Helen Scarsdale Agency

Gnome Life
Big Sur, California, USA

Thin Wrist Records/ Vin du Select Qualitite
Los Angeles, USA

Superior Viaduct
San Francisco, USA

Tompkins Square

Recital

Caldo Verde Records

Awesome Tapes from Africa

Not Not Fun

Delmark
Chicago, USA

International Anthem

Thrill Jockey

Kranky

Numero Uno

Drag City

Hausu Mountain

Students of Decay
Cincinnati, USA

Scissor Tail Editions
Tulsa, USA

Flaming Biscuit Records
Hartsville, USA

Dust-to-Digital
Atlanta, Georgia, USA

Paradise of Bachelors
Chapel Hill, USA

Three Lobed Recordings
Jamestown, USA

Studio One
Jamaica

Treasure Isle

Family Vineyard
Indianapolis, USA

Orange Milk
Columbus, USA

Spectrum Spools
Cleveland, USA

No Quarter
Philadelphia, USA

Feeding Tube Records
Florence, USA

Eremite
Northampton, USA

Important
Groveland, USA

Matador
Manhattan, USA

Unseen Worlds

Temporary Residence
Brooklyn, USA

RVNG Intl

Ba Da Bing/ Grapefruit

Northern Spy

Root Strata

Norton
New York, USA

Amish

Olde English Spelling Bee

Wackies

Woodist

GENRES

- ● ALT COUNTRY
- ○ AMBIENT
- ● BLUES & FOLK
- ○ CLASSICAL
- ● DANCE
- ● DUB
- ● ELECTRONIC
- ○ EXPERIMENTAL
- ● EXPERIMENTAL FOLK
- ● GLOBAL
- ● GUITAR
- ● HIP-HOP
- ● JAZZ
- ○ LOST CLASSICS
- ● NOISE
- ● PUNK
- ● REGGAE
- ● SKA
- ● SOUL & R'N'B

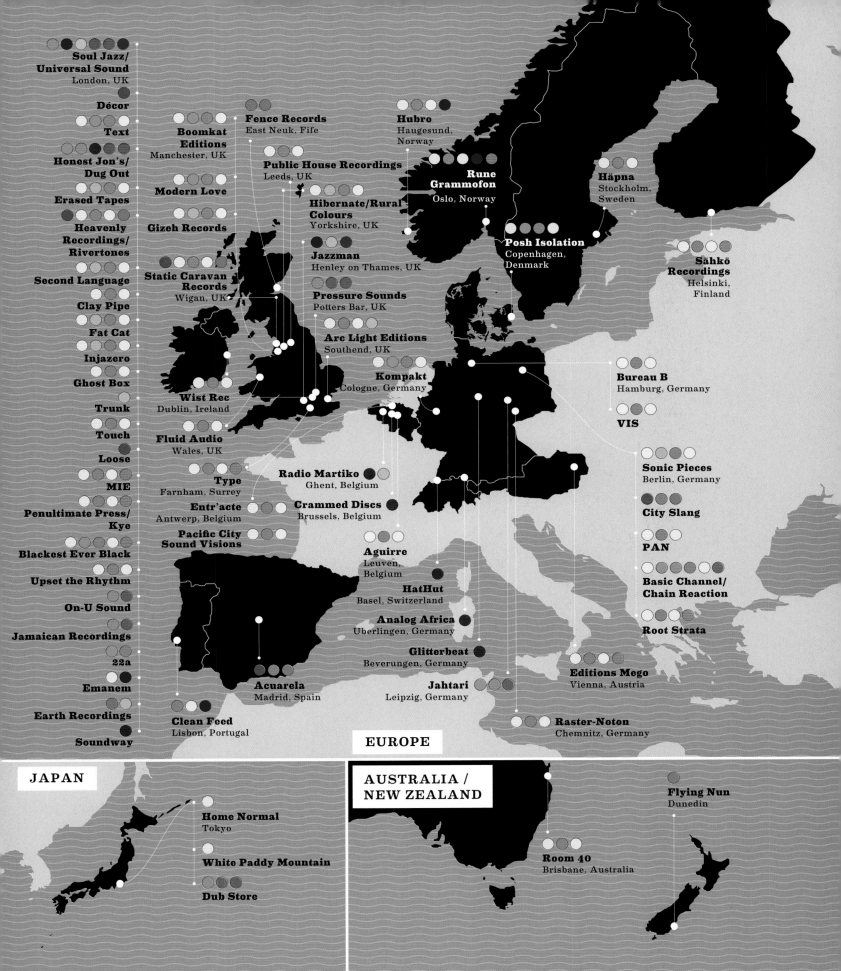

**Soul Jazz/
Universal Sound**
London, UK

Décor

Text

**Honest Jon's/
Dug Out**

Erased Tapes

**Heavenly
Recordings/
Rivertones**

Second Language

Clay Pipe

Fat Cat

Injazero

Ghost Box

Trunk

Touch

Loose

MIE

**Penultimate Press/
Kye**

Blackest Ever Black

Upset the Rhythm

On-U Sound

Jamaican Recordings

22a

Emanem

Earth Recordings

Soundway

**Boomkat
Editions**
Manchester, UK

Modern Love

Gizeh Records

**Static Caravan
Records**
Wigan, UK

Wist Rec
Dublin, Ireland

Fluid Audio
Wales, UK

Type
Farnham, Surrey

Entr'acte
Antwerp, Belgium

**Pacific City
Sound Visions**

Fence Records
East Neuk, Fife

Public House Recordings
Leeds, UK

**Hibernate/Rural
Colours**
Yorkshire, UK

Jazzman
Henley on Thames, UK

Pressure Sounds
Potters Bar, UK

Arc Light Editions
Southend, UK

Kompakt
Cologne, Germany

Radio Martiko
Ghent, Belgium

Crammed Discs
Brussels, Belgium

Aguirre
Leuven,
Belgium

HatHut
Basel, Switzerland

Analog Africa
Uberlingen, Germany

Glitterbeat
Beverungen, Germany

Jahtari
Leipzig, Germany

Acuarela
Madrid, Spain

Clean Feed
Lisbon, Portugal

Hubro
Haugesund,
Norway

**Rune
Grammofon**
Oslo, Norway

Posh Isolation
Copenhagen,
Denmark

Häpna
Stockholm,
Sweden

**Sähkö
Recordings**
Helsinki,
Finland

Bureau B
Hamburg, Germany

VIS

Sonic Pieces
Berlin, Germany

City Slang

PAN

**Basic Channel/
Chain Reaction**

Root Strata

Editions Mego
Vienna, Austria

Raster-Noton
Chemnitz, Germany

EUROPE

JAPAN

Home Normal
Tokyo

White Paddy Mountain

Dub Store

**AUSTRALIA /
NEW ZEALAND**

Flying Nun
Dunedin

Room 40
Brisbane, Australia

•49

WHAT'S UP WITH THE 27 CLUB?

The number of popular musicians who have died at the age of 27 is unusually high. Their deaths were occasionally a result of drug and alcohol abuse, or due to violence such as homicide or suicide. However, more often than not, accidents are to blame.

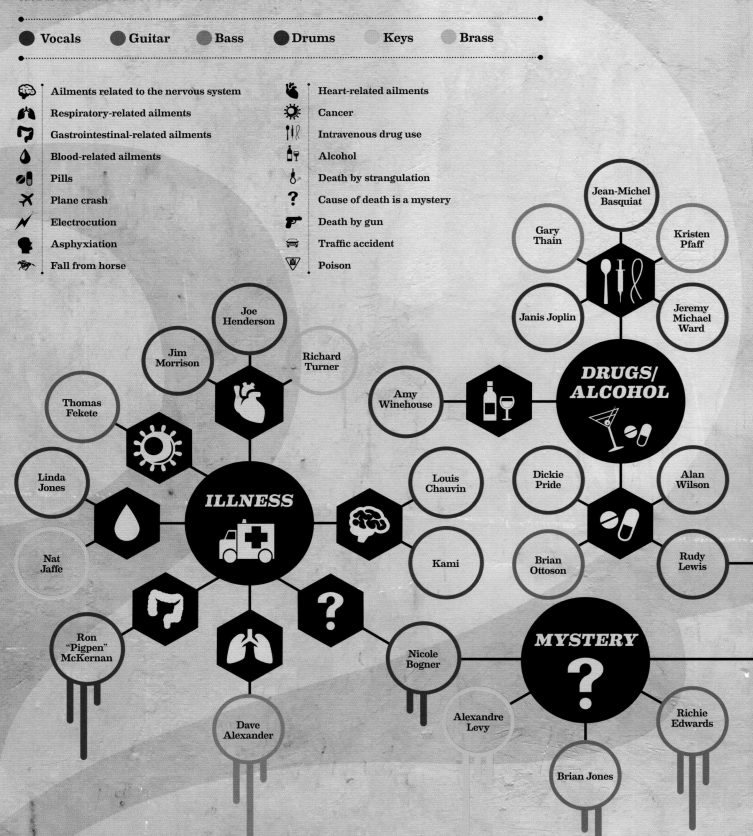

● Vocals ● Guitar ● Bass ● Drums ● Keys ● Brass

🧠 Ailments related to the nervous system
🫁 Respiratory-related ailments
Gastrointestinal-related ailments
💧 Blood-related ailments
💊 Pills
✈ Plane crash
⚡ Electrocution
Asphyxiation
🐎 Fall from horse

♥ Heart-related ailments
☼ Cancer
Intravenous drug use
🍾 Alcohol
Death by strangulation
? Cause of death is a mystery
🔫 Death by gun
🚗 Traffic accident
☠ Poison

DRUGS/ALCOHOL
Jean-Michel Basquiat
Gary Thain
Kristen Pfaff
Janis Joplin
Jeremy Michael Ward
Amy Winehouse
Dickie Pride
Alan Wilson
Brian Ottoson
Rudy Lewis

ILLNESS
Joe Henderson
Jim Morrison
Richard Turner
Thomas Fekete
Linda Jones
Nat Jaffe
Louis Chauvin
Kami
Ron "Pigpen" McKernan
Dave Alexander
Nicole Bogner

MYSTERY
?
Alexandre Levy
Richie Edwards
Brian Jones

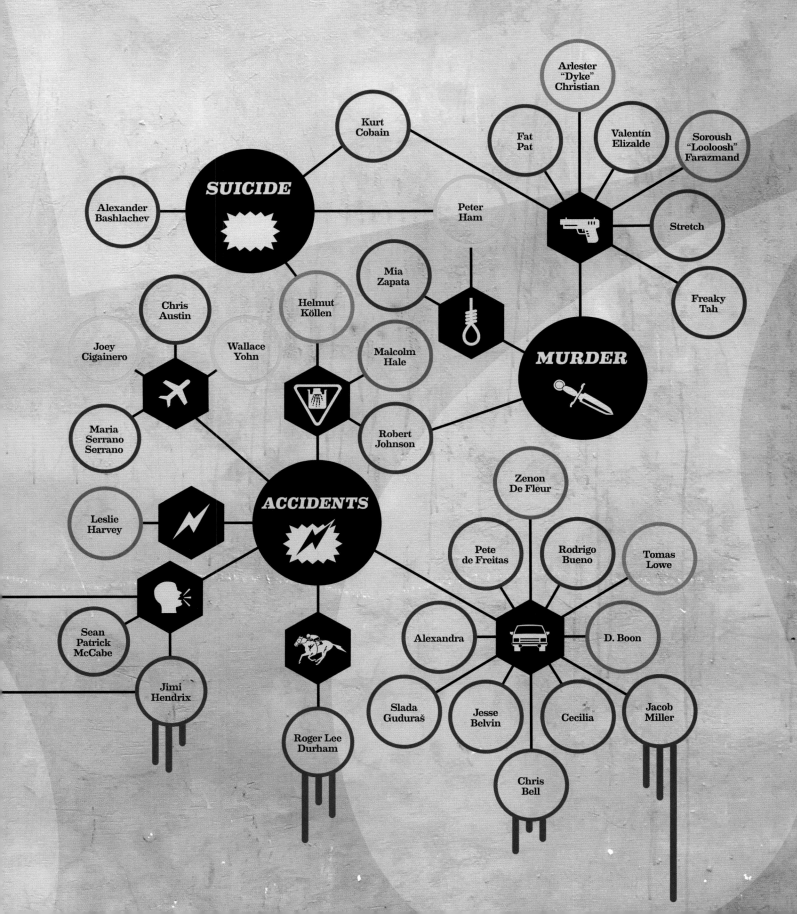

SUICIDE

MURDER

ACCIDENTS

Arlester "Dyke" Christian

Kurt Cobain

Fat Pat

Valentín Elizalde

Soroush "Looloosh" Farazmand

Alexander Bashlachev

Peter Ham

Stretch

Mia Zapata

Freaky Tah

Chris Austin

Helmut Köllen

Joey Cigainero

Wallace Yohn

Malcolm Hale

Maria Serrano Serrano

Robert Johnson

Leslie Harvey

Zenon De Fleur

Pete de Freitas

Rodrigo Bueno

Tomas Lowe

Alexandra

D. Boon

Sean Patrick McCabe

Jimi Hendrix

Roger Lee Durham

Slada Guduraš

Jesse Belvin

Cecilia

Jacob Miller

Chris Bell

LITERARY BAND NAMES

"If music be the food of love, play on." So said Duke Orsino in William Shakespeare's *Twelfth Night* and, whilst no one has taken that character's name for themselves yet, many have taken inspiration from literature and poured it into their work. Here are just a few.

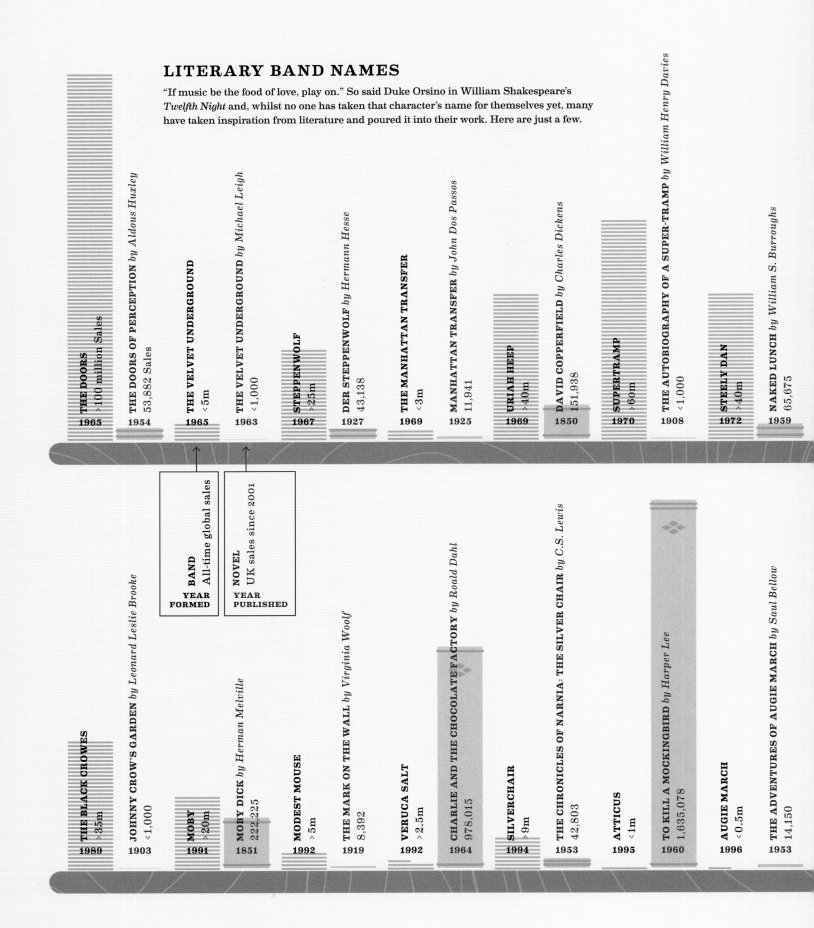

THE DOORS >100 million Sales **1965**
THE DOORS OF PERCEPTION *by Aldous Huxley* 53,882 Sales **1954**
THE VELVET UNDERGROUND <5m **1965**
THE VELVET UNDERGROUND *by Michael Leigh* <1,000 **1963**
STEPPENWOLF >25m **1967**
DER STEPPENWOLF *by Hermann Hesse* 43,138 **1927**
THE MANHATTAN TRANSFER <3m **1969**
MANHATTAN TRANSFER *by John Dos Passos* 11,941 **1925**
URIAH HEEP >40m **1969**
DAVID COPPERFIELD *by Charles Dickens* 151,938 **1850**
SUPERTRAMP >60m **1970**
THE AUTOBIOGRAPHY OF A SUPER-TRAMP *by William Henry Davies* <1,000 **1908**
STEELY DAN >40m **1972**
NAKED LUNCH *by William S. Burroughs* 65,675 **1959**

BAND — All-time global sales / YEAR FORMED
NOVEL — UK sales since 2001 / YEAR PUBLISHED

THE BLACK CROWES >35m **1989**
JOHNNY CROW'S GARDEN *by Leonard Leslie Brooke* <1,000 **1903**
MOBY >20m **1991**
MOBY DICK *by Herman Melville* 222,225 **1851**
MODEST MOUSE >5m **1992**
THE MARK ON THE WALL *by Virginia Woolf* 8,392 **1919**
VERUCA SALT >2.5m **1992**
CHARLIE AND THE CHOCOLATE FACTORY *by Roald Dahl* 978,015 **1964**
SILVERCHAIR >9m **1994**
THE CHRONICLES OF NARNIA: THE SILVER CHAIR *by C.S. Lewis* 42,803 **1953**
ATTICUS <1m **1995**
TO KILL A MOCKINGBIRD *by Harper Lee* 1,635,078 **1960**
AUGIE MARCH <0.5m **1996**
THE ADVENTURES OF AUGIE MARCH *by Saul Bellow* 14,150 **1953**

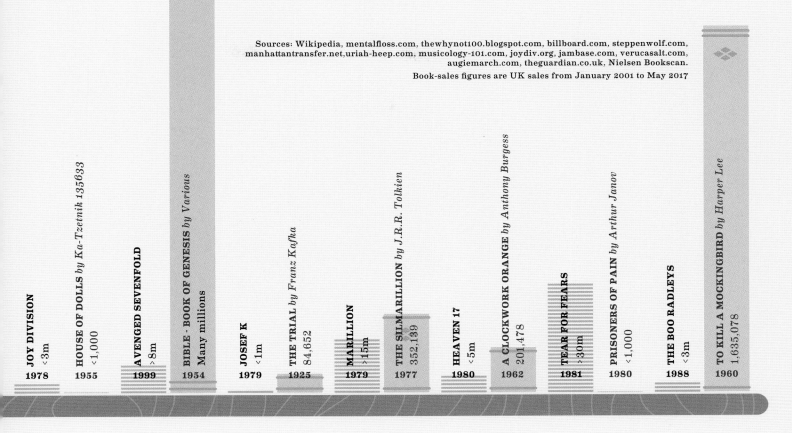

Sources: Wikipedia, mentalfloss.com, thewhynot100.blogspot.com, billboard.com, steppenwolf.com, manhattantransfer.net, uriah-heep.com, musicology-101.com, joydiv.org, jambase.com, verucasalt.com, augiemarch.com, theguardian.co.uk, Nielsen Bookscan.

Book-sales figures are UK sales from January 2001 to May 2017

JOY DIVISION
<3m
1978

HOUSE OF DOLLS *by Ka-Tzetnik 135633*
<1,000
1955

AVENGED SEVENFOLD
>8m
1999

BIBLE - BOOK OF GENESIS *by Various*
Many millions
1954

JOSEF K
<1m
1979

THE TRIAL *by Franz Kafka*
84,652
1925

MARILLION
>15m
1979

THE SILMARILLION *by J.R.R. Tolkien*
352,139
1977

HEAVEN 17
<5m
1980

A CLOCKWORK ORANGE *by Anthony Burgess*
201,478
1962

TEAR FOR FEARS
>30m
1981

PRISONERS OF PAIN *by Arthur Janov*
<1,000
1980

THE BOO RADLEYS
<3m
1988

TO KILL A MOCKINGBIRD *by Harper Lee*
1,635,078
1960

BELLE & SEBASTIAN
<3m
1996

BELLE ET SÉBASTIAN *by Cécile Aubry*
<1,000
1967

ARTFUL DODGER
<1m
1997

OLIVER TWIST *by Charles Dickens*
358,463
1838

COLDPLAY
>80m
1998

CHILD'S REFLECTIONS: COLD PLAY *by Philip Horky*
<1,000
1997

AS I LAY DYING
<3m
2001

AS I LAY DYING *by William Faulkner*
38,284
1930

MY CHEMICAL ROMANCE
>6m
2001

ECSTASY: THREE TALES OF CHEMICAL ROMANCE *by Irvine Welsh*
31,278
1996

TITUS ANDRONICUS
<1m
2005

TITUS ANDRONICUS *by William Shakespeare*
12,607
1590s

OF MICE & MEN
>1m
2009

OF MICE AND MEN *by John Steinbeck*
1,546,534
1937

ONE MAN BAND

Some do it by choice, others because they can find no one else to play with. The one man band has been around since the 1400s, when musicians would play a simple flute with one hand and a drum with the other. Over the years, the instruments have changed and the playing style has been refined but the basics are the same: one man, multiple instruments, making a hell of a din.

With the variations listed here, along with, let's not forget, singing, it's possible to produce a version of pretty much any song.

PENNY WHISTLE

RECORDER

MOUTH

MOUTH ORGAN

HORN

KAZOO

UKELELE

GUITAR

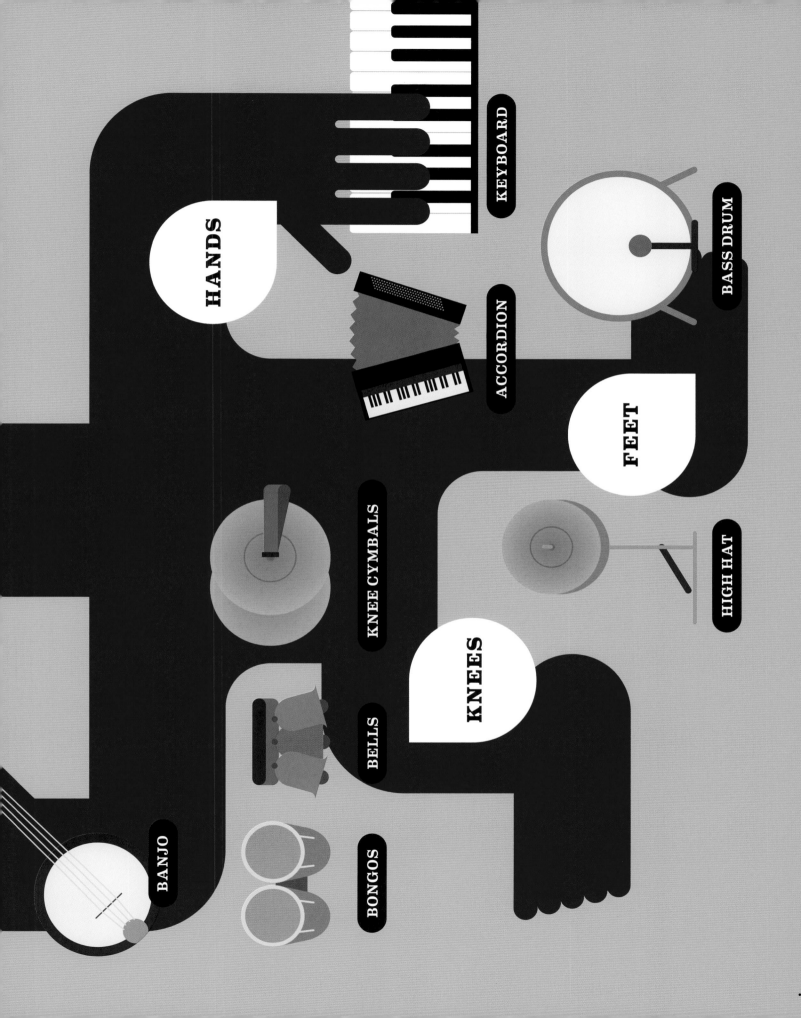

KEYBOARD

HANDS

BASS DRUM

ACCORDION

FEET

KNEE CYMBALS

HIGH HAT

BELLS

KNEES

BANJO

BONGOS

IT WASN'T ALL IN THE DELIVERY:
9 FAILED MUSIC FORMATS

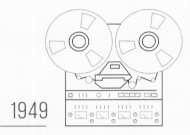

1949

REEL-TO-REEL TAPES

Pre-recorded reels were first released in America in 1949 – and by EMI into the UK market in 1952 – at a time when most homes were coming to terms with the Dansette record player. Take-up was slow, recorders expensive and bulky and, despite superior sound quality, general fiddliness and problems with mangled tape meant the reel-to-reel tapes never really seriously challenged vinyl as a pre-recorded device. It remains the choice format for a select few audiophiles. By the mid-1960s a loop-tape cartridge, which was enclosed in moulded plastic and did not need re-threading midway through a concerto, had been developed.

1950s

PORTABLE TURNTABLES

Although they have appeared periodically through the ages – from pastel-coloured Dansettes popping out of a suitcase on a 1950s picnic through to the Audio Technica AT-727 Sound Burger turntable, and even present-day retro models – it's unlikely sales will ever threaten the portability of the mp3, or even the radio-cassette. Why lug all that vinyl out into the countryside, where it will only warp in the sun? And it proved a bit difficult keeping the needle on the record as the Jag took a sharp bend.

1964

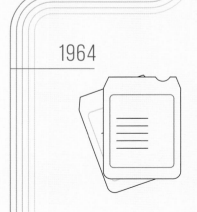

8-TRACK TAPE

Developed in 1964 by, among others, the Lear Jet Corporation. The dashboard of an aircraft or Cadillac was big enough to house an 8-track tape player, and the format was popular in 1960s America (more space in America meant larger refrigerators too and, generally speaking, the States led the rest of the world in tape adoption), but the bulky cartridges were soon superseded by the more compact cassette, which had actually been devised a year earlier. A similar 4-track tape never really got off the ground. RCA developed the quadraphonic 8-track, which also crashed with quad sound.

Sources: *How Music Got Free*, Stephen Witt
(2015, Bodley Head/Vintage), "Atco's Collections", YouTube,
listverse.com, www.youtube.com, theguardian.com, 1001blocks.com

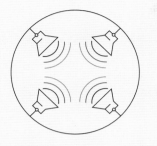

1971 QUADRAPHONIC SOUND

Introduced in 1971, this doubled the use of stereo channels to create a
simulation of the sound experience of a live gig – with four speakers
positioned in the corners of your living room. Started out as an expensive
reel-to-reel tape format, but the high cost prevented significant sales.
Then, in a faint pre-echo of what would later happen with compressed
digital files, an industry standard for compatible four-channel sound
components for vinyl and 8-track tape could not be agreed upon. Dolby
Surround Sound today pretty much replicates this experience.

SELECTAVISION VIDEO DISC AND LASER DISC

Both formats resembled a sort of 12" version of the CD or DVD, and the Laser Disc was used
primarily for storing film, but the SelectaVision Video Disc, a capacitance electronic disc, was
developed by RCA, a record company, and was basically a video phonograph – an analogue device
with crammed-in audio signals like an LP, but at a much greater density. The varying depths of the
grooves (rather than the cuts in the groove vibrating the stylus – see analogue v digital sound on
pp.112-13) stored the audio information. RCA had been developing its SelectaVision format since
the late 1960s, but both ultimately failed as consumers would need to install a significant bank of
playback equipment and essentially convert their front rooms into something resembling a 1970s
mobile TV control unit.

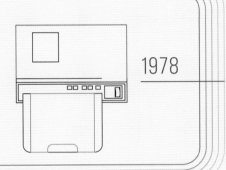

1978

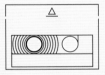

1987

CD CAROUSEL/CHANGER

Still on the market, but many are simply not sturdy enough
and break after heavy use. A combination of the vinyl
renaissance and heavy streaming surely looks to see off this
1990s convenience device.

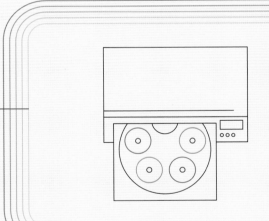

DAT

Smaller cassette developed to
replace the standard cassette,
with enhanced recording clarity.
In fact, recording clarity of such
an enhanced high calibre that
concerns over piracy effectively
spelled the end for this device.
As Listverse.com points out, this
technology later paved the way for
the all-digital mp3. Piracy was not
an issue there, of course.

1993

1992

SONY MINIDISC

CD Walkman convenience allied
to high quality recording function
– but too expensive to usurp home
taping on a cassette and, ten years
on, just as the world embraced
digital file sharing, the MiniDisc
itself became obsolete in the face
of the mp3 revolution.

MP2

Despite the MUSICAM group, a
consortium of inventors funded by
Dutch corporation Philips, bulldozing
their way to having the mp2 adopted
as a trade standard, the superior
compressing capacity of rival mp3
technology won out – with a little
help from NAPSTER. Mp2 digital
European radio, interactive CD-
ROMs, video compact discs and DAT
tape all went the way of the 8-track.

WE ARE WAVING

The sound of a musical instrument, or voice, reaches our ears because it creates waves, or "vibrations". These vibrations travel away from the source of the sound, moving the vibration from particle to particle. These vibrations cause a change in pressure – if sound is travelling through the air, it causes a change in air pressure.

Imagine sound as if it was a stone falling into water. When the stone hits the surface, it disturbs it and sends waves (water waves in this case) away from the point where the stone landed. The bigger the stone, the bigger the waves. In the same way, the louder a noise is, the bigger the sound wave, and it both travels further and we hear it louder.

But what is it that makes different instruments sound different, or allows us to create sounds with different notes? What is it, simply, that allows music to be made?

SOUND WAVE

A sound wave has three main variables:

AMPLITUDE
How loud it is.

FREQUENCY
How often the wave repeats.

WAVELENGTH
How long the wave is.

The last two are inversely proportional – as frequency increases, the wavelength decreases.

Changes in these enable different sounds to be created: increasing the amplitude makes a sound louder, while increasing the frequency of the wave increases the pitch.

HOW SOUND WAVES WORK

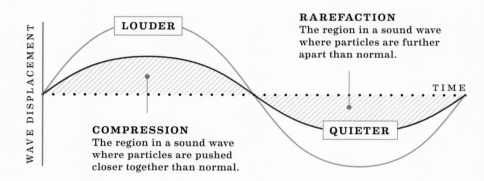

RAREFACTION
The region in a sound wave where particles are further apart than normal.

COMPRESSION
The region in a sound wave where particles are pushed closer together than normal.

LOUDER/QUITER
This sound wave shows a note of the same pitch being produced but in the lighter blue curve it is louder. The amplitude has been increased, increasing the pressure and thus the volume.

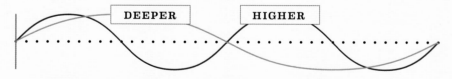

DEEPER/HIGHER
Here the volume, or amplitude, remains the same but the wavelength has shortened in the dark blue curve, thus increasing the frequency and, therefore, the pitch. This means the note goes up the scale.

FREQUENCY & WAVE LENGTH

Frequency and wave length defines the pitch of a note. The graph shows the frequencies of three notes: A3, A4 and A5. (A4 is the middle A on a piano, and is the note that orchestras tune to.) Every octave, the frequency of the note doubles.

Hertz – hertz measure the frequency of a sound wave. One hertz is equal to one cycle per second. A4 is, therefore, equivalent to a sound wave that cycles 440 times every second.

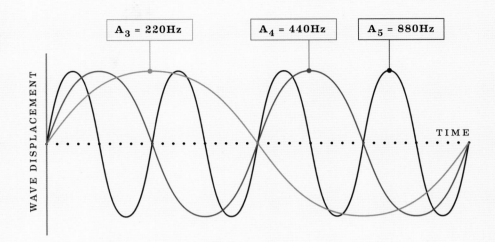

$A_3 = 220Hz$ $A_4 = 440Hz$ $A_5 = 880Hz$

WAVE DISPLACEMENT

TIME

INSTRUMENTS

If instruments produce sounds at the same amplitude and frequency, why do they not all sound the same? This is because of something called overtones (also called harmonics and pitch). The pitch and loudness of these overtones give the notes unique sounds, which are the timbre of the instrument. The graph shows a sample of the irregularities created in the sound waves of various instruments.

PLAYING THE SAME NOTE

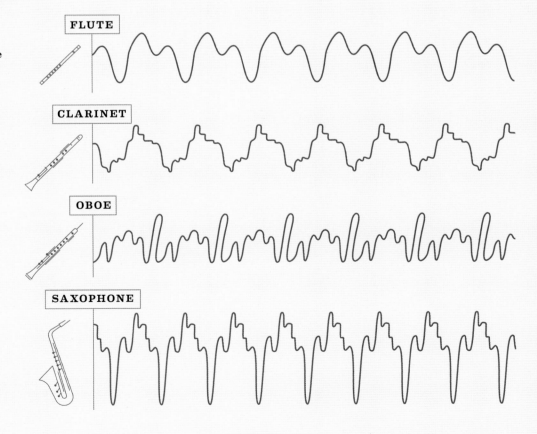

FLUTE

CLARINET

OBOE

SAXOPHONE

FOR QUEEN AND COUNTRY

A good national anthem has a strong melody, meaningful lyrics and a rousing chorus, unless you're Spanish, in which case, sorry, no lyrics at all. You'll just have to hum. It should also not be too long, which is why it is very rare to hear all 15 verses of the Netherland's Wilhelmus: that would take well over ten minutes. As well as being the longest, the Dutch anthem is also the oldest.

No. of verses

KEY

Year Adopted
COUNTRY
Name of Anthem
(Lyrics by / Music by)

PRIMARY DEDICATION
- The Flag
- The Country
- The People
- The Ruler
- The Deity
- No Lyrics

1926   1 Verse
REPUBLIC OF IRELAND
The Soldier's Song
(Peader Kearney. Liam Ó Rinn [Irish translation] / Patrick Heeney)

1745   3 Verses
UNITED KINGDOM
God Save the Queen (or King)
(Author unknown)

1931   4 Verses
UNITED STATES OF AMERICA
Star-Spangled Banner
(Francis Scott Key / John Stafford Smith)

1761   1 Verse
SPAIN
Marcha Real
(No lyrics / Manuel de Espinosa de los Monteros, Bartolomé Pérez Casa)

1978   2 Verses
NIGERIA
Arise. O Compatriots
(John A. Ilechukwu, Eme Etim Akpan, B. A. Ogunnaike, Sota Omoigui and P. O. Aderibighe / The Police Band, led by B. E. Odiase)

1948   6 Verses
ECUADOR
¡Salve. Oh Patria!
(Juan León Mera / Antonio Neumane)

BRAZIL   2 Verses
Hino Nacional
(1922 . Osório Duque-Estrada / 1831 . Francisco Manuel da Silva)

1813   3 Verses
ARGENTINA
Himno Nacional Argentina
(Vicente López y Planes / Blas Parera)

1997   2 Verses
SOUTH AFRICA
Nkosi Sikelel' iAfrika/Die Stem van Suid-Afrika
(Enoch Sontonga, C . J. Langenhoven / Afezekile Malonde, Marthinus Lourens de Villiers)

Sources: seatgeek.com,
Wikipedia, nationalanthems.
me, gov.ca, loc.gov.

1932   **15 Verses**
NETHERLANDS
Wilhelmus
(Unknown / Adrianus Valerius)

2000   **3 Verses**
RUSSIA
State Anthem of the Russian Federation
(Sergey Mikhalkov / Alexander Alexandrov)

1795   **7 Verses**
FRANCE
La Marseillaise
(Claude Joseph Rouget de Lisle)

1982   **1 Verse**
CHINA
March of the Volunteers
(Tian Han / Nie Er)

1999   **1 Verse**
JAPAN
Kimigayo
(Unknown / Hiromori Hayashi)

1922   **1 Verse**
GERMANY
Deutschlandlied
(August Heinrich Hoffman
von Fallersleben /
Joseph Haydn)

1954   **3 Verses**
PAKISTAN
Qaumi Taranah
(Hafeez Jullundhri / Ahmad G Chagla)

1950   **1 Verse**
INDIA
Jana Gana Mana
(Rabindranath Tagore)

1946   **6 Verses**
ITALY
Il Canto degli Italiani
(Goffredo Mameli / Michele Novaro)

1945   **3 Verses**
INDONESIA
Indonesia Raya
(Wage Rudolf Supratman)

**SAUDI
ARABIA**   **1 Verse**
Sārī
(1984 . Ibrahim Khafaji /
1950 . Abdul Rahman Al-Khateeb)

1984   **2 Verses**
AUSTRALIA
Advance Australia Fair
(Peter Dodds McCormick)

WORLD CUP SONGS

When a football match finishes, the players jog off and head for the showers – the very place where most people who can't sing choose to do so. Which leads us very nicely to World Cup songs. Some are sung by the players themselves on camera, while some players, we imagine, only belt them out in the safety of the post-game shower. There's no known link between football ability and singing prowess, as proven by this selection.

WORLD CUP POSITION

SONG CHART POSITION

○ BETTER THAN TEAM

● WORST THAN TEAM

WINNERS

NUMBER 1

(W) #1

2014
Germany
Auf Uns

#1

1962
Chile
El Rock del Mundial

(Sold over 2 million)

RUNNERS UP

NUMBERS 2-5

(RU)

2010
Holland
Oranje Oranje

#1

1990
England
World in Motion

#3

SEMI-FINALS

NUMBERS 6-15

(SF)

(SF)

#6

Sources: Wikipedia, newyorker.com, thesun.co.uk

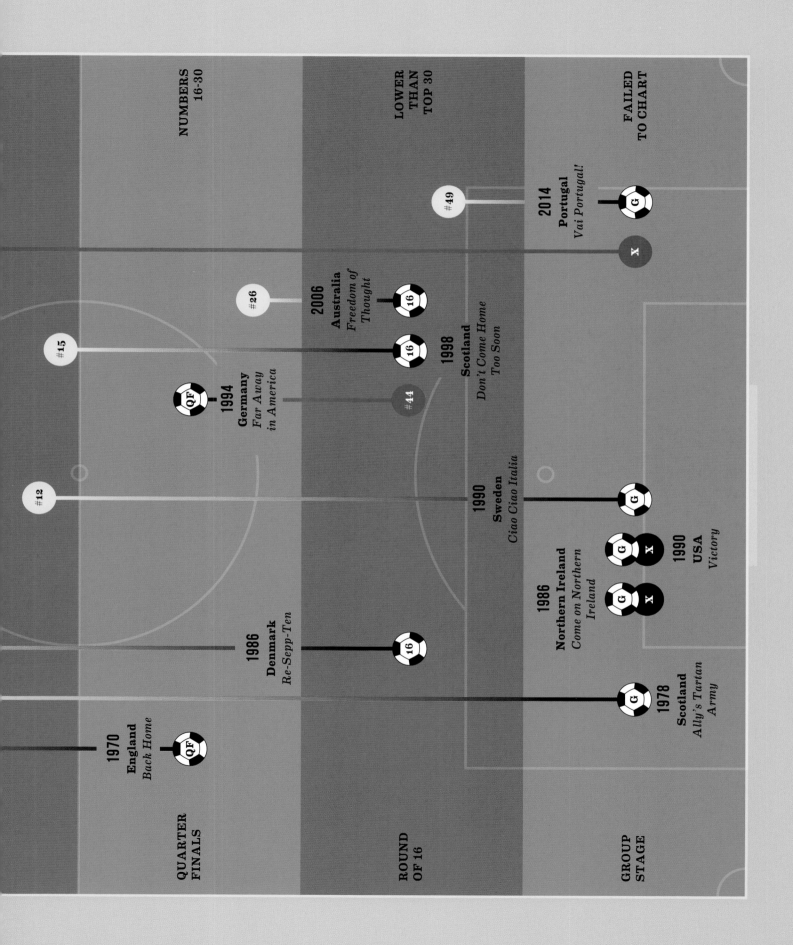

NUMBERS 16-30

LOWER THAN TOP 30

FAILED TO CHART

#49

2014
Portugal
Vai Portugal!

#26

2006
Australia
Freedom of Thought

#15

1998
Scotland
Don't Come Home Too Soon

1994
Germany
Far Away in America

#44

#12

1990
Sweden
Ciao Ciao Italia

1990
USA
Victory

1986
Northern Ireland
Come on Northern Ireland

1986
Denmark
Re-Sepp-Ten

1978
Scotland
Ally's Tartan Army

1970
England
Back Home

QUARTER FINALS

ROUND OF 16

GROUP STAGE

•63

GOING IT ALONE

Leaving the comfort of a group is a tough decision to make, especially when the band you are leaving has been a major hit. Sometimes it works and even releases extra energy but it can also be very lonely and unsuccessful. Can you escape the baggage of the group and create your own identity or will you be forever linked to your ex-band mates? Below are a few of the more successful.

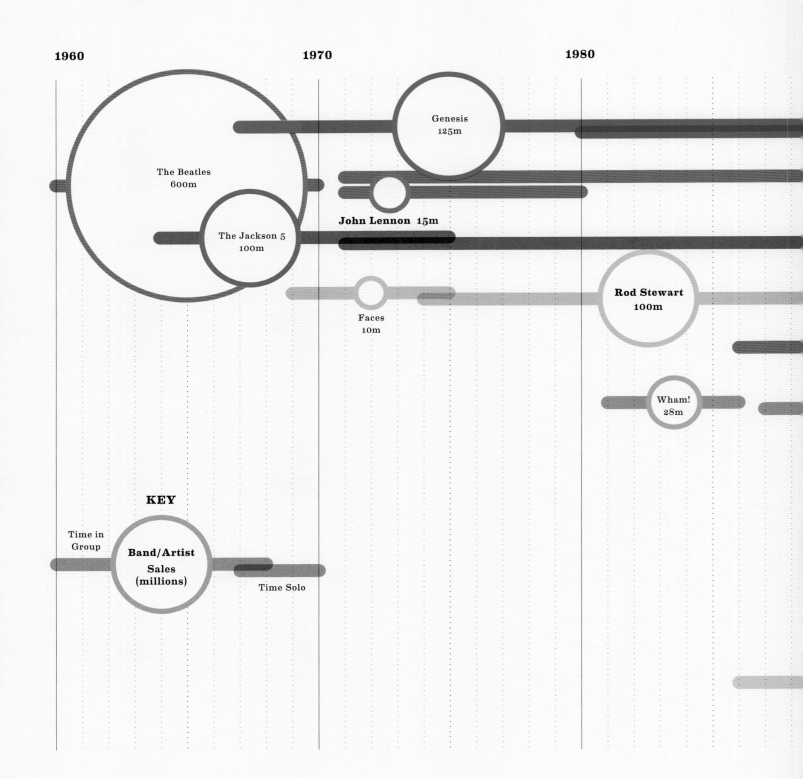

1960

1970

1980

The Beatles
600m

Genesis
125m

The Jackson 5
100m

John Lennon 15m

Faces
10m

Rod Stewart
100m

Wham!
28m

KEY

Time in
Group

**Band/Artist
Sales
(millions)**

Time Solo

Sources: Wikipedia, newyorker.com, thesun.co.uk

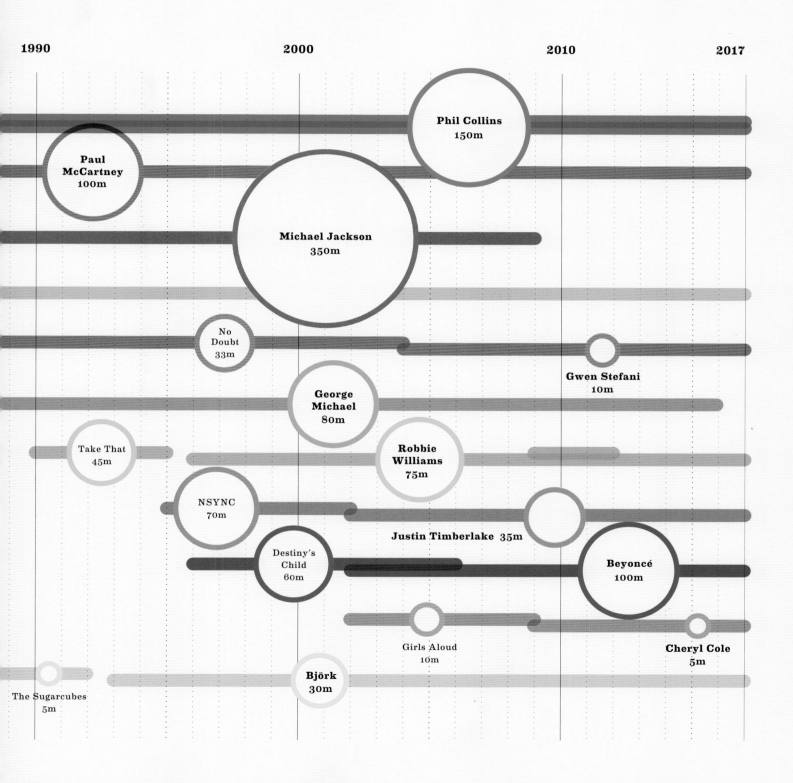

1990   2000   2010   2017

Phil Collins 150m

Paul McCartney 100m

Michael Jackson 350m

No Doubt 33m

Gwen Stefani 10m

George Michael 80m

Take That 45m

Robbie Williams 75m

NSYNC 70m

Justin Timberlake 35m

Destiny's Child 60m

Beyoncé 100m

Girls Aloud 10m

Cheryl Cole 5m

Björk 30m

The Sugarcubes 5m

THE ROOTS OF THE "NEW CLASSICAL"

The December 2016 issue of *Uncut* magazine ran a feature on the "new classical", explaining how a punk and/or an independent ethos had brought together a collective scene of classical musicians capable of filling concert halls with fans of indie music. Here's a timeline of 30 years of the slow percolation of a classical sensibility into "indie", ambient and electronica.

1985

4AD records of west London, home to a distinctive strain of ethereal ambient goth (the Cocteau Twins, This Mortal Coil, The Birthday Party) release *Spleen and Ideal* by Dead Can Dance: "Lisa Gerrard's voice cut through the massed choral drift like a galleon emerging through the fog'.*

1993

Elvis Costello teams up with the Brodsky Quartet on the CD *The Juliet Letters*.

1995

Tindersticks play the Bloomsbury Theatre, London, with a full orchestra (including 14 violins, 6 violas and 4 cellos).

Rachel's, a US post-hardcore "chamber group" formed from the ashes of Louisville Kentucky post-hardcore band Rodan, release their debut LP, *Handwriting*, on Quarterstick records.

The debut Stars of the Lid CD, *Music for Nitrous Oxide*, an album of lengthy ambient electronic drone pieces, possesses a stately, classical undertone.

1997

Stars of the Lid's *The Ballasted Orchestra* released.

Godspeed You! Black Emperor, a Montreal collective, release an apocalyptic record of spoken word, and mournful strings, *F# A#∞*.

1986

Former BBC newsreader-turned-Radio 4 DJ Richard Baker can't stop playing a 4AD promo 7" single, "Poleganala E Todora" by Le Mystère Des Voix Bulgares, the Bulgarian State Radio and Television Female Choir.

Harold Budd introduces piano to the Cocteau Twins on their collaborative LP, *The Moon and the Melodies*.

1994

The compilation CD from the late-night Radio 3 programme *Mixing It* features Conlon Nancarrow and the Penguin Café Orchestra alongside the Royal Stockholm Philharmonic Orchestra and the Aphex Twin.

Jan Garbarek and The Hilliard Ensemble's *Officium*, chamber jazz reworking of Gregorian chant, achieves crossover appeal, selling upwards of 1.5 million copies for "jazz" label ECM.

1996

Rachel's *Music for Egon Schiele* and *The Sea and the Bells* released.

Harold Budd and Hector Zazou's album of drifting ambient piano, spoken-word samples and jazzy trip-hop-style beats, *Glyph*, is given a drum & bass remix.

1998

Stockholm-based chamber orchestra, the Nàu Ensemble release *The Eternal: Variations on Joy Division*, a "suite of loose adaptations" of the themes and atmospheres of Joy Division's "Eternal", "Atmosphere" and "Decades".

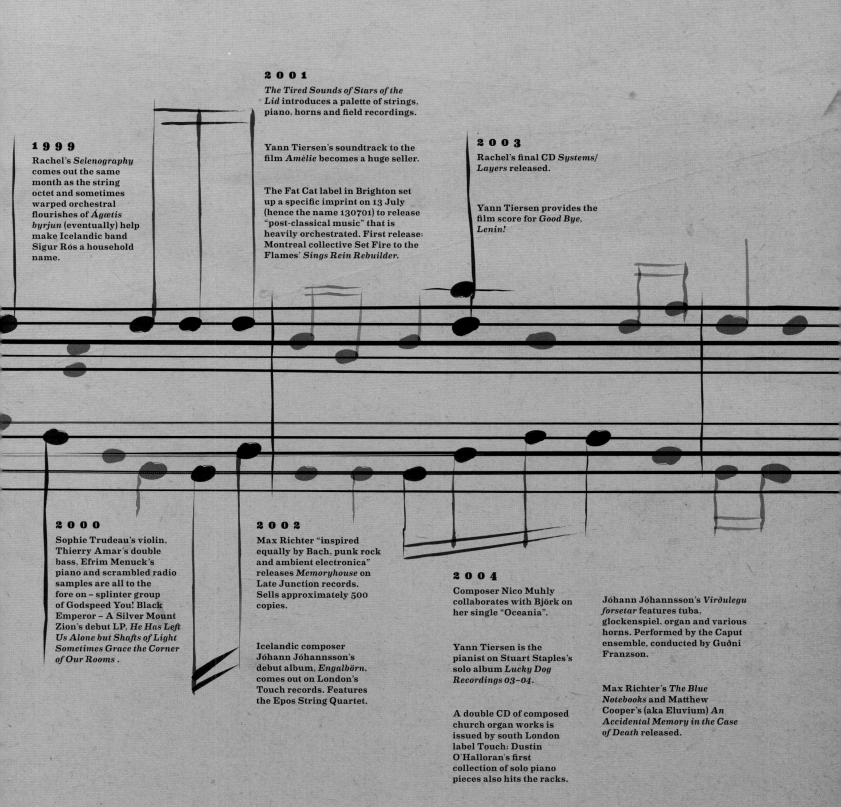

Sources: *Facing the Other Way: the Story of 4AD*, Martin Aston (2013), The Friday Project/HarperCollins)*,
secondlanguagemusic.com†, *Uncut* magazine, bedroomcommunity.net, thequietus.com, brainwashed.com,
fat-cat.co.uk, theartsdesk.com

2001

The Tired Sounds of Stars of the Lid introduces a palette of strings, piano, horns and field recordings.

Yann Tiersen's soundtrack to the film *Amèlie* becomes a huge seller.

The Fat Cat label in Brighton set up a specific imprint on 13 July (hence the name 130701) to release "post-classical music" that is heavily orchestrated. First release: Montreal collective Set Fire to the Flames' *Sings Rein Rebuilder.*

1999

Rachel's *Selenography* comes out the same month as the string octet and sometimes warped orchestral flourishes of *Ágætis byrjun* (eventually) help make Icelandic band Sigur Rós a household name.

2003

Rachel's final CD *Systems/Layers* released.

Yann Tiersen provides the film score for *Good Bye, Lenin!*

2000

Sophie Trudeau's violin, Thierry Amar's double bass, Efrim Menuck's piano and scrambled radio samples are all to the fore on – splinter group of Godspeed You! Black Emperor – A Silver Mount Zion's debut LP, *He Has Left Us Alone but Shafts of Light Sometimes Grace the Corner of Our Rooms* .

2002

Max Richter "inspired equally by Bach, punk rock and ambient electronica" releases *Memoryhouse* on Late Junction records. Sells approximately 500 copies.

Icelandic composer Jóhann Jóhannsson's debut album, *Engalbörn*, comes out on London's Touch records. Features the Epos String Quartet.

2004

Composer Nico Muhly collaborates with Björk on her single "Oceania".

Yann Tiersen is the pianist on Stuart Staples's solo album *Lucky Dog Recordings 03–04.*

A double CD of composed church organ works is issued by south London label Touch: Dustin O'Halloran's first collection of solo piano pieces also hits the racks.

Jóhann Jóhannsson's *Virðulegu forsetar* features tuba, glockenspiel, organ and various horns. Performed by the Caput ensemble, conducted by Guðni Franzson.

Max Richter's *The Blue Notebooks* and Matthew Cooper's (aka Eluvium) *An Accidental Memory in the Case of Death* released.

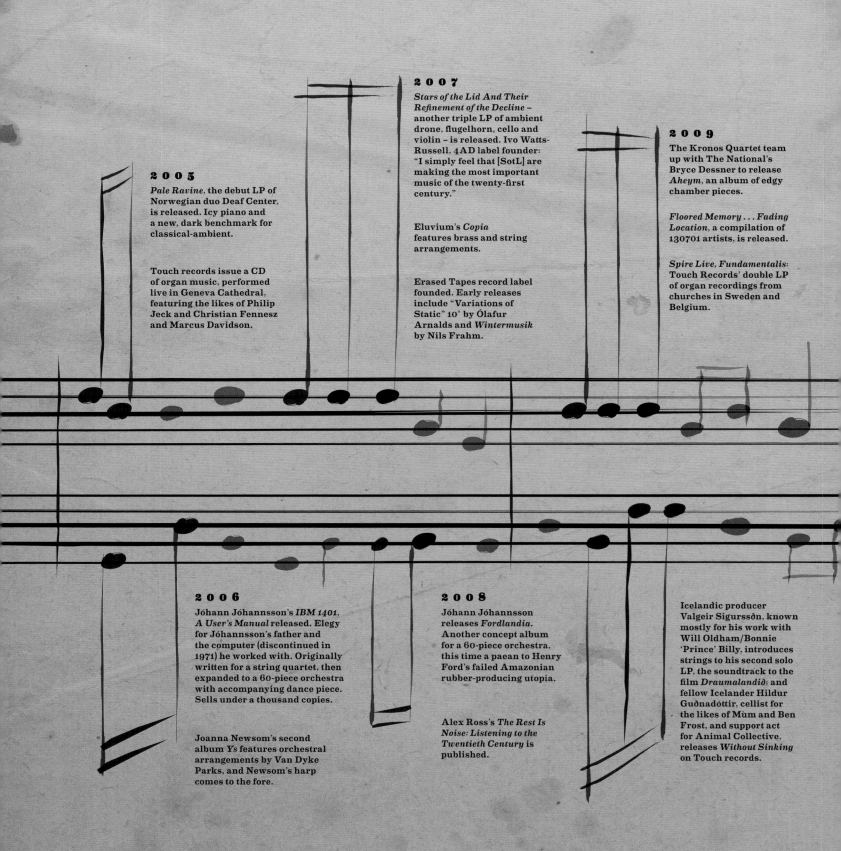

2 0 0 5

Pale Ravine, the debut LP of Norwegian duo Deaf Center, is released. Icy piano and a new, dark benchmark for classical-ambient.

Touch records issue a CD of organ music, performed live in Geneva Cathedral, featuring the likes of Philip Jeck and Christian Fennesz and Marcus Davidson.

2 0 0 7

Stars of the Lid And Their Refinement of the Decline – another triple LP of ambient drone, flugelhorn, cello and violin – is released. Ivo Watts-Russell, 4AD label founder: "I simply feel that [SotL] are making the most important music of the twenty-first century."

Eluvium's *Copia* features brass and string arrangements.

Erased Tapes record label founded. Early releases include "Variations of Static" 10" by Ólafur Arnalds and *Wintermusik* by Nils Frahm.

2 0 0 9

The Kronos Quartet team up with The National's Bryce Dessner to release *Aheym*, an album of edgy chamber pieces.

Floored Memory . . . Fading Location, a compilation of 130701 artists, is released.

Spire Live, Fundamentalis: Touch Records' double LP of organ recordings from churches in Sweden and Belgium.

2 0 0 6

Jóhann Jóhannsson's *IBM 1401, A User's Manual* released. Elegy for Jóhannsson's father and the computer (discontinued in 1971) he worked with. Originally written for a string quartet, then expanded to a 60-piece orchestra with accompanying dance piece. Sells under a thousand copies.

Joanna Newsom's second album *Ys* features orchestral arrangements by Van Dyke Parks, and Newsom's harp comes to the fore.

2 0 0 8

Jóhann Jóhannsson releases *Fordlandia*. Another concept album for a 60-piece orchestra, this time a paean to Henry Ford's failed Amazonian rubber-producing utopia.

Alex Ross's *The Rest Is Noise: Listening to the Twentieth Century* is published.

Icelandic producer Valgeir Sigurssðn, known mostly for his work with Will Oldham/Bonnie 'Prince' Billy, introduces strings to his second solo LP, the soundtrack to the film *Draumalandið*; and fellow Icelander Hildur Guðnadóttir, cellist for the likes of Mùm and Ben Frost, and support act for Animal Collective, releases *Without Sinking* on Touch records.

2010

Pianist David Moore assembles a Brooklyn-based ensemble of 11 players to record Bing and Ruth's debut album *City Lake*.

Featuring acoustic and electric guitars and vintage synthesizers, Yann Tiersen's *Dust Lane* completes the new classical-rock crossover – albeit in the other direction.

2011

Jóhann Jóhannsson's soundtrack to Bill Morrison's film of archival footage, *The Miners' Hymns,* features a brass orchestra recorded in Durham Cathedral.

2013

Nils Frahm's live collection, *Spaces*, propels the Hamburg-born pianist onto the arena circuit. Where he once played London's Café Oto, he now fills the Barbican.

2015

Max Richter releases *Sleep*, an eight-hour suite that goes on to be performed in real time overnight in various concert venues from Berlin to London to the Sydney Opera House.

Nils Frahm's soundtrack *Music from the Motion Picture Victoria*, and Mary Lattimore's contemporary harp albums *Luciferin' Light* and *At the Dam* see the light of day.

Áine O'Dwyer's *Music for Church Cleaners, Volumes I & II* is re-released on MIE records. Features O'Dwyer's improvised pipe-organ pieces and the cleaners of St Mark's church, Islington, enjoying the music while they work.

2012

Joanna Newsom becomes indie rock's most famous harpist with the release of the triple album *Have One on Me*.

A Young Person's Guide to Kyle Bobby Dunn, piano and classical instrumentation processed into lengthy ambient drone pieces by Canadian composer Kyle Bobby Dunn, and *Celestial King for a Year*, for voice, strings and electronics, by Richard Moult, a composer and painter based in the Outer Hebrides, are released.

The 40-piece London Contemporary Orchestra perform *The Disintegration Loops* live, the ambient tape music of New York musician William Basinski, at the Royal Festival Hall, London.

Hildur Guðnadóttir plays cello as A Winged Victory for the Sullen (Adam Wiltzie and pianist Dustin Halloran) complete their set at London's Cecil Sharp House with a rendition of Arvo Pärt's "Fratres for Cello and Piano".

Michael Tanner's The Cloisters, a self-titled CD on Second Language featuring harp, cello and church harmonium, was "conceived during a time of deep personal dissatisfaction with the drone/ambient/classical/minimalist 'scene' – one seemingly populated by the same 30 blokes making the same music, more often than not sporting the same beard."‡

2014

Pinô by Otto A Totland, Satie-like solo piano released on Sonic Pieces from Berlin.

2016

France becomes the home of "new classical" solo piano works: Christine Ott, *Only Silence Remains*; Jean Michel-Blais, *II*; and Yann Tiersen, *Eusa* (an album of solo piano and field recordings from Tiersen's Breton island home).

From New York label Temporary Residence, Eluvium's *False Readings On* features operatic vocals.

"Another band formed in art school" has almost become a cliche when writing about music. Of course, by no means all bands did – just take a look at the Musicians' Other Jobs graphic for evidence of that. Judas Priest's Glenn Tipton said of his own "Heavy Metal" upbringing in a metal-works factory, "The factory I worked in was a massive steelwork labyrinth, riddled with polluted canals, massive grimy workshops, foundries and steam hammers. It doesn't take a great leap of imagination to realise why metal ended up sounding the way it did."*

But while British death metal stalwarts Bolt Thrower may have formed in a Coventry pub toilet, far more bands and musicians have learned their trade in a somewhat more genteel setting. Here's something of a breakdown of the roots of art school musicians.

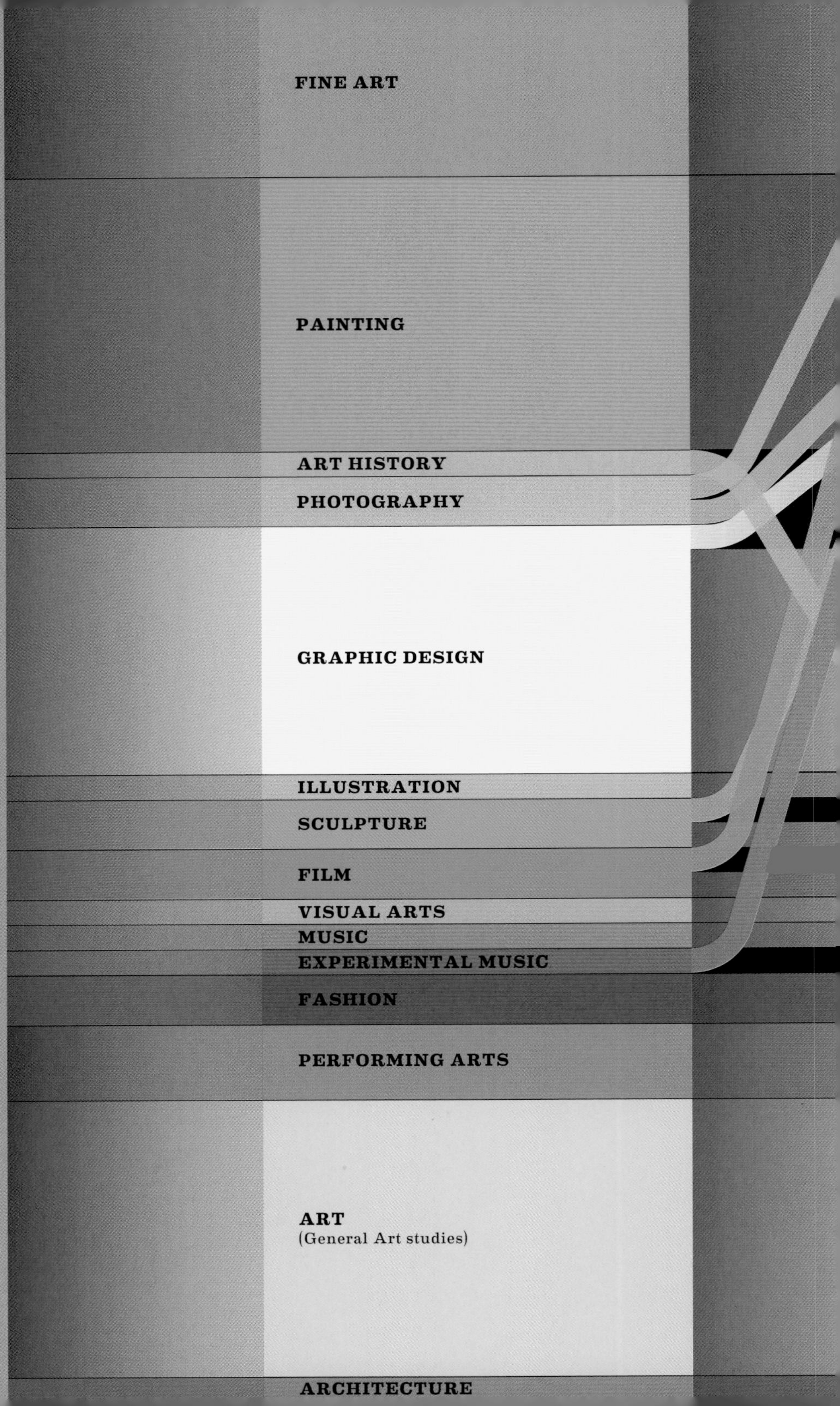

FINE ART

PAINTING

ART HISTORY

PHOTOGRAPHY

GRAPHIC DESIGN

ILLUSTRATION

SCULPTURE

FILM

VISUAL ARTS

MUSIC

EXPERIMENTAL MUSIC

FASHION

PERFORMING ARTS

ART
(General Art studies)

ARCHITECTURE

Bryan Ferry | Roxy Music | *Newcastle College of Art*

Michael Chapman | Musician | *Leeds University*

Jarvis Cocker | Pulp | *Central St Martins*

Gerald Casale, Mark Mothersbaugh | Devo | *Kent State University art school*

Florence Welch | Florence and the Machine | *Camberwell College of Arts*

Graham Coxon | Blur | *Goldsmiths College*

Green Gartside, Tom Morley | Scritti Politti | *Leeds Polytechnic*

David Byrne, Chris Frantz, Tina Weymouth | Talking Heads | *Rhode Island School of Design*

Brian Eno | Roxy Music | *Ipswich Art School and Winchester School of Art*

Bob Hardy | Franz Ferdinand | *Glasgow School of Art*

Syd Barrett | Pink Floyd | *Cambridge Technical College and Camberwell College of Arts*

Michael Stipe | R.E.M. | *University of Georgia*

Georgia Hubley | Yo La Tengo | *Maryland Institute College of Art*

Paul Simonon | The Clash | *Byam Shaw School of Art*

John Lennon | The Beatles | *Liverpool College of Art*

Jimmy Page | Led Zeppelin | *Sutton Art College*

Joni Mitchell | Singer-songwriter | *Alberta College of Art*

Billy Childish | Musician | *Central St Martins*

Chuck D | Rapper | *Adelphi University*

Toro Y Moi | Singer-songwriter | *University of South Carolina*

Freddie Mercury | Queen | *Ealing Art College*

Pete Townshend | The Who | *Ealing Art College*

Ronnie Wood | The Rolling Stones | *Ealing Art College*

Keith Richards | The Rolling Stones | *Sidcup Art College*

Charlie Watts | The Rolling Stones | *Harrow Art School*

Adam Ant | Adam and the Ants | *Hornsey College of Art*

Kano | Rapper | *Barking College*

Faris Badwan | The Horrors | *Central St Martins*

Laurie Anderson | Musician/Composer | *Barnard College and Columbia University*

MIA | Singer-songwriter | *Central St Martins*

PJ Harvey | Singer-songwriter | *Yeovil Art College*

John Cale | Velvet Underground | *Goldsmiths College*

A$AP Ferg | Rapper | *High School of Art & Design, Manhattan*

Sade | Singer-songwriter | *Central St Martins*

Marc Almond | Soft Cell | *Leeds Polytechnic*

2Pac | Rapper | *Baltimore School of Arts*

Nicki Minaj | Rapper/Singer | *La Guardia High School*

David Bowie | Singer-songwriter | *Bromley Technical High School*

Joe Strummer | The Clash | *Central School of Art & Design*

Mick Jones | The Clash | *Hammersmith School of Art*

Ray Davies | The Kinks | *Hornsey College of Art*

Malcolm Mclaren | Musician/Manager | *Central St Martins and Goldsmiths College (among others)*

Viv Stanshall | Singer-songwriter | *Central St Martins*

Eric Clapton | Cream | *Kingston College of Art*

Jerry Dammers | The Specials | *Lanchester Polytechnic*

Patti Smith | Singer-songwriter | *Glassboro State College*

Dougie Payne, Fran Healy, Andy Dunlop | Travis | *Glasgow School of Art*

Andy Gill, Jon King | Gang of Four | *Leeds University*

Ice Cube | Rapper | *Phoenix Institute of Technology*

of the canvass and you can't judge a song by its length. Of course
anyway. Bing Crosby's "White Christmas" is the best-selling single
ads, it is probably the perfect length. The longest single to top the
und the World", coming in at 9 minutes 38 seconds. It's worth noting
all came out in 1959. Was there a vinyl shortage?

Best-selling Singles

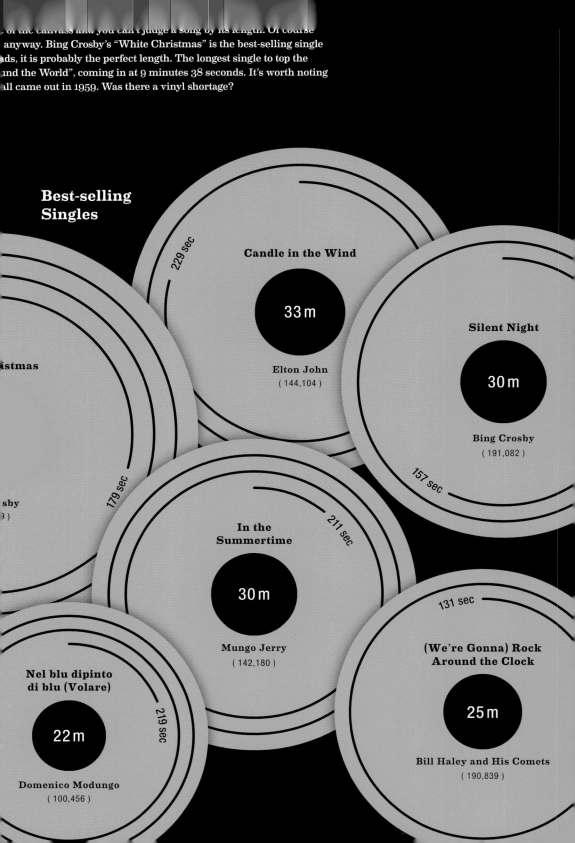

229 sec

Candle in the Wind

33 m

Elton John
(144,104)

istmas

Silent Night

30 m

Bing Crosby
(191,082)

157 sec

sby
))

179 sec

In the Summertime

211 sec

30 m

Mungo Jerry
(142,180)

131 sec

(We're Gonna) Rock Around the Clock

25 m

Bill Haley and His Comets
(190,839)

Nel blu dipinto di blu (Volare)

219 sec

22 m

Domenico Modungo
(100,456)

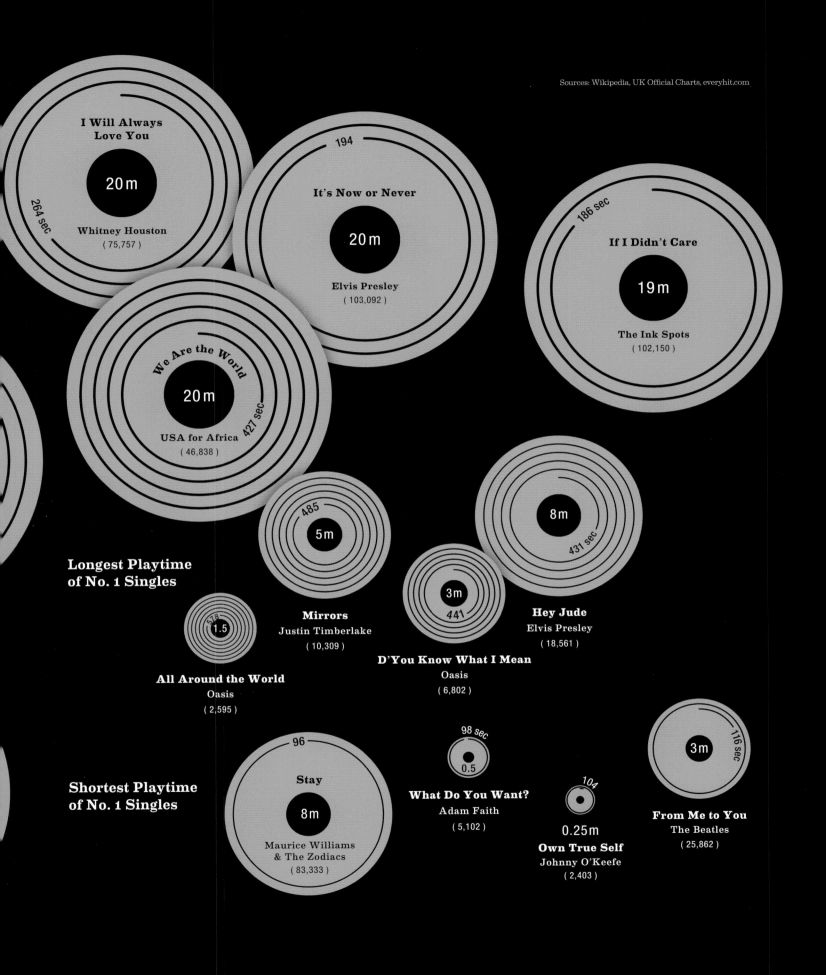

I Will Always Love You

20m

264 sec

Whitney Houston
(75,757)

194

It's Now or Never

20m

Elvis Presley
(103,092)

186 sec

If I Didn't Care

19m

The Ink Spots
(102,150)

We Are the World

20m

427 sec

USA for Africa
(46,838)

485

5m

Mirrors
Justin Timberlake
(10,309)

8m

431 sec

Hey Jude
Elvis Presley
(18,561)

3m

441

D'You Know What I Mean
Oasis
(6,802)

Longest Playtime of No. 1 Singles

1.5

All Around the World
Oasis
(2,595)

Shortest Playtime of No. 1 Singles

96

Stay

8m

Maurice Williams
& The Zodiacs
(83,333)

98 sec

What Do You Want?
Adam Faith
(5,102)

0.5

104

0.25m

Own True Self
Johnny O'Keefe
(2,403)

116 sec

3m

From Me to You
The Beatles
(25,862)

GET YOUR GROOVE ON

The Beatles' *Sgt. Pepper's Lonely Hearts Club Band* was a ground-breaking album in many ways, one of which came right at the very end. On the inner groove of side two, the Fab Four laid down a repeating message: "never could see any other way". Not a hidden track as such, but a little treat. Since then easter eggs, as they have become known, have cropped up regularly. Some are well hidden and others are hiding in plain sight.

Sources: Wikipedia, eeggs.com, whatculture.com, bbc.co.uk, discogs.com, beatlesbible.com

	ARTIST	RECORD	WHAT IS THE HIDDEN MESSAGE/TRACK	WHERE ON TRACK	HOW TO PLAY IT
01	Ozzy Osbourne	Bloodbath in Paradise	Your mother sells whelks in Hull.	0.05	Backwards
02	Nelly Furtado	Big Hoops	Oh my God! Descending to the 13th floor, 14th, descending to the 12th floor.	Intermittent throughout	Backwards
03	Franz Ferdinand	Michael	She's worried about you. Call your mother.	1.34	Backwards
04	Moby	Machete	I have to say goodbye.	1.40	Backwards
05	Chumbawamba	Look! No Strings!	Oh fuck me, Jesus.	5.00	Backwards
06	Frank Zappa	Hot Poop	Better look around before you say you don't care. Shut your fucking mouth about the length of my hair. How would you survive if you were alive, shitty little person?	0.16	Backwards
07	Weird Al Yankovic	Nature Trail to Hell	Satan Eats Cheese Whiz.	3.41	Backwards
08	ELO	Fire on High	The music is reversible but time i not. Turn back!	0.26	Backwards
09	Pink Floyd	Empty Spaces	Congratulations, you've just discovered the secret message. Please send your answer to Old Pink, care of the funny farm, Chalfont.	1.15	Backwards
10	The Beatles	Rain	The sun shines. Rain. When the rain comes, they run and hide their heads.	2.55	Backwards
11	Nirvana	Nevermind	Endless, Nameless.	End of the album	After 10 minutes, silence
12	The Adverts	Crossing the Red Sea with the Adverts	Gary Gilmore's eyes, bored teenagers, safety in numbers and we who wait	At the start of the album	Before the first official track
13	Ben Folds Five	Song for the Dumped	Argument ending with "shut the fuck up".	Before the track starts	Sound is kept low
14	Ben Folds Five	Whatever and Ever Amen	I've got your hidden track right here, Ben Folds is a fucking asshole.	At the start of the album	Before the first official track
15	The Beatles	Abbey Road	Her Majesty.	End of album after 18" of silence	Unlisted
16	The Beatles	Sgt. Pepper's Lonely Hearts Club Band	Never could see any other way.	At the end of side two	On the inner groove, repeats ad infinitum
17	Avril Lavigne	Goodbye Lullaby	Alice (Extended Version).	End of the album	After a minute's silence following the track "Goodbye"
18	David Bowie	Blackstar	Galaxy of stars.	The vinyl album cover	Revealed when left in the sun

POP OF THE POPS

Where would we be without charts? When musicians compose songs, they just want to make music people want to listen to but, inevitably, there comes a point where they look to the top 10 and dream of making it. There are charts all over the world, the earliest of which was based on sales of sheet music, whilst the latest are a combination of downloads, vinyl and CD sales, and various other measures.

Sources: officialcharts.com, westword.com, poparchives.com, lanet.lv, radio2.be, wikipedia, bac-lac.gc.ca, olt20.com, www.top40.nl, chartsaroundtheworld.com

NEWEST CHARTS

COUNTRY	FIRST CHART	FIRST NUMBER 1	LONGEST NUMBER 1
Russia	23 Nov 2003	Via Gra & Valery Meladze *Okean i Tri Reki (Ocean and three Rivers)*	6 WEEKS **LOBODA** *40 градусов (40 Degrees)*
Sweden	14 Nov 1975	George Baker Selection *Paloma Blanca (White Dove)*	20 WEEKS **Baccara** *Yes Sir, I Can Boogie*
Belgium	2 May 1970	Norman Greenbaum *Spirit in the Sky*	16 WEEKS **Fixkes** *Kvraagetaan (I Request)*
Japan	2 Nov 1967	Jackey Yoshikawa & his Blue Comets *Kitaguni no Futari (In a Lonesome City)*	16 WEEKS **Shiro Miya** *Onna no Michi (The Way of a Woman)*
Australia	5 Oct 1966	The Beatles *Yellow Submarine/Eleanor Rigby*	15 WEEKS **Ed Sheeran** *Shape of You*
Netherlands	2 Jan 1965	The Beatles *I Feel Fine*	15 WEEKS **Ed Sheeran** *Shape of You*

COUNTRY		FIRST CHART		FIRST NUMBER 1		LONGEST NUMBER 1
Canada		**1 Sep 1964**		**Supremes** *Where Did Our Love Go*		**The Black Eyed Peas** *I Gotta Feeling* — 16 WEEKS
Ireland		**1 Oct 1962**		**Elvis Presley** *She's Not You*		**Bill Whelan** *Riverdance* — 18 WEEKS
Spain		**5 Jan 1959**		**Ana Maria Parra** *Las Chicas de la Cruz Roja (The Red Cross Girls)*		**Carlos Baute ft. Marta Sachez** *Colgando en Tus Manos (Hanging in Your Hands)* — 27 WEEKS
Italy		**20 Dec 1958**		**Domenico Modugno** *Io (the)*		**Vasco Rossi. Vasco** *Extended Play* — 21 WEEKS
France		**5 Oct 1955**		**Jacqueline Francois** *Les Lavandières du Portugal*		**Pharrell Williams** *Happy* — 22 WEEKS
Germany		**Dec 1953**		**Kilima Hawaiians** *There Is a Horse Halter Hanging on the Wall*		**Boney M.** *Rivers of Babylon* — 17 WEEKS
UK		**14 Nov 1952**		**Al Martino** *Here in My Heart*		**Frankie Laine** *I Believe* — 18 WEEKS
USA		**4 Jan 1936**		**Joe Venuti** *Stop, Look and Listen*		**Mariah Carey and Boyz II Men** *One Sweet Day* — 16 WEEKS

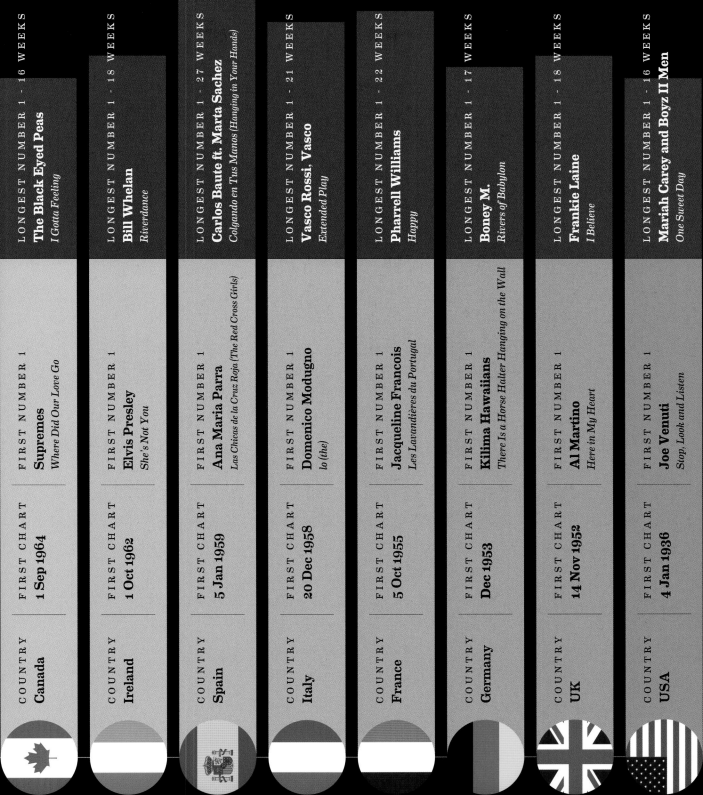

INTERESTING RADIO STATIONS ACROSS AMERICA

At the 1912 international conference on 'Radiotelegraphs', America was awarded the call signs 'W', 'K', 'A' and 'N'. The latter two were assigned to the military. W and K were awarded for commercial radio stations and, henceforth, affixed to a mind-boggling number of acronyms – W for radio stations to the east of the Mississippi; K for those to the west. It's impossible to list all 13- to 14,000 radio stations broadcasting in America, but here are a few interesting stations for anyone travelling across the country. (Warning for European listeners: many of these stations are community funded – i.e. they will most likely be attempting to secure your 'pledge' with alarming regularity. But once you get over that, there are musical treasures to be mined.)

WNUR 89.3 FM
Chicago, Illinois
Founded: 1950 / Facebook likes: 3,988
Chicago's sound experiment: freeform station.
Sample: jazz all morning, more underground rock and experimental sounds as the sun crosses the yardarm. Breakfast with Coleman Hawkins and the Bill Evans trio; evening meal with Ryley Walker, Fennesz, Sonic Youth and Yo La Tengo. Saturday afternoon: Milton Babbitt "String Quartet-No.2" and DJ Senseless "Sex with a Robot"

KUPS 90.1 FM
University of Puget Sound,
Seattle, Washington
Founded: 1968
Facebook likes: 2,380

KAOS 89.3 FM
Olympia, Washington
Founded: 1973
Facebook likes: 4,290

KEXP 90.3 FM
Seattle, Washington
Founded: 1972
Facebook likes: 324,455
Cutting edge indie from the University of Washington

KOSW 91.3 FM
Ocean Shores, Washington
Founded: 2004
Facebook likes: 348

KBOO Community Radio 90.7 FM
Portland, Oregon
Founded: 1968 / Facebook likes: 16,903
Sample: nice music mix. From Queen Makedah to Townes van Zandt and Patti Smith. Also, intense current affairs discussion of post-capitalist life

KCOU 88.1 FM
University of Missouri, Missouri
Founded: 1963 / Facebook likes: 4,535
Sample: Miles Davis's, "Drad Dog" followed by "You Gotta Fight for Your Right to Party", by the Beastie Boys; simultaneously an intense discussion of college football on the sports stream

KWVA 88.1 FM
University of Oregon, Oregon
Founded: 1993 / Facebook likes: 2,580
Sample: playing the Beastie Boys, Talking Heads and Throbbing Gristle through the night; programmes include *Banjo for Breakfast*, presented by Banjo Tony, *Trout Fishing in Eugene*: *Please Forgive Me for My Synths*: the *No Pants Party*, presented by Billy Dibble, and *Blood on the Saddle* presented by the Kranky Kowboy

KRCC 91.5 FM
Colorado Springs, Colorado
Founded: 1951 / Facebook likes: 6,372
NPR station of documentaires TED radio hour and carries the BBC World Service in the middle of the night

KUSF 90.3 FM
San Francisco, California
Founded: 1963-2011 / Facebook likes: 1,285
Since 2011 run "in exile" as an online only station

KRSC 91.3 FM
Tulsa, Oklahoma
Founded: 1985 / Facebook likes: 2,618
Sample programmes: *Hillbilly Happy Hour*, *Bluegrass on the Hill*, *Rude Boy Radio* and *Riot Radio*

KCSB 91.5 FM
Santa Barbara, California
Founded: 1961 / Facebook likes: 5,114

KCRW 89.9 FM
Santa Monica, Southern California
Founded: 1945 / Facebook likes: 191,909
Sample: famous for the *Morning Becomes Eclectic* show, anything and everything from Al Dobson Jnr, Chance the Rapper, Thundercat and Bjork

KOOP 91.7 FM
Austin, Texas
Founded: 1994
Facebook likes: 5,349
Community station features crate-digging and a show of oddities picked up at thrift stores

KOPO 88.9 FM
Hawaii
Founded: 2006
No Facebook page. Folk, funk, rap, reggae, punk and rock

KVRX 91.7 FM
Austin, Texas
Founded: 1994 / Facebook likes: 8,416
Student-run station takes over from KOOP in the evenings – "None of the hits all of the time"

Sources: pastemagazine.com, wow247.co.uk, pigeonsandplanes.com, indieonthemove.com, primermagazine.com. Data correct as of April 2017.

GENRES

BLUES • COUNTRY • BLUEGRASS • PUNK • METAL • ROCK • INDIE • ALT ROCK • COLLEGE ROCK • FOLK • LATIN
CLASSICAL • LOUNGE • JAZZ • ROOTS • REGGAE • R'N'B • FUNK • MOTOWN • SOUL • GOSPEL • AFRICAN
DANCEHALL • ECLECTIC • TECHNO • CAJUN • RAP • HIP-HOP • EXPERIMENTAL • UNDERGROUND • BOOKS

KUOM, 100.7 FM
Radio K, Minneapolis, Minnesota
Founded: 1922 / Facebook likes: 9,307
The twin cities are soaked in good music. Afternoon sample:
Silver Apples, Car Seat Headset, Burial and Thundercat

WBMX.com
Chicago, Illinois
Founded: 1981
Facebook likes: 6,205
Old school hip-hop
and Chicago house

WYMS 88.9 FM
Radio Milwaukee, Milwaukee, Wisconsin
Founded: 1973 / Facebook likes: 38,207

WNMC 90.7 FM
Michigan College Radio,
Traverse City, Michigan
Founded: 1967 / Facebook likes: 2,261

WCBN 88.3 FM
University of Michigan,
Ann Arbor, Michigan
Founded: 1952
Facebook likes: 3,908

WOBC 91.5 FM
Cleveland, Ohio
Founded: 1949
Facebook likes: 2,382
Punk, hip-hop, metal
sit alongside classical
broadcasts from the
onsite conservatoire
at Oberlin College

WRUV 90.1 FM
Burlington, Vermont
Founded: 1955 / Facebook likes: 3,041
Sample: Saturday afternoon show
of "downtempo ambient, elevator
music and electronic"

WERS 88.9 FM
Emerson College, Boston
Founded: 1949
Facebook likes: 14,851

WFMU 91.1 FM
East Orange, New Jersey
Founded: 1958
Facebook likes: 62,699
Legendary New Jersey
independent station playing John Cale's
"Paris 1919" on a random listen

**WBGO Jazz Radio
88.3 FM**
Newark, New Jersey
Founded: 1979
Facebook likes: 41,358
Public radio broadcasting
jazz in New York.
Sample: Saturday afternoon
with Milt Jackson, Art
Farmer, Jimmy Smith's
"Got my Mojo Workin'"
and Cannonball Adderley's
"Why Am I Treated So Bad!"

WFHB 91.3 FM
Bloomington, Indiana
Founded: 1993
Facebook likes: 3,803

WVMW 91.7 FM
Scranton, Pennsylvania
Founded: 1975
Facebook likes: 951

WEVL 89.9 FM
Memphis, Tennessee
Founded: 1976
Facebook likes: 8,230

WPTS 92.1 FM
Pittsburgh, Pennsylvania
Founded: 1984
Facebook likes: 4,722

WKDU 91.7 FM
Philadelphia, Pennsylvania
Founded: 1958
Facebook likes: 5,118
Sample: Wednesday afternoon
Philly Jazz Show featured an hour
of music by Lee Morgan; Sunday
morning broadcast, *Metal and
Coffee*; reggae on Saturday nights

WNYU 89.1 FM
New York City, New York
Founded: 1949
Facebook likes: 4,647

Clocktower.org Radio
Brooklyn, New York
Founded: 1972 / Facebook likes: 6,780
Experimental arts, music and theatre
station based in Brooklyn

WBAI 99.5 FM
Free Speech Radio, New York
Founded: 1960 / Facebook likes: 9,490
Sample: random tuning into Sunday
morning discussion of the ethics of
organic chocolate manufacturing

**WRLT Lightning
100.1 FM**
Nashville, Tennessee
Founded: 1986
Facebook likes: 40,051

WNRN 91.9 FM
Charlottesville, Virginia
Founded: 1996 / Facebook likes: 9,020

WXYC 89.3 FM
Chapel Hill, North Carolina
Founded: 1977 / Facebook likes: 4,474
Sample: in amongst the Cajun and
doo-wop Mary Halvorson Octect's
"Spirit Splitter" picked up on a
random listen

WFUV 90.7 FM
New York City, New York
Founded: 1947 / Facebook likes: 40,376
Fordham University station, the Bronx.
Sample: features the likes of Bronx-born
Alynda Segarra of Hurray for the Riff Raff
talking about her favourite Lou Reed song.

WWOZ 90.7 FM
New Orleans, Louisiana
Founded: 1980 / Facebook likes: 89,343
"Guardians of the groove"

WUSC 90.5 FM
University of South Carolina, South Carolina
Founded: 1946 / Facebook likes: 4,069

JANUARY TO DECEMBER

Songs written about specific times, by their nature, are usually about the past. The writer is thinking back to a specific event, a season or moment, which has touched his or her life and left a mark. Because of this, if you listen to the songs detailed here, you will go on a roller-coaster of emotions: from the depths of a dead pet to the highs of a first love.

January

January Git Gilbert O'Sullivan
B-side of the single "Matrimony" which only charted in the Netherlands.

January Pilot
The Scottish rockers' only UK number 1.

January 28th J. Cole
It's the day he was born.

January-February Barbara Dickson
Released in January 1980, it took until April to peak in the charts.

February

February Stars Foo Fighters
Tenth track from the album The Colour and The Shape.

February Winds Billy Talent
From the Canadian band originally known as Pezz.

February Smith & Thell
The duo won Rookie of the Year at the 2015 Denniz Pop Awards.

February Song Josh Groban
The singer was born on the 27th February 1981.

March

March Madness Future
Went gold in the States following its release in 2015.

Waters of March Marisa Monte, David Byrne
This track was for an Aids Benefit album.

The Ides of March Iron Maiden
An instrumental track from the album Killers.

Spring Affair Donna Summer
Part of a concept album about the seasons of the year.

April

April Come She Will Simon & Garfunkel
As well as appearing on Sounds of Silence, it is on the soundtrack of The Graduate.

The April Fools Dionne Warwick
One of five singles released in 1969.

Sometimes It Snows in April Prince
The singer died on 21st April 2016 and, consequently, this song hit the charts around the globe 30 years after its release.

April in Paris Frank Sinatra
A much covered song, Frank's version appears on his Live in Paris album.

May

First of May Bee Gees
Barnaby, Barry Gibb's dog's, birthday.

Autumn to May Peter, Paul and Mary
The B-side to "Don't Think Twice, It's All Right".

My Girl the Month of May Dion & The Belmonts
This single failed to chart in the States but reached number 9 in the UK in 1966.

Night of the 4th of May Al Stewart
This track is about the events surrounding a party Stewart went to with his girlfriend Mandi in 1969.

June

June is Bustin' Out All Over Rodgers and Hammerstein
From Rodgers and Hammerstein's Carousel, definitely about the month, not a character called June.

June Hymn The Decemberists
From the bands only number 1 album, The King is Dead.

June in January Dean Martin
Martin was born on 7th June 1917.

The Last Day of June 1934 Al Stewart
A song about the infamous Night of the Long Knives or Röhm-Putsch.

Sources: Wikipedia, Spotify

July

4th of July, Asbury Park (Sandy) Bruce Springsteen
Asbury Park is a 20-minute drive south from Long Branch, where Springsteen was born and raised.

Cold Day in July Dixie Chicks
The song refers to the type of day it would be when a lover would leave.

June, July, and August Freddy Cannon
This was the B-side to "Palisades Park", and was Freddy's best-selling single.

Hotter than July (Album) Stevie Wonder
This was Wonder's best-performing album in the UK.

August

Time for August Julie London
From her album Calendar Girl, *where every song relates to a different month of the year. Nice idea.*

August October Robin Gibb
A single from Gibb's first album as a solo artist.

August Holland Beirut
The band, named after the city, are from the States.

August Twelve Khruangbin
From Houston, Texas, the band's name means aeroplane (literally engine fly) in Thai.

September

September Morn Neil Diamond
From the eponymous album released in December 1979.

It Might as Well Rain Until September Carole King
King wrote this for Bobbie Vee but he didn't release it as a single. She did and had her biggest UK hit.

September Earth, Wind & Fire
Slightly re-written and re-recorded as "December" for the Holiday album.

September Song JP Cooper
Released in September 2016.

October

October Song Amy Winehouse
Written as a lament about Winehouse's pet canary Ava after it died.

October George Ogilvie
Ogilvie began his music career by uploading videos and songs to Youtube.

October Icarus
Bristol-based brothers Tom and Ian Griffiths.

Autumn Leaves Eva Cassidy
A song written in 1945, it appears on Songbird, *the compilation album released two years after Cassidy's death in 1996.*

November

November Rain Guns N' Roses
Coming in at just under 9 minutes, it is the longest song to get into the Billboard Top Ten.

November Has Come Gorillaz
A cartoon band co-created by Damon Albarn and Jamie Hewlett.

Mr November The National
The group is made up of two sets of brothers who back up the lead singer, Matt Berninger.

Gone Till November Wyclef Jean
Bob Dylan makes a silent appearance in the video for this single.

December

December, 1963 (Oh What a Night!) The Four Seasons
The original title was 5th December 1933 and, rather than a song about early love, it was about the repeal of Prohibition.

Cold December Night Michael Bublé
The twelfth track on Bublé's 2011 Christmas album.

December Ariane Grande
Released in December 2015 on Grande's Christmas & Chill album.

Merry X'mas Everybody Slade
Although the title of the song has the word X'mas, the lyrics employ the full word on what is the greatest Christmas song of all time. The "S" of X'mas is reversed on the cover and label of the original single.

THE PIRATE RADIO STATIONS
OF 1980S AND 1990S LONDON

From the 1970s to the dawn of the Internet, there were hundreds
of pirate radio stations in London, often moving decks and
transmitters every couple of weeks to stay ahead of the authorities.
Here's a sound map of some of the most vital. Some are recalled
from fond memories of moving to south London in the late 1980s;
others are taken from the definitive account of pirate radio in
London in the 1970s and 1980s: Stephen
Hebditch's *London's Pirate Pioneers*.

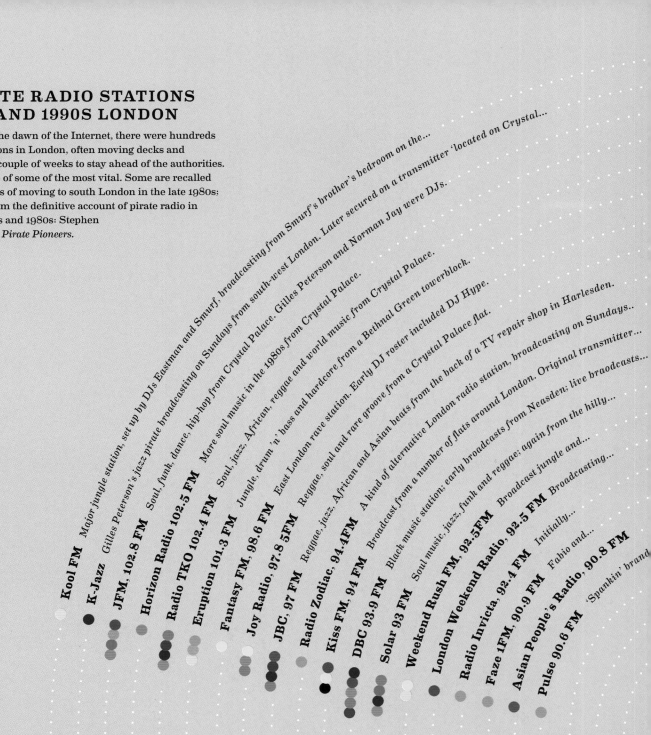

Kool FM Major jungle station, set up by DJs Eastman and Smurf, broadcasting from Smurf's brother's bedroom on the...

K-Jazz Gilles Peterson's jazz pirate broadcasting on Sundays from south-west London. Later secured on a transmitter 'located on Crystal...

JFM, 102.8 FM Soul, funk, dance, hip-hop from Crystal Palace. Gilles Peterson and Norman Jay were DJs.

Horizon Radio 102.5 FM More soul music in the 1980s from Crystal Palace.

Radio TKO 102.4 FM Soul, jazz, African, reggae and world music from Crystal Palace.

Eruption 101.3 FM Jungle, drum 'n' bass and hardcore from a Bethnal Green towerblock.

Fantasy FM, 98.6 FM East London rave station. Early DJ roster included DJ Hype.

Joy Radio, 97.8 5FM Reggae, jazz, African and rare groove from a Crystal Palace flat.

JBC, 97 FM Reggae, jazz, African and Asian beats from the back of a TV repair shop in Harlesden.

Radio Zodiac, 94.4FM A kind of alternative London radio station, broadcasting on Sundays..

Kiss FM, 94 FM Broadcast from a number of flats around London. Original transmitter...

DBC 93.9 FM Black music station; early broadcasts from Neasden; live braodcasts...

Solar 93 FM Soul music, jazz, funk and reggae; again from the hilly...

Weekend Rush FM, 92-5FM Broadcast jungle and...

London Weekend Radio, 92.5FM Broadcasting...

Radio Invicta, 92.4 FM Initially...

Faze 1FM, 90.9 FM Fabio and...

Asian People's Radio. 90.8 FM Broadcasting...

Pulse 90.6 FM 'Spankin' brand

G E N R E S

● JAZZ ● SOUL ● REGGAE ● FUNK
○ JUNGLE ● ECLECTIC ○ RAVE ● DRUM 'N' BASS
● HIP-HOP ● AFRICAN ● ASIAN

Sources:
Wikipedia, thepiratearchive.net, vice.com, allcrew.co.uk,
fantazia.org.uk, amfm.org.uk: *London's Pirate Pioneers:
The Illegal Broadcasters Who Changed British Radio,
Stephen Hebditch (2015, TX Publications).

...Banister House estate, Clapton. Still running today online.

...Palace's famous pirate row'. *

...Listings and performances from the Kentish Town studio by the likes of Misty in Roots and Scritti Politti.

...on Shooters Hill, then Crystal Palace. Late-1980s house and rare groove from the likes of Trevor Nelson.

...from the Notting Hill Festival. Home of Rankin Miss P before her move to Radio 1.

...district of Crystal Palace, south-east London. Jez Nelson (later Jazz FM, Kiss FM and Radio 3) broadcast here in the mid-late 1980s.

...hardcore rave from inside a concrete barricade on the top floor of a block of council flats on the Nightingale Estate, Hackney. DJs allegedly abseiled in.

...from a council flat in Sydenham. Tim Westwood started his hip-hop career here.

...broadcasting soul late into the south London night from a bedroom in Mitcham, kept going in one form or another until the mid-1980s.

...Grooverider had early shows on this late-1980s Brixton dance/black music station.

...Broadcast Asian music from above a newsagent's on Holloway Road.

...new tunes coming from LTJ Bukem. Big shout to the Peas and Chips Gang, Mad Liquorice and the Bushurst Hill Crew.

Sunrise FM 88.75 FM   East London station that could be picked up south of the river. Still going as soul-led Internet station.

Centreforce, 88.3 FM   Old-skool rave from the Balfron Tower, east London's Trellick Tower.

Rude FM, 88.2 FM   Jungle and drum 'n' bass from Islington.

...hip-hop from Tim Westwood. (Launched as an official station in September 1990.)

DAH DAH DAH DAAAAAAAH!

Kaikhosru Shapurji Sorabji is generally credited with writing the longest symphony. His Organ Symphony No. 2 takes over 8 hours to perform, without a break. It is not much of a surprise that, having been completed in 1932, no one was brave enough to try to play it for some time. It was not until 1994 that it finally had a public performance. Anyone considering buying the music to play at home should take note that it covers 350 pages. Here are a selection of the longest and shortest symphonies from the most eminent composers.

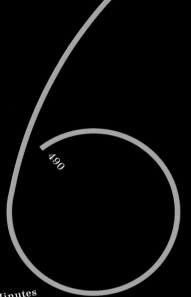

490

Symphony Length in Minutes

Composer	Symphony	Length
Mozart	Symphony No. 5	10
Haydn	Symphony No. 2	10
Benjamin Britten	Simple Symphony	18
Franz Schubert	Symphony No. 3	23
Beethoven	8th Symphony	24
Shostakovich	Symphony No. 9	26
Vaughan Williams	Symphony No. 8	29
Brahms	Symphony No. 3	30
Hector Berlioz	Grande symphonie funèbre et triomphale	31
Haydn	Symphony No. 56	32
Tchaikovsky	Symphony No. 2	35
Mozart	Symphony No. 41	
Benjamin Britten	Spring Symphony	
Edward Elgar	Symphony No. 1	
Brahms	Symphony No. 2	
Franz Schubert	Symphony No. 9	
Edward Elgar	Symphony No. 2	
Tchaikovsky	Symphony Manfred	
Beethoven	9th Symphony	
Vaughan Williams	A Sea Symphony	
Shostakovich	Symphony No. 7	
Mahler	Symphony No. 2	
Hector Berlioz	Roméo et Juliette	
Mahler	Symphony No. 3	
Brian	Symphony No. 1 "The Gothic"	
Sorabji	Organ Symphony No. 2	

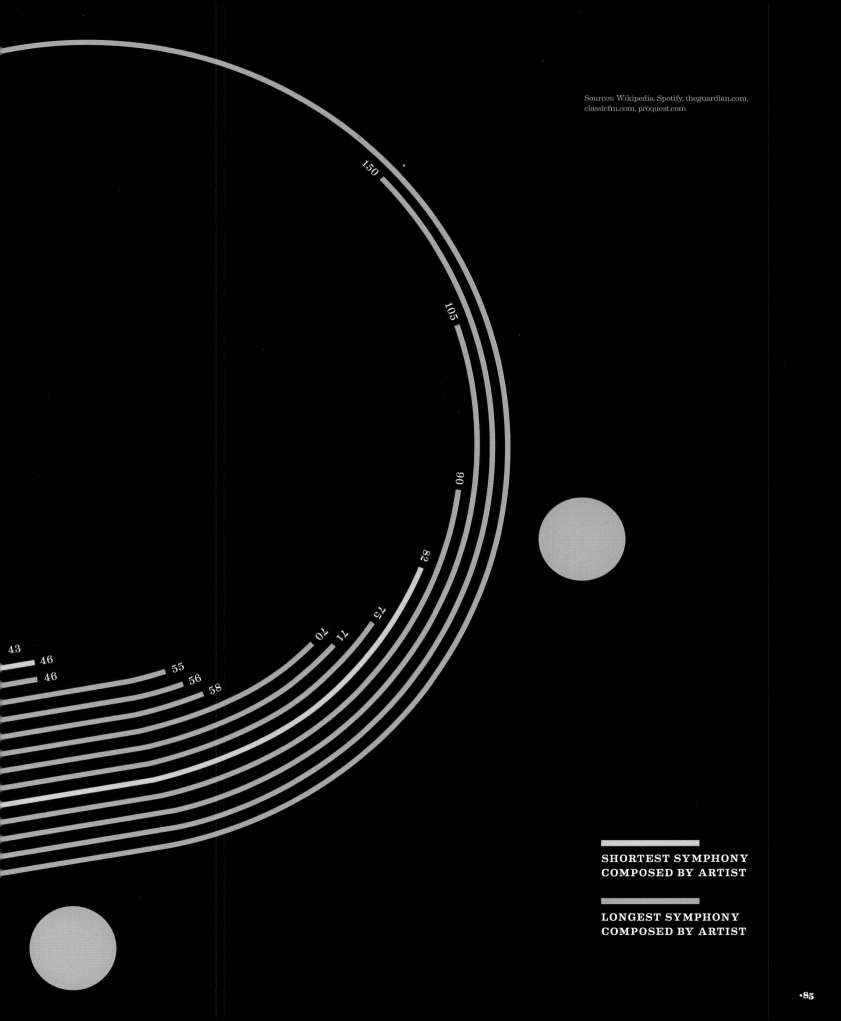

Sources: Wikipedia, Spotify, theguardian.com, classicfm.com, proquest.com

150

105

90

82

75

71

70

43

46

46

55

56

58

SHORTEST SYMPHONY COMPOSED BY ARTIST

LONGEST SYMPHONY COMPOSED BY ARTIST

CLASSIC NUMBER 2s

Who remembers who finished second? In some cases, the records below were scandalously robbed of the top spot by some terrible novelty song and/or appaling schmaltz. Below are records which should have been a place higher, or are generally assumed to have been.

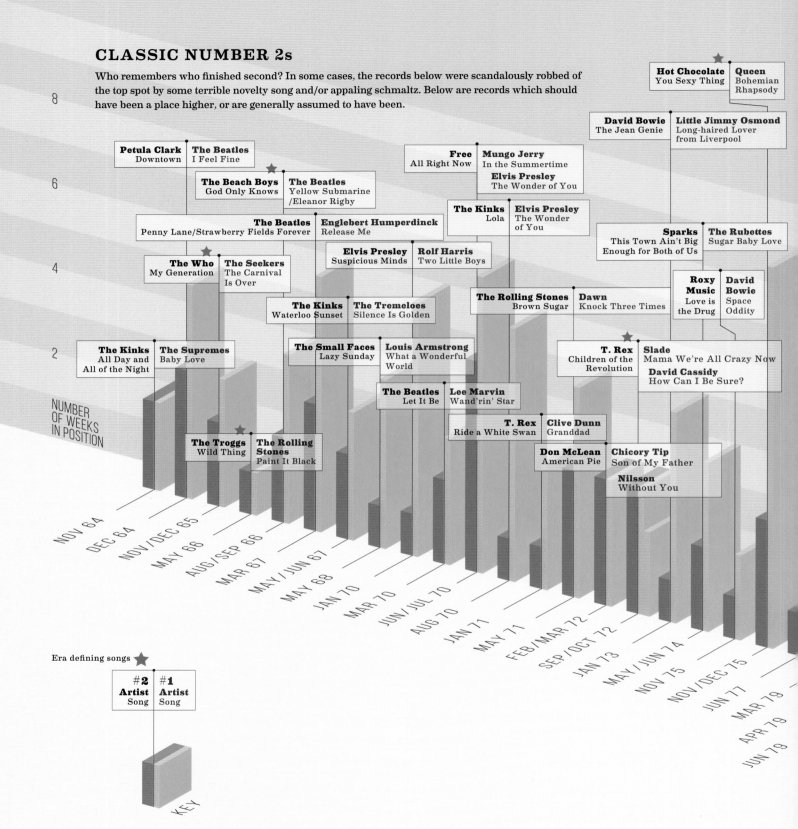

NUMBER OF WEEKS IN POSITION

8

6

4

2

Hot Chocolate
You Sexy Thing | **Queen**
Bohemian Rhapsody

David Bowie
The Jean Genie | **Little Jimmy Osmond**
Long-haired Lover from Liverpool

Petula Clark
Downtown | **The Beatles**
I Feel Fine

Free
All Right Now | **Mungo Jerry**
In the Summertime

Elvis Presley
The Wonder of You

The Beach Boys
God Only Knows | **The Beatles**
Yellow Submarine /Eleanor Rigby

The Kinks
Lola | **Elvis Presley**
The Wonder of You

Sparks
This Town Ain't Big Enough for Both of Us | **The Rubettes**
Sugar Baby Love

The Beatles
Penny Lane/Strawberry Fields Forever | **Englebert Humperdinck**
Release Me

Elvis Presley
Suspicious Minds | **Rolf Harris**
Two Little Boys

The Who
My Generation | **The Seekers**
The Carnival Is Over

Roxy Music
Love is the Drug | **David Bowie**
Space Oddity

The Rolling Stones
Brown Sugar | **Dawn**
Knock Three Times

The Kinks
Waterloo Sunset | **The Tremeloes**
Silence Is Golden

The Kinks
All Day and All of the Night | **The Supremes**
Baby Love

The Small Faces
Lazy Sunday | **Louis Armstrong**
What a Wonderful World

T. Rex
Children of the Revolution | **Slade**
Mama We're All Crazy Now

David Cassidy
How Can I Be Sure?

The Beatles
Let It Be | **Lee Marvin**
Wand'rin' Star

T. Rex
Ride a White Swan | **Clive Dunn**
Granddad

The Troggs
Wild Thing | **The Rolling Stones**
Paint It Black

Don McLean
American Pie | **Chicory Tip**
Son of My Father

Nilsson
Without You

NOV 64
DEC 64
NOV/DEC 65
MAY 66
AUG/SEP 66
MAR 67
MAY/JUN 67
MAY 68
JAN 70
MAR 70
JUN/JUL 70
AUG 70
JAN 71
MAY 71
FEB/MAR 72
SEP/OCT 72
JAN 73
MAY/JUN 74
NOV 75
NOV/DEC 75
JUN 77
MAR 79
APR 79
JUN 79

Era defining songs ★

| #2 Artist Song | #1 Artist Song |

KEY

86•

Sources: BBC, *NME*, *Daily Mail*, Official Charts

★ **Sex Pistols**
God Save the Queen | **Rod Stewart**
I Don't Want to Talk About It

The Pogues and Kirsty MacColl
Fairytale of New York | **Pet Shop Boys**
Always on My Mind

Elvis Costello and the Attractions
Oliver's Army | **The Bee Gees**
Tragedy
Gloria Gaynor
I Will Survive

★ **Pulp**
Common People | **Robson & Jerome**
Unchained Melody

Squeeze
Cool for Cats | **Art Garfunkel**
Bright Eyes

The Jam
The Bitterest Pill | **Survivor**
Eye of the Tiger
Musical Youth
Pass the Dutchie

Pulp
Mis-Shapes/Sorted for Es and Wizz | **Simply Red**
Fairground

Squeeze
Up the Junction | **Tubeway Army**
Are Friends Electric?

Ultravox
Vienna | **Joe Dolce**
Shaddupa You Face
John Lennon
Woman

Heaven 17
Temptation | **Spandau Ballet**
True

★ **Underworld**
Born Slippy | **The Fugees**
Killing Me Softly

Blur
Song 2 | **R Kelly**
I Believe I Can Fly

Laurie Anderson
O Superman | **Dave Stewart with Barbara Gaskin**
It's My Party

Prince
1999/Little Red Corvette | **Foreigner**
I Want to Know What Love Is

The Verve
Bittersweet Symphony | **Puff Daddy & Faith Evans**
I'll Be Missing You

The Stranglers
Golden Brown | **The Jam**
A Town Called Malice

The B-52s
Love Shack | **Beats International**
Dub Be Good to Me
Snap
The Power

The Libertines
Can't Stand Me Now | **3 Of a Kind**
Baby Cakes

Yazoo
Only You | **Nicole**
A Little Peace

★ **Oasis**
Wonderwall | **Robson & Jerome**
I Believe/Up on the Roof

Soft Cell
Torch | **Adam Ant**
Goody Two Shoes

★ **Eminem**
My Name Is . . . | **Mr Ozio**
Flat Beat

10

8

6

4

2

FEB 81
OCT 81
FEB 82
MAY 82
JUN 82
SEP 82
MAY 83
JAN 85
DEC 87
MAR 90
MAY / JUN 95
OCT 95
NOV 95
JUL 96
APR 97
JUL 97
APR 99
AUG 04

EARLY STARTERS, LATE FINISHERS

Everyone knows that Mozart was the earliest of early starters, composing his first work at just five years old when most people can only just about sing a nursery rhyme. Maybe he knew he didn't have long, because he died at the very young age of 35. Another early starter was Richard Strauss but he lived to 85 and worked pretty much up until his last day. This is true for many of the great composers, with many leaving work unfinished.

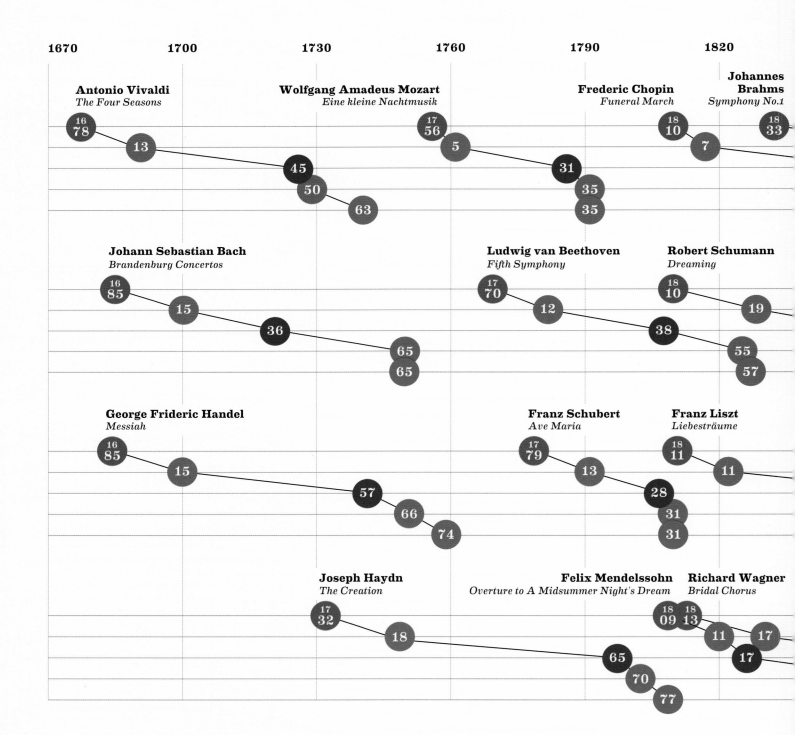

1670 **1700** **1730** **1760** **1790** **1820**

Antonio Vivaldi
The Four Seasons
16 78 · 13 · 45 · 50 · 63

Wolfgang Amadeus Mozart
Eine kleine Nachtmusik
17 56 · 5

Frederic Chopin
Funeral March
18 10 · 7 · 31 · 35 · 35

Johannes Brahms
Symphony No.1
18 33

Johann Sebastian Bach
Brandenburg Concertos
16 85 · 15 · 36 · 65 · 65

Ludwig van Beethoven
Fifth Symphony
17 70 · 12 · 38

Robert Schumann
Dreaming
18 10 · 19 · 55 · 57

George Frideric Handel
Messiah
16 85 · 15 · 57 · 66 · 74

Franz Schubert
Ave Maria
17 79 · 13 · 28 · 31 · 31

Franz Liszt
Liebesträume
18 11 · 11

Joseph Haydn
The Creation
17 32 · 18 · 65 · 70 · 77

Felix Mendelssohn
Overture to A Midsummer Night's Dream
18 09

Richard Wagner
Bridal Chorus
18 13 · 11 · 17 · 17

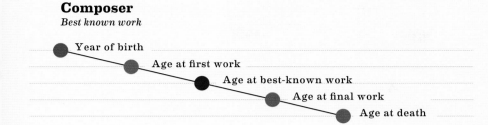

Composer
Best known work

Year of birth
Age at first work
Age at best-known work
Age at final work
Age at death

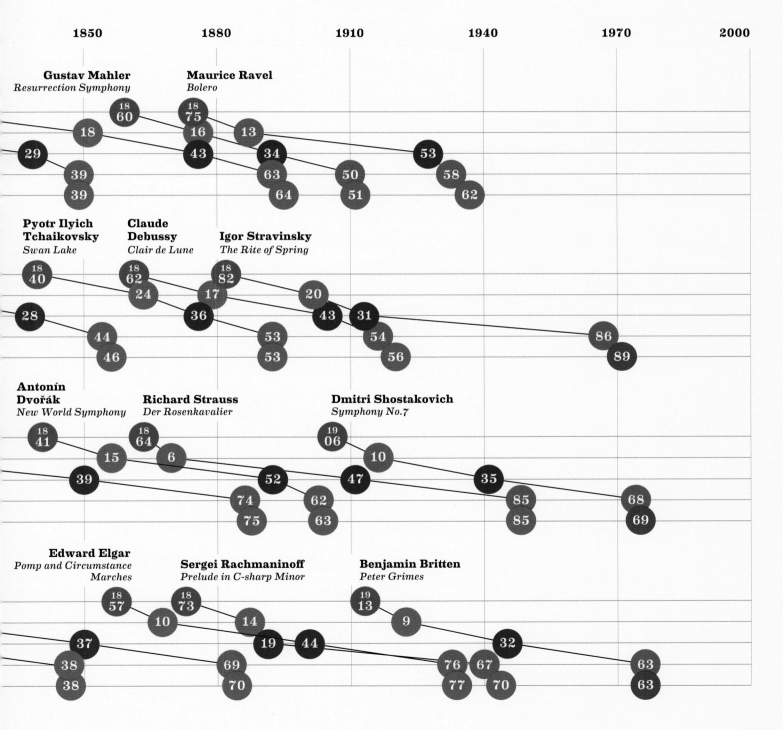

1850   1880   1910   1940   1970   2000

Gustav Mahler
Resurrection Symphony

Maurice Ravel
Bolero

Pyotr Ilyich Tchaikovsky
Swan Lake

Claude Debussy
Clair de Lune

Igor Stravinsky
The Rite of Spring

Antonín Dvořák
New World Symphony

Richard Strauss
Der Rosenkavalier

Dmitri Shostakovich
Symphony No.7

Edward Elgar
Pomp and Circumstance Marches

Sergei Rachmaninoff
Prelude in C-sharp Minor

Benjamin Britten
Peter Grimes

Sources: Wikipedia, Spotify

•89

FROM MEDIEVAL TO MASHUP

There are over 350 breeds of dog and, if you go back to the beginning, all these variations came from one breed. It's the same with music, although there are many many more than 350 "breeds" of music. For every major genre there are numerous sub-genres and sub-sub-genres and that is before you start to consider regional sub-genres. From banging bones on rocks to creating artificial sound with 0s and 1s, it's been a long and winding road.

800	1400	1500	1600	1700	1750	1800	1850	1900	1910

CLASSICAL

Medieval *Gregorian chants*

Renaissance
Josquin des Prez

Baroque *J S Bach*

Classical *Mozart*

Romantic *Beethoven*

Impressionist

20th Century

AFRICAN AMERICAN

Blues

Jazz

KEY

Genre	*Most Popular Artist*

90•

Sources: Wikipedia, classicalmusic.about.com, rateyourmusic.com

1920	1930	1940	1950	1960	1970	1980	1990	2000	2010	2020

Maurice Ravel

Benjamin Britten

BB King

Country *Merle Haggard*

Louis Armstrong

Reggae *Bob Marley*

POPULAR

Pop *Michael Jackson*

Rock and Roll *Elvis Presley*

Rock *Led Zeppelin*

Disco *Donna Summer*

ALTERNATIVE

Hip Hop *Tupac Shakur*

Punk *Ramones*

Rap *Eminem*

Drum and Bass *Noisia*

Indie Rock *The White Stripes*

Indie Pop *Wedding Present*

Funk *James Brown*

Rockabilly *Buddy Holly*

Ska *The Specials*

Electronic *Kraftwerk*

Death Metal *Slayer*

House *Frankie Knuckles*

New Wave *Talking Heads*

Glam *David Bowie*

Grunge *Nirvana*

Northern Soul *Gloria Jones*

Ambient *Brian Eno*

Trance *Armin van Buuren*

Heavy Metal *Black Sabbath*

Madchester *Stone Roses*

Mashup *Danger Mouse*

1960S PIRATE RADIO SHIPS

Ahead of the 1967 Marine Broadcasting Offences Act, the North Sea off the east coast of the UK was full of vessels floating in "international waters" broadcasting pop music to beat-crazy teenagers in England and Scotland. Here's a map of some of the stations.

Sources: thefw.com, theguardian.com
shootfarken.com.au

Radio Mercur (1958) then Radio Sid (from 1961)

First pirate radio. Programmes made on land in Copenhagen, then the *Cheeta Mercur*, a basic fishing vessel (later the *Cheeta II*, an old ferry) would sail out into open water and start running the tapes. Broadcast to Denmark and southern Sweden.

1958 - 62 ✕✕✕✕✕

Radio 270

Transmitting from a Dutch trawler off Scarborough: the signal can be picked up from Newcastle to Nottingham. Pop music interrupted by preacher Garner Ted Armstrong's nightly evangelical broadcast. Suffering a bout of sea-sickness, DJ Paul Burnett once threw up live on air.

1966- 67 ✕✕

January 1966, MV *Mi Amigo* loses its anchor in a storm and washes up at Frinton: Radio Caroline (South) eventually continues to broadcast from the *Cheeta II* which sails south from Sweden.

Radio Veronica

Broadcasts from the *Borkum Riff*, a lighthouse boat/lightship, in the North Sea off the coast of the Netherlands. Holland's most popular radio station.

1960 - 74 ✕✕✕✕✕✕✕
✕✕✕✕✕✕✕

Cheeta Mercur FISHING VESSEL

Cheeta II FERRY

Oceaan VII DUTCH-BUILT LUGGER

LV Comet LIGHTSHIP

Radio Scotland

Broadcasts from the LV *Comet*, initially off Dunbar (on the east coast) in 1965, then in April 1966 sails round to Troon off the west coast.

1965 - 67 ✕✕✕

MV Caroline
(Radio Caroline North)

Sails around the UK and drops anchor off Ramsay Bay, the Isle of Man – the whole of the UK is now covered.

1964 ✕

MV Caroline PASSENGER/CARGO SHIP

Radio Caroline (1964)

The MV *Caroline*, anchored off Felixstowe. Early theme tune: Jimmy McGriff's "Round Midnight"; DJs include Emperor Rosko and Tommy Vance.

1964–Present ✕✕✕✕✕✕✕✕✕
✕✕✕✕✕✕✕✕
✕✕✕✕✕✕✕
✕✕✕✕✕✕

Radio Invicta (1964) then KING Radio (1965) then Radio 390

Broadcast from Red Sands Fort in the Thames Estuary (Radio City's neighbour) off Whitstable. DJ Graham Gill remembers spinning Herb Alpert and Tijuana Brass, "Music to Watch Girls Go By" by Andy Williams, and Bert Kaempfert and his Orchestra (presumably, in 1967, "A Swingin' 'Safari") among the final records before the signal was turned off in July of that year.

1964 - 67 ✕✕✕✕

Radio City

Screaming Lord Sutch establishes Radio City, broadcasting from Shivering Sands army fort, 10 miles off Whitstable in the Thames Estuary in Kent. Long-time pirate radio *éminence grise* – and veteran of Caroline and Radio City among others – Bob Le-Roi remembers surviving on a diet of "meat puddings steam-cooked in a bucket of boiling sea water" and tea with canned milk.

1964 - 67 ✕✕✕✕

Borkum Riff
LIGHTSHIP

Radio North Sea International

The psychedelically painted *Mebo II* sails from the Dutch coast and puts down its anchor five miles off Clacton in March 1970. The British Labour government jam the signal in June of that year: RNI respond by broadcasting pro-Tory messages on a different frequency. DJs include Roger 'Twiggy' Day, and Mark Wesley (later of Radio Luxembourg).

1970 - 74 ✕✕✕✕✕

Caroline merges with Radio Atlanta, a station broadcasting off the MV *Mi Amigo* anchored off Frinton-on-Sea, to form Radio Caroline (South) – remains off Frinton-on-Sea, broadcasting to the east of England.

Mebo II
DUTCH FREIGHTER

Radio London

3.5 miles from Frinton-on-Sea. Supplied future Radio 1 DJs like John Peel, Tony Blackburn, Ed Stewart, Pete Drummond and Kenny Everett. The Beatles' "A Day in the Life" was the last record played before the bailiffs came aboard in August 1967.

1964 - 67 ✕✕✕✕

MV Galaxy
WWII US NAVY MINESWEEPER

MV Caroline
PASSENGER/CARGO SHIP

WWII Sea Fort

•93

COUNTRY MUSICIANS NOT ENTIRELY FROM THE COUNTRY

Johnny Cash was born in Kingsland, Arkansas in 1932 (population: 447) before the family moved to Dyess (population: 515). By the age of 5, Johnny was picking cotton in the fields; no real surprise Johnny Cash turned into a country singer. "From" is a loose term. A few musicians are genuinely from the country: the Carter Family hail from the green fields of Virginia; Gene Autry worked on his father's ranch in southern Oklahoma. But it's not always black and white: Emmylou Harris grew up in the small town of Woodbridge, Virginia, but worked as a waitress in Greenwich Village. Overall, a rural upbringing is not entirely typical of country musicians. We're not suggesting there's something inauthentic about country musicians who aren't from the countryside, just that it's interesting how many of them were shaped by the big city. Perhaps the yearning for a rural idyll tells us much about life in America. (Musicians born around Nashville aren't included in the graphic below too, of course.)

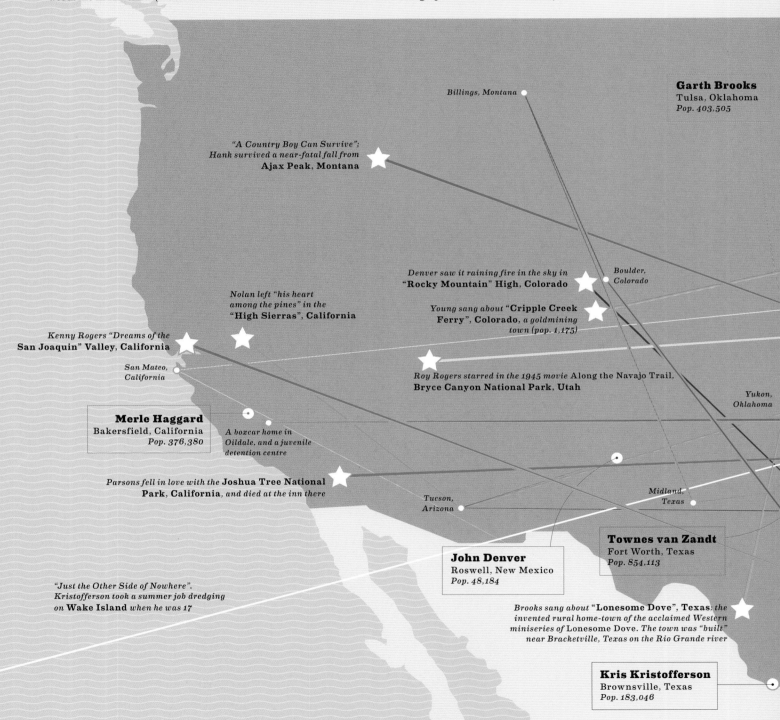

Bob Nolan
Winnipeg, Manitoba
Pop. 705,244

Billings, Montana

Garth Brooks
Tulsa, Oklahoma
Pop. 403,505

"A Country Boy Can Survive"; Hank survived a near-fatal fall from **Ajax Peak, Montana**

Denver saw it raining fire in the sky in **"Rocky Mountain" High, Colorado**

Boulder, Colorado

Nolan left "his heart among the pines" in the **"High Sierras", California**

Young sang about **"Cripple Creek Ferry", Colorado,** *a goldmining town (pop. 1,175)*

Kenny Rogers "Dreams of the **San Joaquin" Valley, California**

San Mateo, California

Roy Rogers starred in the 1945 movie Along the Navajo Trail, **Bryce Canyon National Park, Utah**

Yukon, Oklahoma

Merle Haggard
Bakersfield, California
Pop. 376,380

A boxcar home in Oildale, and a juvenile detention centre

Parsons fell in love with the **Joshua Tree National Park, California,** *and died at the inn there*

Tucson, Arizona

Midland, Texas

John Denver
Roswell, New Mexico
Pop. 48,184

Townes van Zandt
Fort Worth, Texas
Pop. 854,113

"Just the Other Side of Nowhere". Kristofferson took a summer job dredging on **Wake Island** *when he was 17*

Brooks sang about **"Lonesome Dove", Texas**; *the invented rural home-town of the acclaimed Western miniseries of Lonesome Dove. The town was "built" near Bracketville, Texas on the Rio Grande river*

Kris Kristofferson
Brownsville, Texas
Pop. 183,046

Sources: *David Hadju, *Love For Sale: Pop Music in America* – Hadju also writes that Rodgers' namesake, Roy, was "good with a horse". Other sources: various Wikipeida entries; John Nova Lomax on TVZ (www.themayborn.com/article/my-life-tvz); *Dance of Death, The Life of John Fahey, American Guitarist* by Steve Lowenthal (2014, Chicago Review Press); *Are You Ready for the Country* by Peter Doggett (2000, Viking).

Bob Dylan
Duluth, Minnesota
Pop. 86,293

Roy Rogers
Cincinnati, Ohio
Pop. 298,800

KEY

Artist

Major childhood home of artist ●

Other childhood homes of artist ·

"Country" location of significance to artist ★

Hibbing,
Minnesota

Neil Young
Toronto, Ontario
Pop. 2,731,571

Alison Krauss
Decatur, Illinois
Pop. 72,706

Omemee, Ontario

Pickering, Ontario

Boston, Massachusetts

Champaign, Illinois

Oxford University,
where he won a Blue
for boxing

Lucasville,
Ohio

Portsmouth,
Ohio

John Fahey
Takoma Park, Maryland
Pop. 17,765

Nashville, Tennessee

Parents Flossie May &
Jim Haggard moved from
Checotah, Oklahoma
to escape the Dust Bowl

Krauss performed on the award-winning
Cold Mountain *soundtrack,* **North Carolina**

Van Zandt lived in a shack in the 1970s
in the **Little Harpeth River Valley, Tennessee** *(approx. pop. 2)*

Greenville, South Carolina

"If I'd known then what I do
now," said Bob Dylan in 1978,
"I probably would have taken off
when I was 12 and followed Bill
Monroe." The founding father of
bluegrass, Monroe was born in
Rosine, Kentucky *(pop. 41)*

Montgomery,
Alabama

A young Fahey, known for
record-sourcing trips in the deep
South, finally tracked down
legendary lost-bluesman Skip
James, who lived near **Bentonia,**
Mississippi *(pop. 423)*

Waycross, Georgia

Jacksonville, Florida

New Smyrna Beach, Florida

Hank Williams Jr
Shreveport, Louisiana
Pop. 194,920

Gram Parsons
Winter Haven, Florida
Pop. 38,953

Kenny Rogers
Houston, Texas
Pop. 2,303,482

STUDIO KINDA CLOUDY. THE RECORDING STUDIOS OF KINGSTON, JAMAICA, MID-1970S

Engineers and producers like Sylvan Morris, Scientist, King Tubby, Coxsone Dodd (as Dub Specialist), Augustus Pablo, Clive Chin and Lee Perry were behind some of the finest records of the twentieth century. Here's a sound map of the various studios, and just a handful of key records (many mixed, recorded and mastered in different locations) of Kingston, Jamaica, in the mid-seventies, arguably the heyday of dub.

Sources: Sleevenotes to various editions of the LPs mentioned; *Dub: Soundscapes and Shattered Songs in Jamaican Reggae*, Michael E. Veal (Wesleyan, 2007); *The Rough Guide to Reggae*, Steve Barrow and Peter Dalton (Penguin, 2004); *The Small Axe Guide to Dub*, Jim Dooley (Muzik Tree, 2010).

Lee Perry's Black Ark Studio

Lee Perry worked at Studio One, Dynamic Sounds and Randy's as a producer. A studio upgrade at Randy's prompted him to build his own studio in his back garden. Known for his wild psychedelic layering of sounds, "black magic", burning herb and, ultimately, a burning studio. He burnt down a second studio in Switzerland in 2015.

ARTISTS / ALBUM

Lee Perry & the Upsetters *Cloak & Dagger*
Augustus Pablo *East of the River Nile*
The Congos *Heart of the Congos*
Lee Perry *Roast Fish, Collie Weed and Cornbread*
The Upsetters *Return of the Super Ape*
Lee 'Scratch' Perry *The Return of Pipecock Jackson*

King Tubby's Studio

In 1972 jazz-loving electrician Osbourne "King Tubby" Ruddock moved a four-track MCI mixing console picked up from Byron Lee's Dynamic Sound into the tiny front room of his mum's house on Dromilly Avenue, and moved his mum across the road. Bunny Striker Lee and Lloyd "Prince/King Jammy" James, Overton "Scientist" Brown, Lee Perry, Vivian "Yabby You" Jackson, Glen Brown and Horace "Augustus Pablo" Swaby were among the producers who all filed in at various times. The studio/house was so small that it was usually a site of mixing/remixing rather than recording a fully-fledged band. So rough were the surrounding streets that the producers often locked themselves in – recordings of sirens and gunfire mixed into tracks were not such a hyperbole.

ARTISTS / ALBUM

Tommy McCook *Dub*
Tommy McCook *Presenting the Morwells*
Augustus Pablo *Original Rockers*
King Tubby *Dub from the Roots & The Roots of Dub*
Yabby You *Jesus Dread*
Augustus Pablo *King Tubby Meets Rockers Uptown*
Augustus Pablo *Tapper Zukie in Dub*
Augustus Pablo *Original Rockers*
Horace Andy *In the Light/In the Light Dub*
King Tubby *King Tubby Meets the Aggrovators at the Dub Station*
Jackie Mittoo *Champion in the Arena, 1976–1977*

Channel One Studio, the Hoo-Kim Brothers

The Revolutionaries were the house band and the mixing desk went up to 16 channels in 1975. Scientist worked there in the 1980s. Riddims were often laid down at Channel One then taken back and mixed at Tubbys.

ARTISTS / ALBUM

The Morwells *Presenting the Morwells*
Augustus Pablo *Original Rockers*
Jackie Mittoo *Champion in the Arena, 1976–1977*
The Revolutionaries *Earthquake Dub*
The Revolutionaries *Drum Sound, More Gems from the Channel One Dub Room 1974 to 1980*

Joe Gibbs' Recording Studio

Errol Thompson moved here in 1974–75 and mixed in the heavy effects – doorbells, police sirens, barking dogs – that famously characterise the African Dub series of LPs.

ARTISTS / ALBUM

Tommy McCook *Dub*
Well Charge *Vital Dub*
Joe Gibbs and *African Dub,*
the Professionals *Chapters 1–4*

Harry Johnson's Harry J. Studio

ARTISTS / ALBUM

Tommy McCook *Dub*
Augustus Pablo *East of the River Nile*
Keith Hudson *Pick a Dub*
Bob Marley and the Wailers *Natty Dread, Rastaman Vibration*

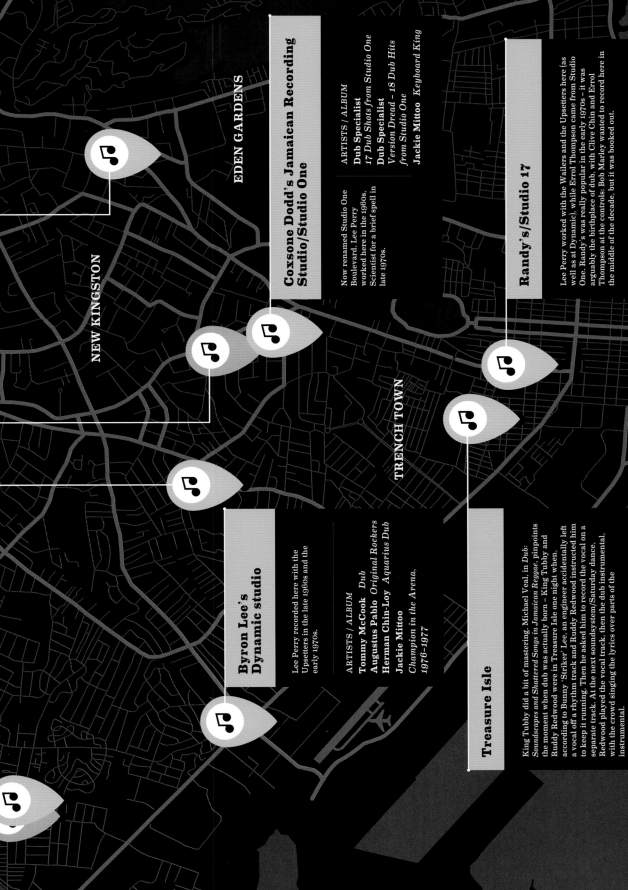

NEW KINGSTON

EDEN GARDENS

TRENCH TOWN

Coxsone Dodd's Jamaican Recording Studio/Studio One

Now renamed Studio One
Boulevard. Lee Perry
worked here in the 1960s.
Scientist for a brief spell in
late 1970s.

ARTISTS / ALBUM
Dub Specialist
17 Dub Shots from Studio One
Dub Specialist
*Version Dread – 18 Dub Hits
from Studio One*
Jackie Mittoo *Keyboard King*

Randy's/Studio 17

Lee Perry worked with the Wailers and the Upsetters here (as
well as at Dynamic), while Errol Thompson came from Studio
One. Randy's was really popular in the early 1970s – it was
arguably the birthplace of dub, with Clive Chin and Errol
Thompson at the controls: Bob Marley wanted to record here in
the middle of the decade, but it was booked out.

ARTISTS / ALBUM
Tommy McCook *Dub*
Tommy McCook *Presenting the Morwells*
Augustus Pablo *This Is Augustus Pablo*
Dub Instrumental *Java, Java, Java*
Joe Gibbs *Dub Serial*

Byron Lee's Dynamic studio

Lee Perry recorded here with the
Upsetters in the late 1960s and the
early 1970s.

ARTISTS / ALBUM
Tommy McCook *Dub*
Augustus Pablo *Original Rockers*
Herman Chin-Loy *Aquarius Dub*
Jackie Mittoo
*Champion in the Arena,
1976–1977*

Treasure Isle

King Tubby did a bit of mastering. Michael Veal, in *Dub:
Soundscapes and Shattered Songs in Jamaican Reggae*, pinpoints
the moment when dub was actually born – King Tubby and
Ruddy Redwood were in Treasure Isle one night when,
according to Bunny 'Striker' Lee, an engineer accidentally left
a vocal off a rhythm track and Ruddy Redwood instructed him
to keep it running. Then he asked him to record the vocal on a
separate track. At the next soundsystem/Saturday dance,
Redwood played the vocal track, then the dub instrumental,
with the crowd singing the lyrics over parts of the
instrumental.

ARTISTS / ALBUM
Errol Brown *Orthodox Dub*

A SOUND TRACK

You shouldn't judge a book by its cover and you can't judge a film by its music. Maybe, though, we should ask: can you judge music by the film it's in? A strong score or even just one memorable song can lift a film from ordinary to extraordinary, and so the people who write that music are justifiably sought after and praised.

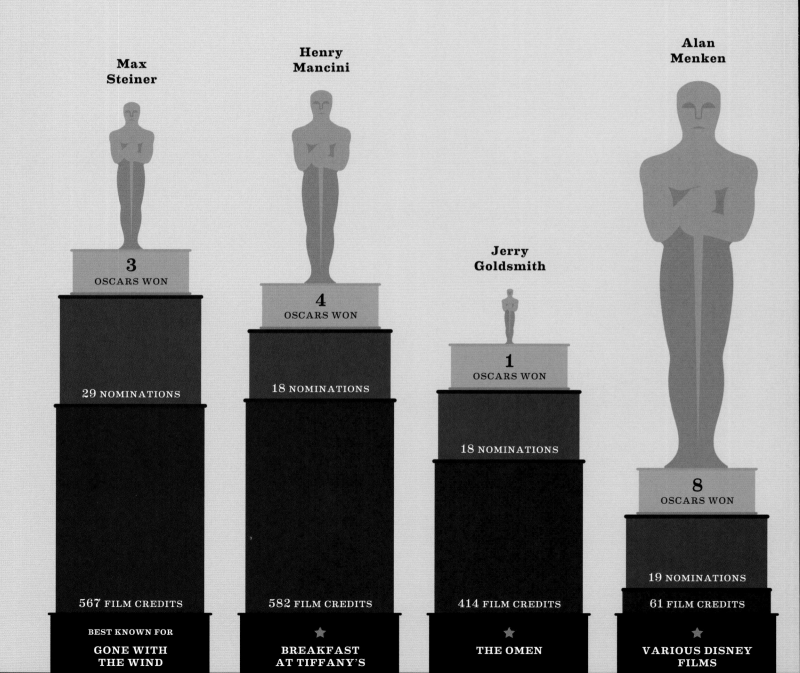

Max Steiner

3
OSCARS WON

29 NOMINATIONS

567 FILM CREDITS

BEST KNOWN FOR
GONE WITH THE WIND

Henry Mancini

4
OSCARS WON

18 NOMINATIONS

582 FILM CREDITS

★
BREAKFAST AT TIFFANY'S

Jerry Goldsmith

1
OSCARS WON

18 NOMINATIONS

414 FILM CREDITS

★
THE OMEN

Alan Menken

8
OSCARS WON

19 NOMINATIONS

61 FILM CREDITS

★
VARIOUS DISNEY FILMS

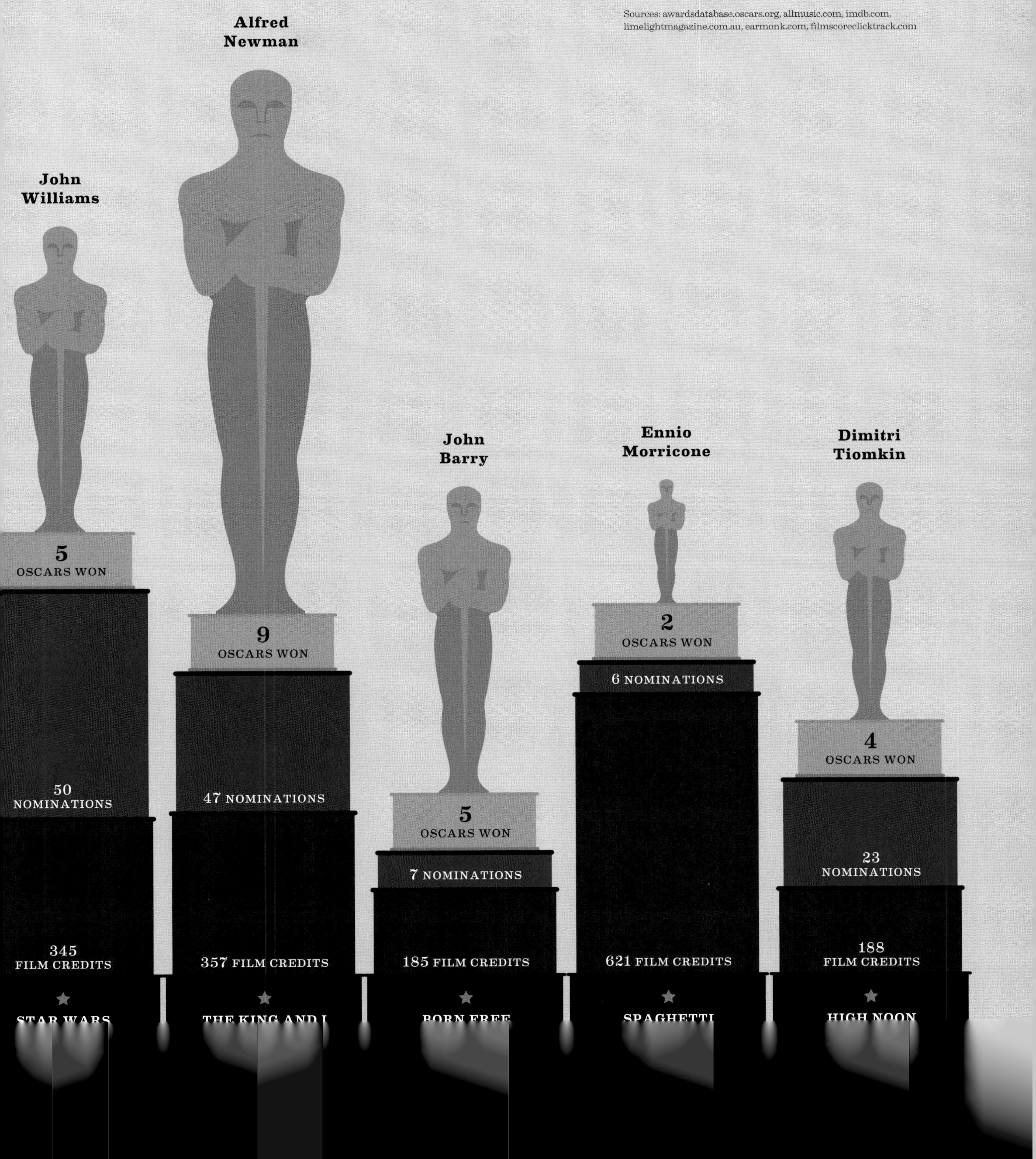
Sources: awardsdatabase.oscars.org, allmusic.com, imdb.com, limelightmagazine.com.au, earmonk.com, filmscoreclicktrack.com
John Williams
5 OSCARS WON
50 NOMINATIONS
345 FILM CREDITS
STAR WARS
Alfred Newman
9 OSCARS WON
47 NOMINATIONS
357 FILM CREDITS
THE KING AND I
John Barry
5 OSCARS WON
7 NOMINATIONS
185 FILM CREDITS
BORN FREE
Ennio Morricone
2 OSCARS WON
6 NOMINATIONS
621 FILM CREDITS
SPAGHETTI
Dimitri Tiomkin
4 OSCARS WON
23 NOMINATIONS
188 FILM CREDITS
HIGH NOON

LOST LONDON MUSIC VENUES

The Music Venue Trust have calculated that 35 per cent of London's grassroots venues have been lost since 2007, mainly due to increasing rents and property redevelopment/gentrification. Here's a ghost map of a few of London's much missed live venues.

1980
KLOOKS KLEEK/ THE MOONLIGHT CLUB/RAT & PARROT

Was the function room of The Railway pub. The pub is still going strong, but the function room is "no longer in use"

Georgie Fame, Howlin' Wolf, Led Zeppelin, John Lee Hooker, U2, Eddie Lockjaw Davis

2013
THE BULL & GATE

Gastropub
(also called Bull & Gate)

Nirvana, Coldplay, Manic Street Preachers

2011
THE LUMINAIRE

Savers
(health, home and beauty store)

Damien Jurado, Jason Molina, Meg Baird, The Felice Brothers

1999
THE KILBURN NATIONAL BALLROOM

Brazilian Univeral Church of the Kingdom of God

The Smiths, New Order, Jesus and Mary Chain, Nirvana

2009
THE WINDSOR CASTLE

Derelict

The Clash, The 101ers, The Jam, The Cure, The Merton Parkas

Early 2000s
SUBTERRANIA

Recently closed nightclub

Eminem, The Wedding Present, The Fall, Primal Scream

2002
THE MEAN FIDDLER

Original venue located in Harlesden. New venue demolished for Tottenham Court Road Crossrail station

Johnny Cash, Nick Cave and the Bad Seeds, Van Morrison, The Triffids, Erasure

1998
BUNJIES COFFEE HOUSE AND FOLK CELLAR

Souk Bazaar Moroccan restaurant

Bob Dylan, Bert Jansch, John Renbourn, Jeff Buckley

2007
HAMMERSMITH PALAIS

Demolished.
Now accommodation

The Beatles, Rolling Stones, The Who, Sex Pistols

2009
THE ASTORIA

Demolished for Tottenham Court Road Crossrail station

Nirvana, The Damned, Madness, LCD Soundsystem

1990
THE FULHAM GREYHOUND

Southern Belle bar
(pool and snooker restaurant)

Status Quo, The Stranglers, The Jam, The Chills

1980
THE NASHVILLE ROOMS

Famous Three Kings pub

Elvis Costello, Dr. Feelgood, Eddie and the Hot Rods, Sex Pistols

1984
THE VENUE

Building site

Iggy Pop, Sun Ra, Charlie Haden's Liberation Orchestra, Ramones

2004

THE SIR GEORGE ROBEY

Demolished / Building site

*The Pogues, U.K. Subs,
Alien Sex Fiend,
The Men they Couldn't Hang*

1982

THE RAINBOW THEATRE

Brazilian Univeral Church
of the Kingdom of God

*David Bowie, The Beatles,
Miles Davis, The Clash*

Sources:
theguardian.com. gigwise.com.
flickr.com. musicvenuetrust.com,
kilburnwesthampstead.blogspot.co.uk

2002

THE CAMDEN FALCON

Residential property

*Tindersticks, The Siddeleys,
Kitchens of Distinction,
The Ecstasy of Saint Theresa*

2010

BARDENS BOUDOIR

Upmarket café,
restaurant and bar
(also called Barden's Boudoir)

Marissa Nadler, Crystal Stilts

2007

STRATFORD REX

Empty. owned by
Newham Council

*Bone Thugs-n-Harmony,
Fugazi, One Nation (raves)*

1999

THE LAUREL TREE

Brewdog Craft Beer bar

*Tortoise, Sparklehorse,
Huggy Bear, Blow-Up (club night)*

1998

THE FOUR ACES

Demolished for Dalston Junction
station & apartments

*Desmond Dekker, Sir Coxsone Dodd,
Prince Jazzbo, The Prodigy*

2010

THE RUSSELL ARMS

Escape Sports bar

Smog, The Palace Brothers

2003

THE BASS CLEFF/
TENOR CLEF/THE BLUE NOTE

Sold to a property developer

*Mark Murphy, Ray Bryant, Norman Jay, Talvin Singh,
Goldie and Metalheadz nights*

2009

THE END

Empty

*Fatboy Slim, Roni Size,
Fabio and Grooverider,
Erol Alkan*

2007

THE SPITZ

Empty

*Cornershop, Squarepusher,
Susanna and the Magical Orchestra,
Sunburned Hand of the Man,*

KEY

YEAR CLOSED

VENUE

What it is now

*Sample artist who
played at venue*

2003

THE MILK BAR /
THE VELVET ROOMS

Demolished for
Tottenham Court Road
Crossrail station

*Carl Cox. The Brand New Heavies,
Fabio, FWD>> (dubstep night)*

2013

CABLE

Seized by Network Rail
as part of redevelopment
of London Bridge Station

Goldie, LTJ Bukem

TYPE OF NEW VENUE

- Derelict/building site
- Transport
- Food/alcohol
- Arts
- Retail
- Residential
- Religious

1985

LYCEUM BALLROOM

Lyceum Theatre
(The Lion King)

*Led Zeppelin, The Rolling Stones,
Joy Division, Fad Gadget*

DO RAY ME ME ME ME

In many ways the most versatile instrument in any musical group is the human voice. Not everyone can do it, but Georgia Brown, an Italian-born Brazilian singer, has a range of 8 octaves, from G2 to G10. Her top note is beyond human hearing and well above that needed to shatter glass. It's not necessary to have someone this versatile in most choirs, and so the norm is to seek out singers with specialist ranges.

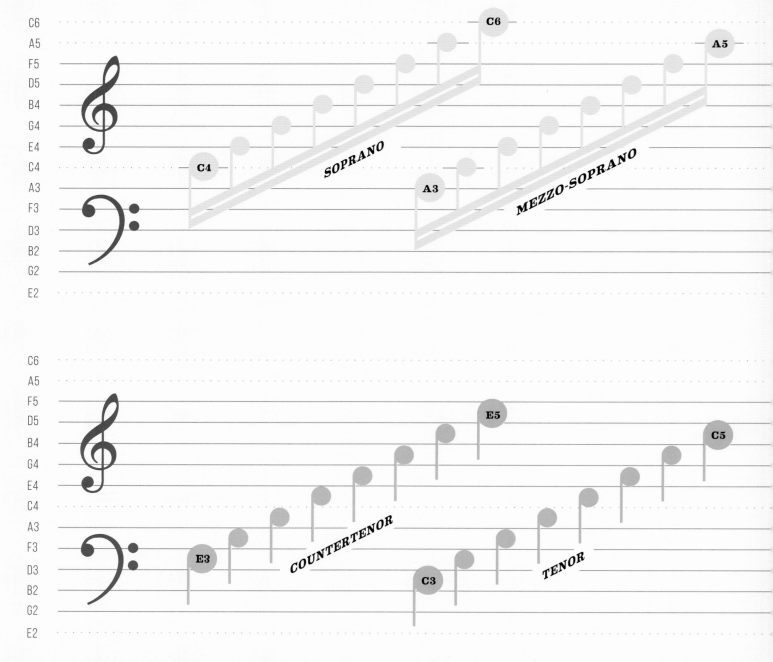

Singers who fall into these voice categories are not necessarily limited to the ranges as listed, but the ranges shown here cover the strongest areas of their voice.

Source: Wikipedia

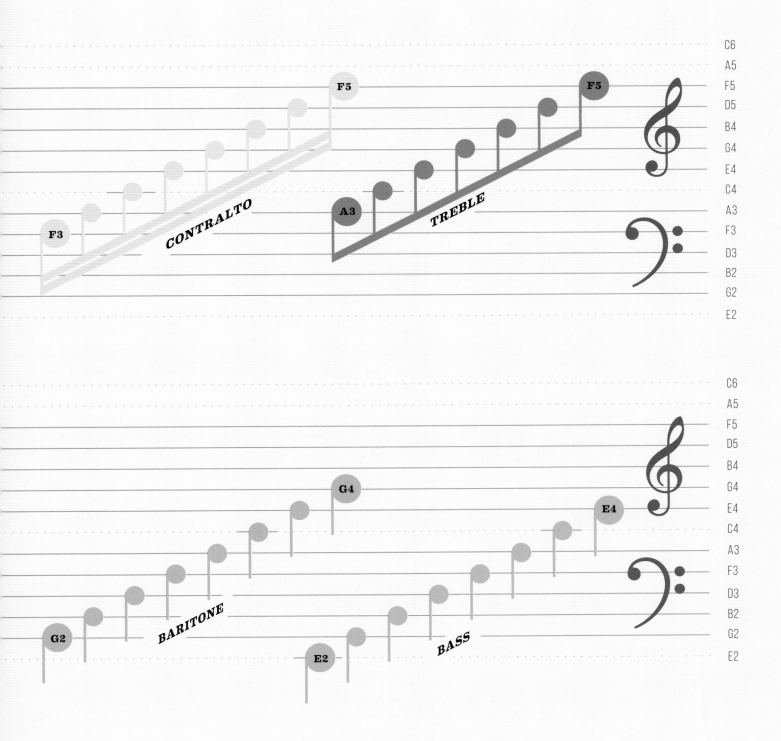

THE "CURSE" OF THE MERCURY PRIZE

In the mid to late-1990s, as Roni Size vanished and Pulp temporarily disappeared after *This Is Hardcore*, talk began of "the curse" of winning the Mercury Prize, the annual music industry award for the best British album of the year. Sales figures, on the whole, don't back up such a notion. Credibility and longevity might be another matter though... Also featured is a "doomed" rating – 1: credibility considerably compromised in the years after the prize win; 5: it's been a rollercoaster; 10: have gone on to achieve/maintain superstar credibility status.

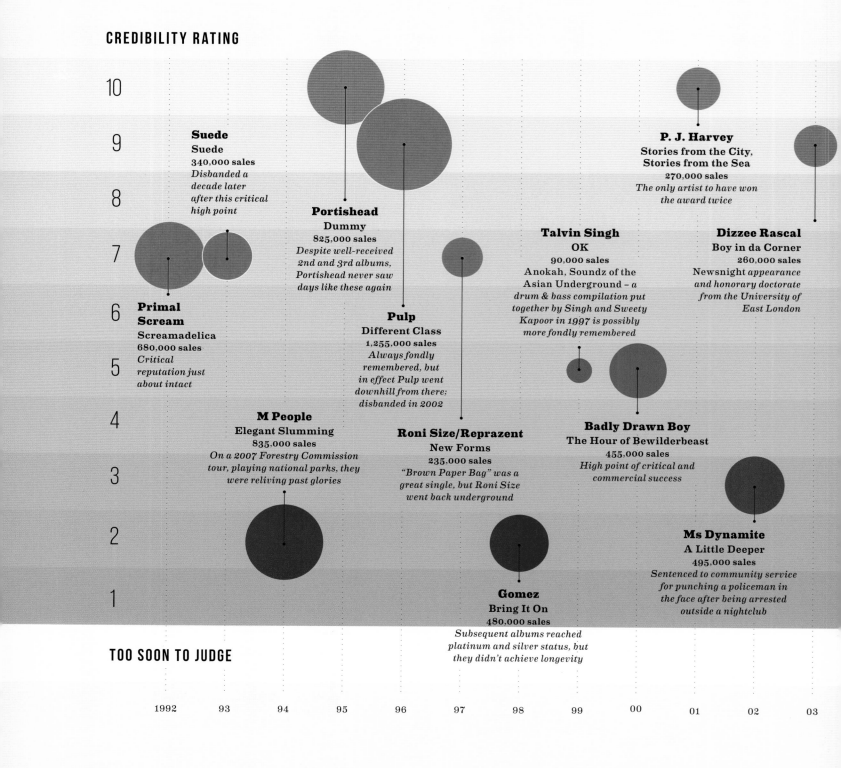

CREDIBILITY RATING

Suede
Suede
340,000 sales
Disbanded a decade later after this critical high point

P. J. Harvey
Stories from the City, Stories from the Sea
270,000 sales
The only artist to have won the award twice

Portishead
Dummy
825,000 sales
Despite well-received 2nd and 3rd albums, Portishead never saw days like these again

Talvin Singh
OK
90,000 sales
Anokah, Soundz of the Asian Underground – a drum & bass compilation put together by Singh and Sweety Kapoor in 1997 is possibly more fondly remembered

Dizzee Rascal
Boy in da Corner
260,000 sales
Newsnight appearance and honorary doctorate from the University of East London

Primal Scream
Screamadelica
680,000 sales
Critical reputation just about intact

Pulp
Different Class
1,255,000 sales
Always fondly remembered, but in effect Pulp went downhill from there; disbanded in 2002

M People
Elegant Slumming
835,000 sales
On a 2007 Forestry Commission tour, playing national parks, they were reliving past glories

Roni Size/Reprazent
New Forms
235,000 sales
"Brown Paper Bag" was a great single, but Roni Size went back underground

Badly Drawn Boy
The Hour of Bewilderbeast
455,000 sales
High point of critical and commercial success

Ms Dynamite
A Little Deeper
495,000 sales
Sentenced to community service for punching a policeman in the face after being arrested outside a nightclub

Gomez
Bring It On
480,000 sales
Subsequent albums reached platinum and silver status, but they didn't achieve longevity

TOO SOON TO JUDGE

10 9 8 7 6 5 4 3 2 1

1992 93 94 95 96 97 98 99 00 01 02 03

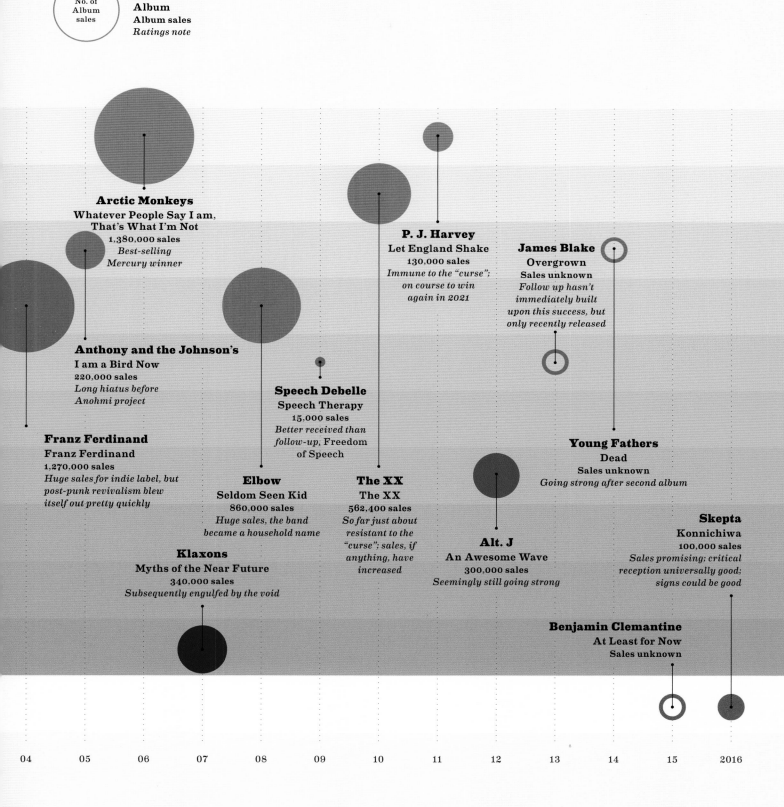

Sources: independent.co.uk, nme.com, theguardian.com, shakenstir.co.uk

KEY

No. of Album sales

Artist
Album
Album sales
Ratings note

Arctic Monkeys
Whatever People Say I am,
That's What I'm Not
1,380,000 sales
*Best-selling
Mercury winner*

P. J. Harvey
Let England Shake
130,000 sales
*Immune to the "curse";
on course to win
again in 2021*

James Blake
Overgrown
Sales unknown
*Follow up hasn't
immediately built
upon this success, but
only recently released*

Anthony and the Johnson's
I am a Bird Now
220,000 sales
*Long hiatus before
Anohmi project*

Speech Debelle
Speech Therapy
15,000 sales
*Better received than
follow-up; Freedom
of Speech*

Young Fathers
Dead
Sales unknown
Going strong after second album

Franz Ferdinand
Franz Ferdinand
1,270,000 sales
*Huge sales for indie label, but
post-punk revivalism blew
itself out pretty quickly*

Elbow
Seldom Seen Kid
860,000 sales
*Huge sales, the band
became a household name*

The XX
The XX
562,400 sales
*So far just about
resistant to the
"curse"; sales, if
anything, have
increased*

Skepta
Konnichiwa
100,000 sales
*Sales promising; critical
reception universally good;
signs could be good*

Klaxons
Myths of the Near Future
340,000 sales
Subsequently engulfed by the void

Alt. J
An Awesome Wave
300,000 sales
Seemingly still going strong

Benjamin Clemantine
At Least for Now
Sales unknown

04 05 06 07 08 09 10 11 12 13 14 15 2016

ONE HIT WONDERS

Andy Warhol famously said that eventually everyone will be famous for 15 minutes. Where music is concerned maybe that should have been 3 minutes. Some bands never make it and some have a lifetime in the charts. But, for a special few, their light shines so brightly but can only be seen around the world just the once.

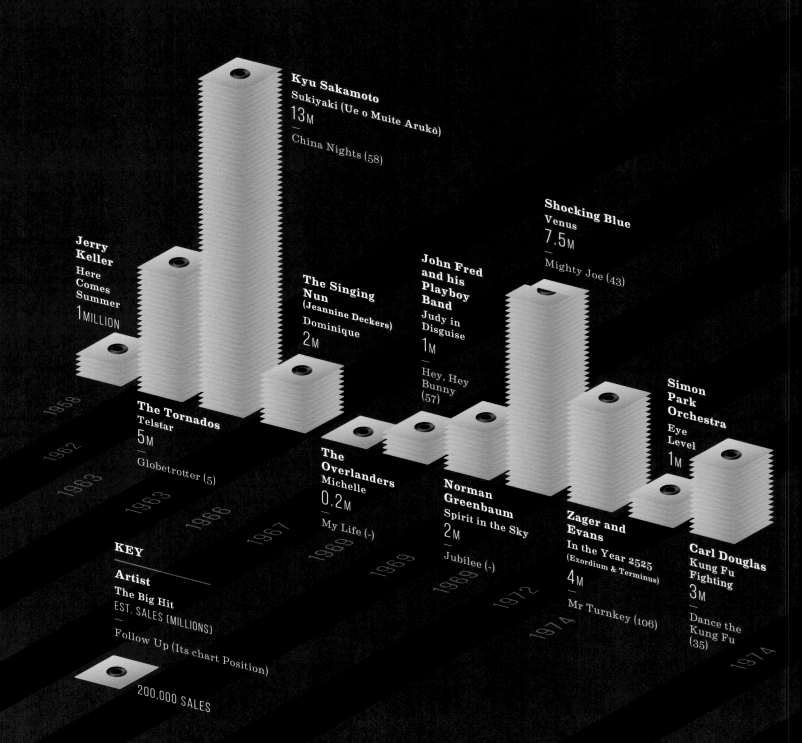

Kyu Sakamoto
Sukiyaki (Ue o Muite Arukō)
13M
—
China Nights (58)

Shocking Blue
Venus
7.5M
—
Mighty Joe (43)

Jerry Keller
Here Comes Summer
1 MILLION

John Fred and his Playboy Band
Judy in Disguise
1M
—
Hey, Hey Bunny (57)

The Singing Nun
(Jeannine Deckers)
Dominique
2M

Simon Park Orchestra
Eye Level
1M

The Tornados
Telstar
5M
—
Globetrotter (5)

The Overlanders
Michelle
0.2M
—
My Life (-)

Norman Greenbaum
Spirit in the Sky
2M
—
Jubilee (-)

Zager and Evans
In the Year 2525
(Exordium & Terminus)
4M
—
Mr Turnkey (106)

Carl Douglas
Kung Fu Fighting
3M
—
Dance the Kung Fu (35)

1958
1962
1963
1963
1966
1967
1969
1969
1969
1972
1974
1974

KEY

Artist
The Big Hit
EST. SALES (MILLIONS)
—
Follow Up (Its chart Position)

200,000 SALES

Terry Jacks
Seasons in the Sun

14M

—

If You Go Away (8)

**Joe Dolce
Music Theatre**
Shaddap You Face

6M

—

If You Want to
Be Happy
(7)

Lipps Inc
Funkytown

5M

—

Designer
Music (-)

Lou Bega
Mambo No.5

6M

—

I Got a
Girl
(55)

Anita Ward
Ring My Bell

2M

—

Make Believe
Lovers (-)

Toni Basil
Mickey

3M

—

Nobody (52)

Baha Men
Who Let
the Dogs Out?

4M

—

You All Dat
(14)

**Typically
Tropical**
Barbados

0.25M

—

Rocket
Now (-)

M
Pop Muzik

2M

—

Moonlight and Muzak
(33)

**DJ Pied Piper
and the
Masters of
Ceremonies**
Do You Really
Like It?

0.5M

Renée and Renato
Save Your Love

0.5M

—

Just One
More Kiss
(48)

1979

1979

1980

1980

1982

1982

1999

2000

2001

•107

DAWN OF THE SYNTHESIZER

The synthesizer has experienced a long and glorious history. Here's a patched timeline of some notable moments from the early days and (overleaf) the subsequent renaissance of the synth.

1967 — *Silver Apples of the Moon* by Morton Subotnick of the San Francisco Tape Center is released. Subnotick playing Buchla synth.

Mort Garson's *The Zodiac Cosmic Sounds* suite, "a musical mindbending trip through the astrological signs" heavily features Paul Beaver on Moog Modular.

Bernie Krauss and Paul Beaver do a roaring trade in Moogs from a booth at the Monterey festival. Many punters are stoned. Beaver ends up playing on *The Trip* and *Point Blank* soundtracks and albums by The Byrds, The Doors and The Monkees.

1969 — *The Well-Tempered Synthesizer* by Wendy/Walter Carlos. Follow-up to *Switched-On Bach*, includes Handel's *Water Music* and other classical compositions rendered on a modular Moog.

Peter Zinovieff develops the VCS3, which features on Roxy Music's early albums and becomes the voice of the Daleks on *Dr Who*.

1952 — Robert Moog graduates from the Bronx High School of Science in New York (and later Cornell University). Early interest in theremins.

1962 — Don Buchla forms Buchla and Associates in Berkeley, California.

1964 — Robert Moog produces the first voltage-controlled Moog Modular Analogue Synthesizer.

1960 — Edward Artemiev, studying at the Moscow Conservatory, sees an advert to work as a volunteer on the newly developed ANZ synthesizer. A decade later, Artemiev meets film director Andrei Tarkovsky at a party, and the soundtrack to the 1972 film *Solaris* is composed on a huge ANZ synthesizer, using sinewaves etched onto glass discs.

1963 — Buchla invents the 100 Series Modular Electronic Music System, having been asked by the San Francisco Tape Center to develop an electronic instrument for live performance.

1966 — Pauline Oliveros, "Once Again/ Buchla Piece".

1968 — Switched-on Bach, by Walter Carlos. The music of Johann Sebastian Bach performed on a modular Moog synthesizer becomes the biggest-selling classical-music record of the year, selling over a million copies.

The debut *Silver Apples* LP is released, recorded on a home-made "primitive" synthesizer.

1970 — Harold Budd, records *The Oak of the Golden Dreams* on their Buchla Electronic Music System.

Florian Fricke's Moog synthesizer "channels the frequencies of the cosmos" on Popol Vuh's debut LP, *Affenstude*.

1972
Brian Eno's VSC3 appears on Roxy Music's self-titled debut LP.

Chicory Tip's "Son of My Father", co-written by Giorgio Moroder, the first number 1 single to feature a modular Moog.

Serge Tcherepnin, a music-composition tutor at the California Institute of Arts, develops his Serge Modular to bring synths to the people (and out of expensive, inaccessible recording studios and laboratories).

Italian composer Piero Umiliani releases his Apollo Moog soundtrack, *L'Uomo Nello Spazio* (The Man in Space), a tribute to the Apollo moon landings.

1974
Suzanne Ciani arrives in New York City with her Buchla 200 series modular synth.

Harmonia release *Live, 1974*.

1977
Giorgio Moroder produces Donna Summer's "I Feel Love" on a huge 1960s Moog Modular. "Will change the sound of club music for the next 15 years," Brian Eno.

Musician Kevin Braheny customises a Serge Modular to produce the Mighty Serge – later features on Michael Stearn's ambient electronic epic *Planetary Unfolding* (1981).

Christopher Franke plays a Moog Modular synth, Projekt Elektronik sequencer, Computerstudio Digital Sequencer, Mellotron, ARP Pro Soloist synthesizer, Elka String synthesizer and an Oberheim sequencer on Tangerine Dream's soundtrack to horror flick *Sorcerer*.

1980
Roland TR-808 is introduced to the market. Invented by Ikutaro Kakehashi, over a three-year period of production, it goes on to feature on Marvin Gaye's "Sexual Healing", Afrika Bambaataa and the Soulsonic Force's "Planet Rock" and Soft Cell's "Tainted Love", among (many) others.

Laurie Spiegel starts feeding Buchla synth and Moog sounds into a GROOVE music computer in New York, resulting in the LP *The Expanding Universe*.

1982
Vangelis's *Blade Runner* soundtrack composed on a Yamaha CS-80.

1983
Moog Source is behind the bassline to New Order's "Blue Monday".

The whole world, it seems, owns a Yamaha DX7 synthesizer.

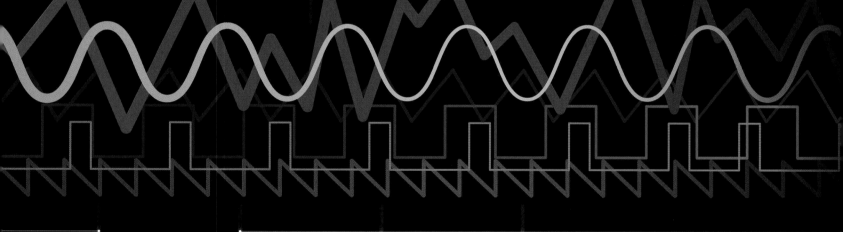

1973
VSC3 – Roxy Music, *For Your Pleasure*; Roland release the compact SH2000 – the synth most commonly seen later in the 1970s and early 1980s on *Top of the Pops*.

1975
Moog Polymoog is released on the market, based on home-organ technology. You could now play the Moog in your front room.

1978
Sun Ra plays a Moog Minimoog on *Languidity*.

1981
Depeche Mode hit the road with a Moog Source synth and a PPG Wave 2.0 synth.

The Human League's *Dare* was recorded using a Casio M10 synth sampler keyboard; a Casio VL-1 monophonic synthesizer and sequencer; a Roland Jupiter-4 analog synth; a Roland System 700 modular synthesizer; Korg Delta and 770 analogue synths; a Yamaha CS-15 analogue synth (also favoured by Marillion on *Script for a Jester's Tear*); a Linn LM-1 drum machine; and a new-fangled Roland MC-8 Microcomposer (a microprocessor and sequencer).

Orchestral Manoeuvres in the Dark release *Architecture & Morality*.

REBIRTH OF THE SYNTHESIZER/
SYNTH IS COOL AGAIN

The synth was always cool in places like Detroit and Chicago. Unfortunately, in Britain it became associated with tacky, mass-produced pop... until it was rediscovered and fetishised anew.

1993 Stereolab, *Transient Random-Noise Bursts with Announcements.*

1998 Boards of Canada, *Music Has the Right to Children.*

2005 Keith Fullerton Whitman's *Multiples* (features "Stereo Music for Serge Modular Prototype, parts 1–3").

1994 Irresistible hazy, ambient synth opening to A Guy Called Gerald's drum & bass 12", "Finley's Rainbow".

2002 James Murphy of LCD Soundsystem sings "I hear you're buying a synthesizer..." on "Losing My Edge".

2008 Benge releases a compilation of tracks played on twenty different synthesizers, *Twenty Systems*. Released as a hardback colour booklet full of circuit diagrams and full-colour, close-up photography of synths, keyboards, trunk cabling, knobs, dials and switches. Highlights include "1975 Moog Polymoog" and "1986 NED Synclavier".

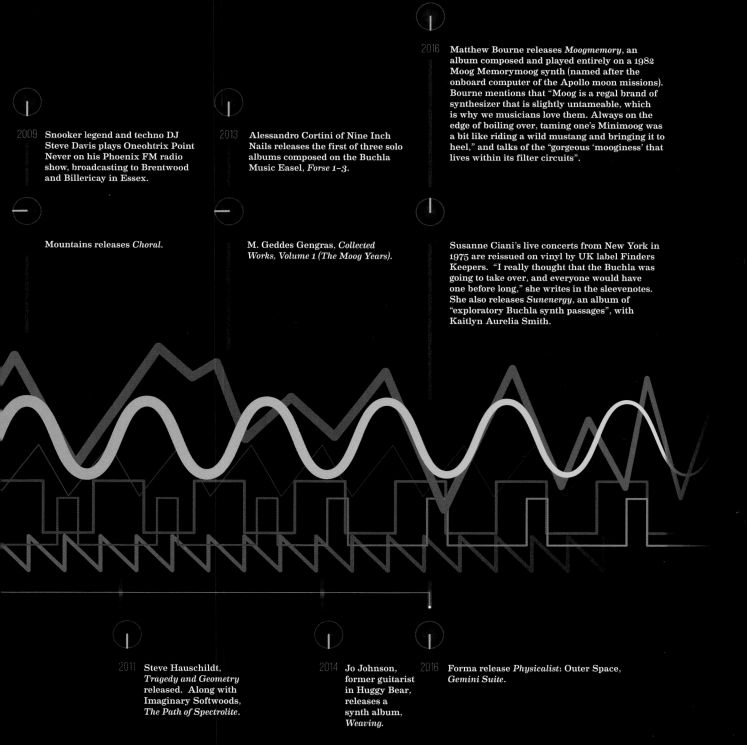

2009 — Snooker legend and techno DJ Steve Davis plays Oneohtrix Point Never on his Phoenix FM radio show, broadcasting to Brentwood and Billericay in Essex.

Mountains releases *Choral*.

2013 — Alessandro Cortini of Nine Inch Nails releases the first of three solo albums composed on the Buchla Music Easel, *Forse 1–3*.

M. Geddes Gengras, *Collected Works, Volume 1 (The Moog Years)*.

2016 — Matthew Bourne releases *Moogmemory*, an album composed and played entirely on a 1982 Moog Memorymoog synth (named after the onboard computer of the Apollo moon missions). Bourne mentions that "Moog is a regal brand of synthesizer that is slightly untameable, which is why we musicians love them. Always on the edge of boiling over, taming one's Minimoog was a bit like riding a wild mustang and bringing it to heel," and talks of the "gorgeous 'mooginess' that lives within its filter circuits".

Susanne Ciani's live concerts from New York in 1975 are reissued on vinyl by UK label Finders Keepers. "I really thought that the Buchla was going to take over, and everyone would have one before long," she writes in the sleevenotes. She also releases *Sunenergy*, an album of "exploratory Buchla synth passages", with Kaitlyn Aurelia Smith.

2011 — Steve Hauschildt, *Tragedy and Geometry* released. Along with Imaginary Softwoods, *The Path of Spectrolite*.

2014 — Jo Johnson, former guitarist in Huggy Bear, releases a synth album, *Weaving*.

2016 — Forma release *Physicalist*; Outer Space, *Gemini Suite*.

Sources: Wikipedia, album sleevenotes from David Stubbs's *Future Days, Krautrock and the Building of Modern Germany* (2014, Faber), *The Wire* 396, moogfoundation. org, pitchfork.com, www.tuug.fi, noisey.vice.com, matthewbourne.com

COMPARING
SOUND
WAVES

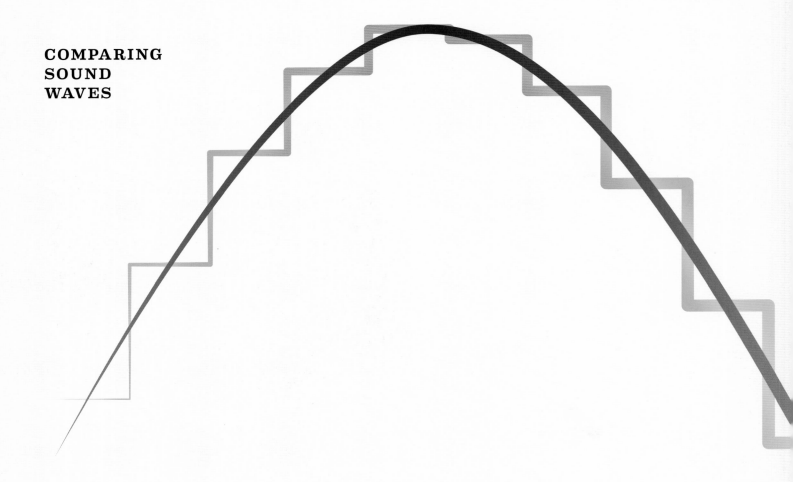

ANALOGUE SOUND

The illustration (right) reveals an electron-microscopic view of a stylus moving between the grooves of a vinyl record. The stylus vibrates between the grooves of the LP – moving from left to right, then back, between the grooves, following the two-channel stereo encoding of audio information. The size of the grooves is directly linked to the notes stored: heavy bass notes require deeper, wider grooves; hence, for reasons of space, techno/hip-hop dance-music 12' singles are cut at 45rpm with fewer grooves on the record but ones which will produce a louder, deeper sound. The vibrations from the needle move a couple of magnets inside the cartridge near a coil, which generates the electricity that is amplified into the audio signal.

AN ELECTRON MICROSCOPIC STYLUS PLAYING A VINYL LP

DIGITAL SOUND

A digital recording only takes a snapshot of an analogue soundwave. On the pitted surface of a CD (right), where there is no data (or pits) on the digital file, there is silence. It's a cleaner, but colder, sound; one that doesn't possess all the warmth, crackle, static, and total range of recorded sound – the perceived "impurity" of vinyl that makes the sound of music on vinyl richer, and so much more attractive to audiophiles. David Byrne noted in *How Music Works* that the history of music could be considered one of convenience triumphing over quality – "crappy sound forever" – the LP (with its tighter grooves closer to the middle) replacing the 45 and 78; the cassette replacing the LP; the CD replacing vinyl: "The spectrum of sound on analogue mediums has an infinite number of gradations, whereas in the digital world everything is sliced into a finite number of slivers. Slivers and bits might fool the ear into believing that they represent a continuous audio spectrum (psychoacoustics at work), but by nature they are still ones and zeros: steps rather than a smooth slope [see main illustration] . . . it's music in pill form, it delivers vitamins, it does the job, but something is missing." But where, in the main, David Byrne is right to scorn convenience, there's nothing like listening to Carl Craig, the Wedding Present or Porter Ricks while burning up a motorway.

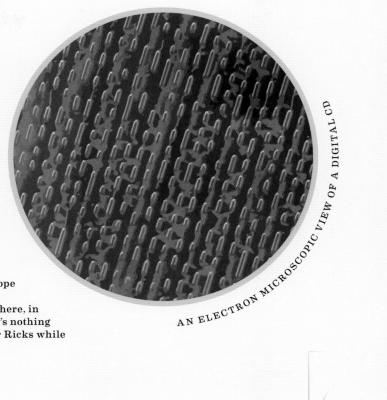

AN ELECTRON MICROSCOPIC VIEW OF A DIGITAL CD

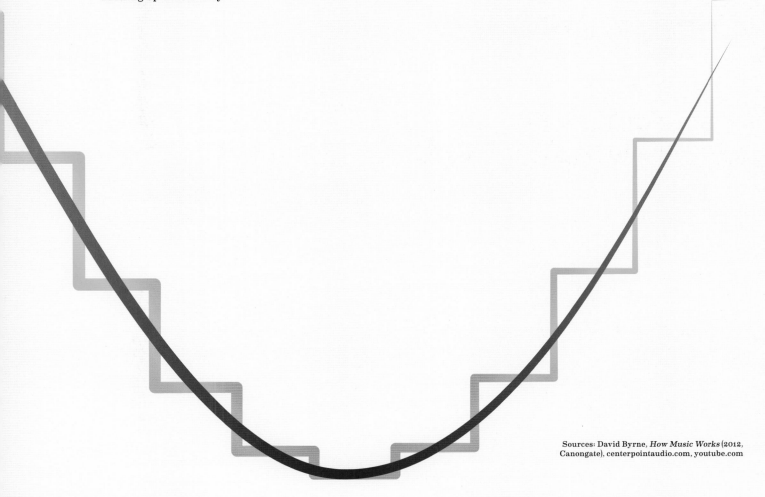

Sources: David Byrne, *How Music Works* (2012, Canongate), centerpointaudio.com, youtube.com

GRIME MAP OF LONDON

London mayor Sadiq Khan is a grime fan, familiar with Wiley, Stormzy and the Section Boyz. At an *NME* Awards ceremony in 2017 he presented Skepta with the Best Male Act award: "This guy is cool, this guy is talented, this guy is a role model, this guy is a Londoner and it's Skepta." Grime is the 21st-century music London is known across the globe for. Here's a map of grime's roots and a few present-day names.

"I was about 18 when I started making music, making beats, my mindset was totally different. It was me, what I knew, Meridian, Tottenham." – Skepta. Skepta, JME, Meridian Dan and others grew up on the Meridian Walk estate forming the original Meridian Crew, before disbanding and splitting to form Boy Better Know and Bloodline Family.‡

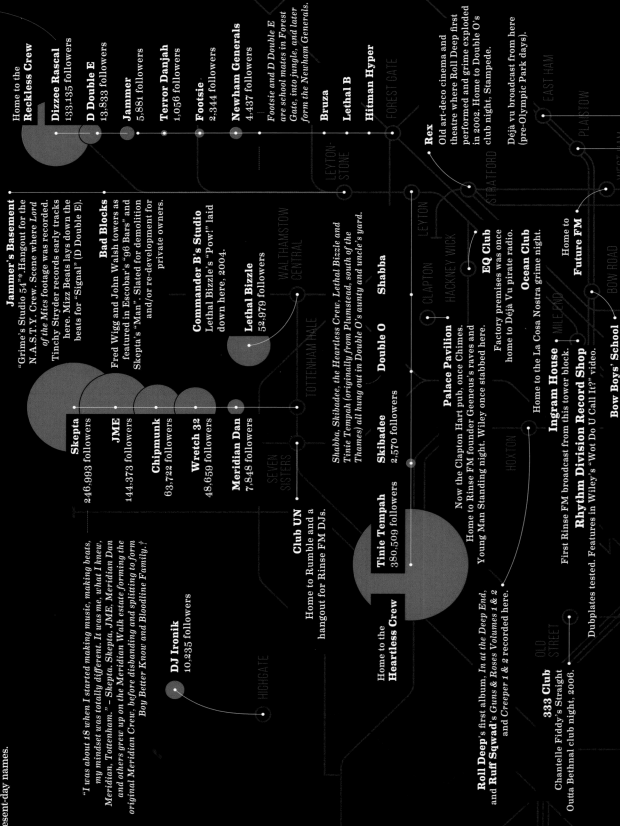

Home to the Reckless Crew

Commonly associated with Roll Deep this guy is also in Forest Gate's Reckless Crew, was also in Forest Gate's Reckless Crew from Bow, was also in Forest Gate's Reckless Crew.

Dizzee Rascal 133,135 followers

D Double E 13,833 followers

Jammer 5,881 followers

Terror Danjah 1,056 followers

Footsie 2,344 followers

Newham Generals 4,437 followers

Footsie and D Double E are school mates in Forest Gate, into jungle, and later form the Newham Generals.

Bruza

Lethal B

Hitman Hyper

FOREST GATE

Rex
Old art-deco cinema and theatre where Roll Deep first performed and grime exploded in 2002. Home to Double O's club night, Stampede.

Déjà vu broadcast from here (pre-Olympic Park days).

EAST HAM

PLAISTOW

WEST HAM

LEYTON-STONE

STRATFORD

Jammer's Basement
"Grime's Studio 54".* Hangout for the N.A.S.T.Y. Crew. Scene where *Lord of the Mics* footage was recorded. Tinchy Stryder records early tracks here. Mizz Beats lays down the beats for "Signal" (D Double E).

Bad Blocks
Fred Wigg and John Walsh towers as featured in Escobar's "96 Bars" and Skepta's "Man". Slated for demolition and/or re-development for private owners.

WALTHAMSTOW CENTRAL

Commander B's Studio
Lethal Bizzle's "Pow!" laid down here, 2004.

Lethal Bizzle 52,979 followers

LEYTON

EQ Club
Factory premises was once home to Déjà Vu pirate radio.

Ocean Club
Home to the La Cosa Nostra grime night.

HACKNEY WICK

CLAPTON

Future FM
Home to

BOW ROAD

Skepta 246,993 followers

JME 144,373 followers

Chipmunk 63,722 followers

Wretch 32 48,659 followers

Meridian Dan 7,848 followers

TOTTENHAM HALE

SEVEN SISTERS

Double O   **Shabba**

Shabba, Skibadee, the Heartless Crew, Lethal Bizzle and Tinie Tempah (originally from Plumstead, south of the Thames) all hung out in Double O's aunty and uncle's yard.

Skibadee 2,570 followers

Palace Pavilion
Now the Clapton Hart pub, once Chimes. Home to Rinse FM founder Geeneus's raves and Young Man Standing night. Wiley once stabbed here.

HOXTON

Ingram House
First Rinse FM broadcast from this tower block.

MILE END

Rhythm Division Record Shop
Dubplates tested. Features in Wiley's "Wot Do U Call It?" video.

Bow Boys' School
alma mater to the likes of Wiley and Slimzee.

Club UN
Home to Rumble and a hangout for Rinse FM DJs.

DJ Ironik 10,235 followers

HIGHGATE

Tinie Tempah 380,509 followers

Home to the Heartless Crew

Roll Deep's first album, *In at the Deep End*, and **Ruff Sqwad**'s *Guns & Roses Volumes 1 & 2* and *Creeper 1 & 2* recorded here.

OLD STREET

333 Club
Chantelle Fiddy's Straight Outta Bethnal club night, 2006.

Line Centre

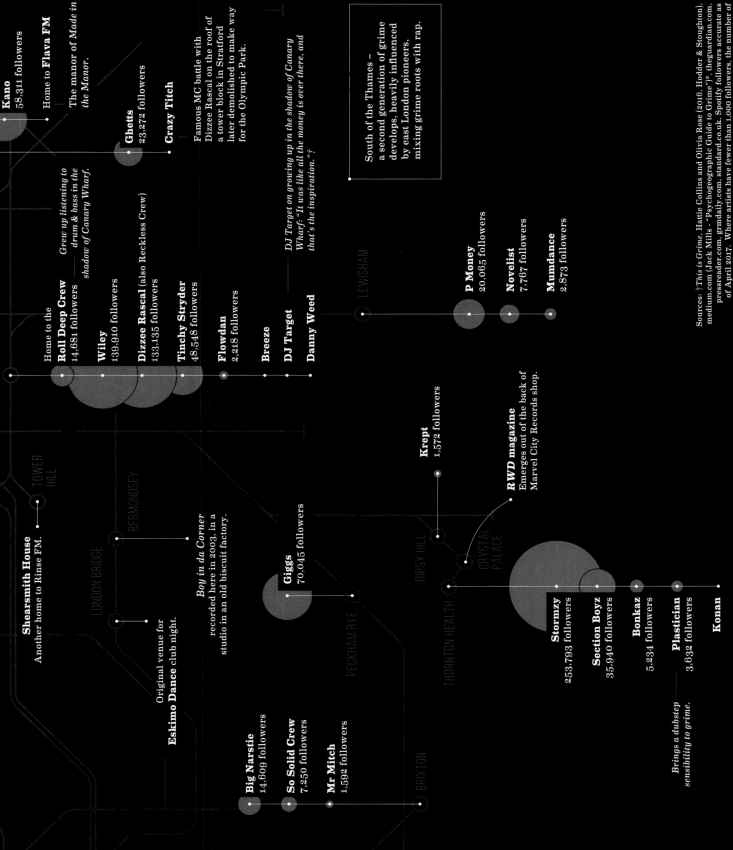

Kano
58,311 followers

Home to **Flava FM**

The manor of *Made in the Manor*.

Ghetts
23,272 followers

Crazy Titch

Famous MC battle with Dizzee Rascal on the roof of a tower block in Stratford later demolished to make way for the Olympic Park.

DJ Target on growing up in the shadow of Canary Wharf: "It was like all the money is over there, and that's the inspiration."†

South of the Thames – a second generation of grime develops, heavily influenced by east London pioneers, mixing grime roots with rap.

Home to the
Roll Deep Crew 14,681 followers

Grew up listening to drum & bass in the shadow of Canary Wharf.

Wiley
139,910 followers

Dizzee Rascal (also Reckless Crew)
133,135 followers

Tinchy Stryder
48,548 followers

Flowdan
2,218 followers

Breeze

DJ Target

Danny Weed

LIMEHOUSE

LEWISHAM

P Money
20,065 followers

Novelist
7,767 followers

Mumdance
2,873 followers

TOWER HILL

Shearsmith House
Another home to Rinse FM.

BERMONDSEY

Original venue for
Eskimo Dance club night.

LONDON BRIDGE

Boy in da Corner recorded here in 2003, in a studio in an old biscuit factory.

Giggs
70,045 followers

PECKHAM RYE

Krept
1,572 followers

RWD magazine
Emerges out of the back of Marvel City Records shop.

GIPSY HILL

CRYSTAL PALACE

THORNTON HEATH

Stormzy
253,793 followers

Section Boyz
35,940 followers

Bonkaz
5,234 followers

Plastician
3,632 followers

Konan

Brings a dubstep sensibility to grime.

Big Narstie
14,609 followers

So Solid Crew
7,250 followers

Mr Mitch
1,592 followers

BRIXTON

Sources: †*This is Grime*, Hattie Collins and Olivia Rose (2016, Hodder & Stoughton), medium.com (Jack Mills – "Psychogeographic Guide to Grime")*, theguardian.com, medium.com, pressreader.com, grmdaily.com, standard.co.uk. Spotify followers accurate as of April 2017. Where artists have fewer than 1,000 followers, the number of followers is unlisted.

BLIND BLUESMEN AND WOMEN

There's no question record companies in 1920s America suddenly hit upon a market for black street singers of a mostly sacred (but sometimes profane) nature. "The labels knew they could sell more records by putting the word 'blind' before the artist's name," blues collector John Tefteller told *Goldmine* in 2013 – before outlining the unforgivable state of race relations back then, black artists being recorded "almost exclusively" by white producers. "I don't know if these singers really wanted to call themselves 'blind' or not. Probably not," Tefteller concluded. Hopefully, though, this spread will inspire future record-shopping trips and deep journeys of musical exploration through the American South.

COMPLETELY BLIND BLUESMEN AND WOMEN

Blind Joe Taggart
1892–1961

Life blind **100%** | from **Birth**

South Carolina country blues and gospel singer and guitarist who also recorded under a wide variety of other "blind" names, as well as, debatably, Six Cylinder Smith. His famous "The Storm is Passing Over" can be found on the excellent Mississippi Records compilation *Fight On, Your Time Ain't Long* – next to a track, "Wouldn't Mind Dying" ("if dying was all"), by Blind Mamie Forehand.

Blind Lemon Jefferson
1893–1929

Life blind **100%** | from **Birth**

Laid down 92 sides for Paramount in Chicago. Either born blind before freezing to death in a snowy Chicago gutter in December 1929* or (Paul Fryer suggests in the sleevenotes to *One Dime Blues*) an overweight Lemon collapsed in the back of his chauffeur-driven car and was also only partially blind: he may have entertained unemployed cotton-pickers while bo-weavil ripped through the crop, but could nevertheless "identify various types of money bills in seconds". "Black Snake Moan" sounds as chilling now as it did in 1927.

Blind Mamie Forehand
1895–1936

Life blind **100%** | from **Birth**

Gospel singer, triangle and finger-symbol player, married A.C. Forehand, a guitar and harmonica player who was also blind. The pair recorded together, but, after Mamie died in 1936, A.C. married a blind pianist and organist, Frances Forest. John Fahey wrote of the Forehands, "Their singing and playing sounds worshipful, adoring and humble... one foot on earth and one in heaven. They never cease to astound me."

Blind Boy Blake
1896–1934

Life blind **100%** | from **Birth**

Fingerpicking, Piedmont blues guitarist from Newport News, Virginia. Amanda Petrusich comes close to finding his much sought after Paramount 78, "Miss Emma Lizer/Dissatisfied Blues" in her book *Do Not Sell at Any Price*.

Blind Willie McTell
1898–1959

Life blind **100%** | from **Birth**

Gifted 12-string guitarist and singer, fêted by Bob Dylan and the White Stripes, responsible for Ralph "Streets of London" McTell's surname and the Allman Brothers' staple "Statesboro Blues". McTell's biographer, Michael Gray, wrote of him never achieving a hit record but being widely loved: "Working clubs and parking lots, playing to blacks and whites, tobacco workers and college kids, human jukebox and local hero [McTell]] enjoyed a modest career and an independent life."

PARTIALLY BLIND BLUESMEN AND WOMEN

Blind Uncle Gaspard
1878–1937

Life blind 88% | **from Unknown**

Partially blind, melancholic Cajun guitarist from Louisiana who apparently suffered with depression and alcoholism. On a 78 like "Mercredi Soir Passé", it's possible to hear the future mournful strumming of a Jackson C. Frank, or even a hint of Karen Dalton.

Reverend Gary Davis
1896–1972

Life blind 90% | **from Ulcers**

A difficult childhood in South Carolina: blind, rejected by his mother, father shot dead by a sheriff. Nevertheless, the young Davis constructed an early guitar from his grandmother's pie pan and taught himself to play. He married, travelled the Carolinas and Tennessee playing on street corners and giving guitar lessons for cash (to, among others, Blind Boy Blake). but left his first wife when he found out that "she wasn't my wife but everybody else's."

Blind Willie Johnson
1897–1945

Life blind 85% | **from Eclipse or lye water**

Texan gospel and blues singer and guitarist. Could have been blinded by a solar eclipse, or accidently doused in lye water (an early drain unclogger) by his stepmother mid-argument with Johnson's father over the former's "infidelity". Disturbingly gravelly voice heard on "John the Revelator" from 1930 contrasts strikingly with Angeline Johnson's vocal (no doubt Lee Hazlewood and Nancy Sinatra were listening). Died of pneumonia contracted after getting soaked in a doomed attempt to put out a house fire.*

Blind Joe Reynolds
1904–1968

Life blind 60% | **from Shot in the face**

Elusive and itinerant Paramount recording artist thought to hail from Tallulah, Louisiana, where he was blinded by a shotgun blast to the face before being picked up performing on a street by renowned talent scout H.C. Speir. Vocal phrasings on "Cold Woman Blues" pre-figure Janis Joplin and Mick Jagger by half a century. Cream covered "Outside Woman Blues" on their *Disraeli Gears* LP.

Blind Teddy Darby
1906–1975

Life blind 71% | **from Glaucoma**

St Louis blues guitarist and pianist who served time for selling moonshine. Also recorded under the names of Blind Blues Darby and Blind Squire Turner. His rare Paramount 78 "Lose Your Mind"/"What am I to Do?" sold for $1000 in 2007.

Blind Boy Fuller
1907–1941

Life blind 44% | **from Untreated neonatal conjunctivitis**

Fingerpicking guitarist and singer from North Carolina who went blind at 19 from untreated neonatal conjunctivitis. Served time after shooting his wife in the leg, and was responsible for "Truckin' My Blues Away" and "Get Your Yas Yas Out". Amanda Petrusich's *Do Not Sell at Any Price* features a great account of contemporary guitarist Nathan Salsburg retrieving a Blind Boy Fuller LP from a dumpster in Kentucky.

Blind Roosevelt Graves
1909–1962

Life blind 79% | **from Unknown physical injury**

Harmonica player who lost his sight in childhood. Woody Guthrie wrote of Terry's harmonica playing, "The tobacco sheds of North Carolina are in it and all of the blistered and hurt and hardened hands cheated and left empty, hurt and left crying."

Sonny Terry
1911–1986

Life blind Unknown | **from Unknown**

Mississippi blues guitarist and singer responsible for "Woke Up This Morning with My Mind on Jesus", included on *American Primitive vol. 1* and described by John Fahey as the "hottest 'religious record' ever made."

Blind Gussie Nesbit
Unknown

Life blind Unknown | **from Unknown**

A preacher/guitarist from Georgia, Nesbit's righteous growl is probably best heard on "Motherless Children", from 1935. Lonnie Donegan would have heard Gussie Nesbit's "Canaan Land".

Sources: *Goldmine*, Mike Greenblatt, 24 April 2013 www.goldminemag.com; listverse.com; Amanda Petrusich, *Do Not Sell at Any Price: the Wild, Obsessive Hunt for the World's Rarest 78rpm Records* (Scribner, 2014)*; *Harry Smith's Anthology of American Folk Music* (sleevenotes); Woody Guthrie quoted in Greil Marcus's *Invisible Republic: Bob Dylan's Basement Tapes* (Picador, 1997); "no one really knows if the whole band was blind," blues collector John Tefteller told *Goldmine* in April 2013, www.goldminemag.com**; *Hand Me My Travellin' Shoes: In Search of Blind Willie McTell*, Michael Gray (Bloomsbury, 2007); sleevenotes to *American Primitive Volume 1, Raw Pre-War Gospel (1926—1936)* by John Fahey, August 1997, Revenant records; Paul Fryer, sleevenotes to *One Dime Blues*, Blind Lemon Jefferson (Aldabra records, late 1980s).

COVERED IN GLORY

Two of the biggest bands of all time started off their careers playing cover versions, but The Beatles' and The Rolling Stones' careers would surely have faltered had they not gone on to write their own material. However, many artists unfortunately find that their cover versions are what they are best known for; Sinead O'Connor, for instance is best-known for the Prince-penned "Nothing Compares 2 U".

For a cover version to succeed, it has to take what's good about the original and spice it up with the covering artist's magic. And while not all cover versions are better than the original (say hello to Mike Flowers Pops' "Wonderwall"), they often still do as well in the charts.

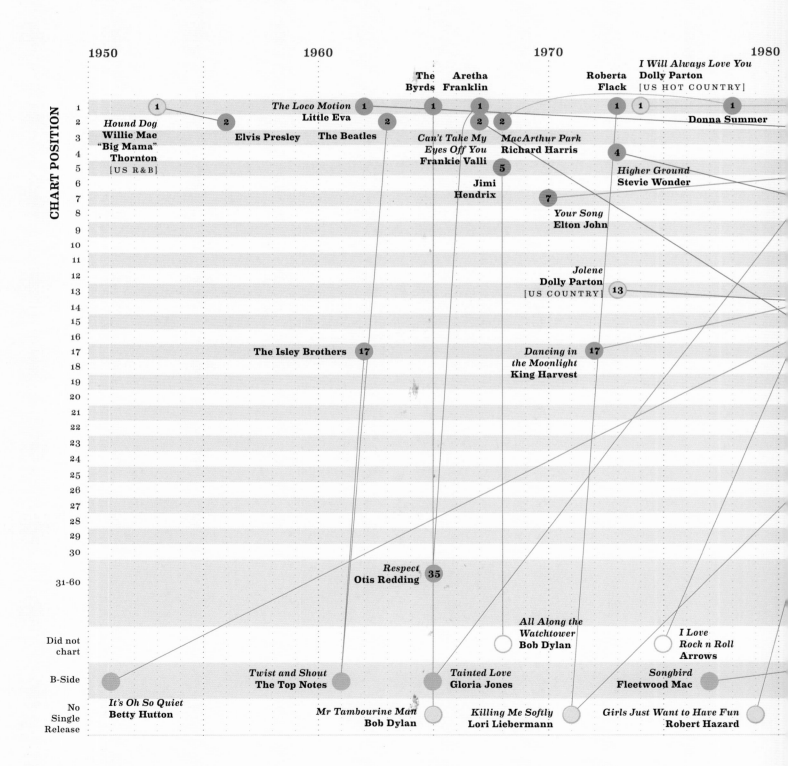

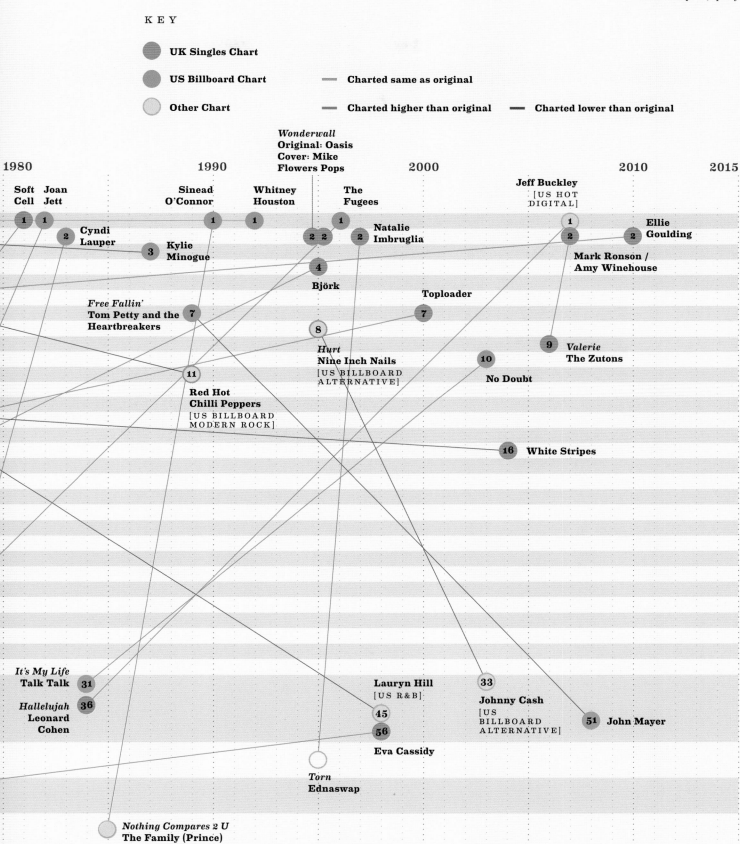

Sources: Wikipedia, Spotify

KEY

⬤ UK Singles Chart

⬤ US Billboard Chart   ▬ Charted same as original

○ Other Chart   ▬ Charted higher than original   ▬ Charted lower than original

1980   1990   2000   2010   2015

Wonderwall
Original: Oasis
Cover: Mike
Flowers Pops

Jeff Buckley
[US HOT DIGITAL]

Soft **Joan**
Cell **Jett**
Sinead **Whitney** **The**
O'Connor **Houston** **Fugees**

①① ① ① ① ①

② **Cyndi**
Lauper
②② ② **Natalie**
Imbruglia
② **Ellie**
Goulding

③ **Kylie**
Minogue
④ **Mark Ronson /**
Amy Winehouse

④ **Björk**

Free Fallin'
Tom Petty and the
Heartbreakers
⑦ **Toploader**
⑦

⑧ ⑨ *Valerie*
The Zutons

Hurt
Nine Inch Nails
[US BILLBOARD ALTERNATIVE]
⑩ **No Doubt**

⑪ **Red Hot**
Chilli Peppers
[US BILLBOARD MODERN ROCK]

⑯ **White Stripes**

It's My Life
Talk Talk ㉛
Lauryn Hill
[US R&B]
㉝

Hallelujah ㊱
Leonard
Cohen
Johnny Cash
[US BILLBOARD ALTERNATIVE]

㊺ � **John Mayer**

㊷ **Eva Cassidy**

○
Torn
Ednaswap

○ *Nothing Compares 2 U*
The Family (Prince)

HOTELS IN SONGS

The life of a musician on tour involves many hours in tour buses or on planes along with many nights away from home in hotels. It's no wonder then that many of the most well-known lyrics relate to those lonely nights staring at four walls.

74 Hastings St W
Vancouver
BC V6B 1G6
Canada

(It was a bar)

2011
GRAND UNION HOTEL
THE DREADNOUGHTS

4020 W.
Lafayette
Boulevard
Detroit, Michigan

(Now a 'flophouse')

2001
HOTEL YORBA
WHITE STRIPES

Stockton Inn
1 Main Street
Stockton
NJ 08559

1949
THERE'S A SMALL HOTEL
ELLA FITZGERALD

1987
BLUE HOTEL
CHRIS ISAAK

Stockton, California

(Ella could be singing about either)

2012
SUN HOTEL
THE MENZINGERS

1974
CHELSEA HOTEL #2
LEONARD COHEN

Montecito Inn 1295
Coast Village Rd
Santa Barbara
CA 93108

410 Cedar Ave
Scranton
PA 18505

(It was a bar)

222 W 23rd St
New York City
NY 10011

1977
HOTEL CALIFORNIA
EAGLES

Elvis Presley Blvd
Memphis, TN 38116

1956
HEARTBREAK HOTEL
ELVIS PRESLEY

Av. Atlântica
1702
Copacabana
Rio de Janeiro
RJ, 22021-001

1986
IMPERIAL HOTEL
STEVIE NICKS

1978
COPACABANA
BARRY MANILOW

120•

Sources: telegraph.co.uk, independent.ie, historicdetroit.org,
wikipedia, procolharum.com, stocktoninn.com, montecitoinn.com

Year of song
HOTEL SONG
BAND/ARTIST

⭐ Hotel exists

Hotel does not exist

Hotel might exist

1969
BALLAD OF JOHN AND YOKO
THE BEATLES

Apollolaan 138
Amsterdam, 1077 BG
Netherlands

London
UK

2008
HOTEL ISTANBUL
ELBOW

Rue d'Italie 1
1800 Vevey
Switzerland

1973
**SITTING IN MY
HOTEL**
THE KINKS

1973
GRAND HOTEL
PROCOL HARUM

Istanbul, Turkey

2001
KARMA HOTEL
SPOOKS

Tibet

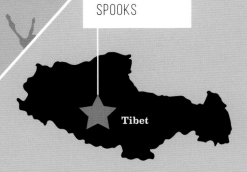

•121

MUSIC FLOODS THE BRAIN

You don't have to be a musician to have a musical brain. In fact, music – traditionally associated with the right hemisphere, which is the creative, perceptive side of the brain – actually floods through all cortical and subcortical areas of your old loaf. "Music-listening, performance, and composition engage nearly every area of the brain that we have so far identified, and involve nearly every neural subsystem," writes record producer turned neuroscientist Daniel Levitin in This Is Your Brain on Music. Indeed, music occupies more areas than language; Levitin even suggests music may have pre-dated and facilitated our ancestors' adoption of the spoken word – before also pointing out that, when the Ramones sang of having "no cerebellum" in "Teenage Lobotomy", they were on suspect ground, anatomically speaking (a lobotomy would remove the higher, frontal, organising lobes of the brain, not the deeper, evolutionarily ancient cerebellum of the lower brain). Here's a very basic visual guide to areas of the brain affected by music.

MOTOR CORTEX
Home of rhythm; listening to music can kickstart a damaged motor system into action. Oliver Sacks recalls the beat of Mendelssohn's *Violin Concerto in E minor* to get him walking again after an accident. Music can also calm the tics and explosions of a Tourette's sufferer and bring calm and release to the spasms and freezes of Parkinson's disease.

SOMATOSENSORY CORTEX
Where normally this would be biased towards the stronger hand, the grey matter is symmetrical in keyboard players.

FRONTAL CORTEX
Damage to left hemisphere here – loss of powers of abstraction and language – has been known to result in a flooding through of creative input from the right-hand side of the brain. Oliver Sacks, in *Musicophilia*, memorably wrote of the orthopaedic surgeon struck by lightning in a phone booth who, on recovering, suddenly became obsessed with piano music – to the extent of mastering Chopin, composing his own pieces and performing as a concert pianist. Music can also be a source of great pleasure and communication for non-verbal autistic children and adults.

MEDIAL PREFRONTAL CORTEX
Thought to be a store of musical memory, particularly from adolescence.

AUDITORY CORTEX/TEMPORAL LOBE
Thicker folds of grey matter discovered in famous composers and musicians. Auditory cortex is responsible for sound processing – found to be generally 102 per cent larger in musicians, giving them a sharper, faster response to sound in general, whether that's tone, pitch or picking out speech in a noisy room.

PROLACTIN
A brain chemical that is released as a curative to grief. Williamson writes of a feel-good subconscious prolactin fix when craving sad music to make the listener feel good again.

Sources: Daniel Levitin, *This Is Your Brain on Music* (Atlantic, 2008)
Oliver Sacks, *Musicophilia* (Picador, 2008), Victoria Williamson, *You Are the Music* (Icon, 2014)
www.popsci.com

HIPPOCAMPUS

Daniel Levitin, in *This Is Your Brain on Music*, locates the amygadala (the seat of memory that has "a strong emotional component") as sitting right next to the hippocampus, where past musical associations are stored. Memory and emotion are intimately connected. As Levitin writes, "As soon as we hear a song that we haven't heard since a particular time in our lives, the floodgates of memory open and we're immersed in memories." Which, if nothing else, explains the continual presence of *Top of the Pops 2* on television schedules.

CORPUS CALLOSUM

A broad band of nerve fibres joining the right and left hemispheres of the brain. Victoria Williamson, in *You are the Music*, writes of studies showing an enhanced corpus callosum in "right-handed keyboard musicians and string musicians". Thicker, denser white matter has been known to coat the neural pathways between the temporal and frontal lobes of musicians – the release of neurotransmitters like dopamine from the deeper, pleasure centres of the brain to the frontal cortex also point to a "brain reward system" that can come into play on hearing both familiar and new music.

NUCLEUS ACCUMBENS

The brain's reward centre. Dopamine released from here; mood generally improved on listening to music.

HOW MUSIC FLOWS AROUND THE BRAIN

AMYGADALA

A subcortical area of the brain, the "emotion centre"; also forms emotional responses to music as part of a complex network of brain wiring, both cortical and subcortical. Someone with frontaltotemporal dementia (FTD), or damage to a more vulnerable part of the brain, may retain the emotional core memory of music. Hence, Alzheimer sufferers can burst into perfectly recalled song. As Victoria Williamson writes in *You Are the Music*, "Musical memories really do, in every sense, become part of our inner being."

CEREBELLUM

Evolutionarily speaking one of the oldest parts of the brain, and a centre for controlling movement and monitoring beat. Lights up in studies when music is played that the listener knows well. Responsible for the "habituation circuit": on walking into the house you instantly detect that something is wrong with the central-heating system as the beat of the boiler firing up is somehow irregular. Ditto that demo version of U2's "Pride (In the Name of Love)" that doesn't sound quite right. Deterioration of the cerebellum in Parkinson's sufferers; enlarged neo-cerebellum in people with Williams Syndrome (often gifted musicians).

SOUND MAP OF AFRICA

Perhaps just a little tired of the guitars and drums, verse–chorus–verse of the Western rock cannon? Here's a great starting list of superb 21st-century albums of unearthed historical and contemporary African recordings.

Sources: Discogs ratings: Discogs.com

KEY

COUNTRY — Year of Release
Album — LABEL NAME
Artist
Description
Discogs rating

MOROCCO

Ecstatic Music of the Jemaa El Fna — 2010
Various — SUBLIME FREQUENCIES
Electrifying compilation of street musicians who play by night in the central square in Marrakesh – working-class oud, banjo and mandolin players playing songs of love, injustice and solidarity, powered by car batteries.
Discogs rating: 4.68 ★★★★

Nuits de Printemps and Nuits de Été — 2016-17
Abdou El Omari — RADIO MARTIKO
Three-volume series of exploratory keyboard LPs from the 1970s.
Discogs rating: 4.68 ★★★★
Discogs rating: 4.79 ★★★★

ALGERIA

1970's Algerian Proto-Rai Underground — 2008
Various — SUBLIME FREQUENCIES
Mournful trumpet and electric guitar with wah-wah pedal to add to the storm, whipped up on this superb compilation.
Discogs rating: 4.85 ★★★★

SENEGAL

Yiilo Jaam — 2011
Lewlewal de Podor — SAHEL SOUNDS/ MISSISSIPPI
Beautiful mellow guitar and hoddu album recorded in Podor.
Discogs rating: 4.43 ★★★☆

Waande Kadde — 2017
Amadou Binta Konté and Tidiane Thiam — SAHEL SOUNDS
Trance-like hoddu and acoustic-guitar music from the eponymous fishing village on the banks of the Senegal River; a follow-up of sorts to Yiilo Jaam from two members of Lewlewal de Podor.
Discogs rating: 4.17 ★★★☆

MALI

The Original Sound of Mali — 2017
Various — MR BONGO
Mostly 1970s groove-based compilation championed by BBC 6 Music's Lauren Laverne.
Discogs rating: 4.83 ★★★★

Le Super Biton National de Ségou — 2012
Le Super Biton — KINDRED SPIRITS
National de Ségou
Traditional instruments and electric guitars in seminal 1977 LP from Malian orchestra.
Discogs rating: 4.88 ★★★★

L'Orchestre Kanaga de Mopti — 2011
L'Orchestre — KINDRED SPIRITS
Kanaga de Mopti
Intense balafon and hand-drum freakout – superb sax and organ too.
Discogs rating: 4.91 ★★★★

Music from Saharan Cellphones — 2011
Various — SAHEL SOUNDS
Fine compilation of music made with cheap drum machines and pirated PC-based beat-making programs recorded on phones.
Discogs rating: 4.42 ★★★☆

Laila Je T'Aime: Guitar Music from the Western Sahel — 2012
Various — SAHEL SOUNDS
Atmospheric collection of largely acoustic guitar and desert blues from the dusty plains and scrubland of northern Mali; includes a superior version of The Police's "Message in a Bottle".
Discogs rating: 4.24 ★★★☆

Bush Taxi Mali — 2004
Various — SUBLIME FREQUENCIES
Contemplative guitar, balafon and flute recordings interspersed with some Bamako radio.
Discogs rating: 3.88 ★★★

NIGER

A Story of Sahel Sounds — 2016
Various — TEPPICH RECORDS
Terrific raw-sounding soundtrack of mostly live recordings for the documentary about the eponymous label.
Discogs rating: 4.50 ★★★★☆

Torodi — 2015
Hama — SAHEL SOUNDS
Tuareg synth album; incorporates hip-hop beats.
Discogs rating: 4.47 ★★★★☆

Agrim Agadez — 2017
Various — SAHEL SOUNDS
Another fine guitar compilation from the Sahel region, largely minimal and acoustic but includes a blistering cover of Jimi Hendrix's "Hey Joe" by Anza de L'Ader.
Discogs rating: 4.67 ★★★★

Les Filles de Illighadad — 2016
Fatou Seidi Ghali and — SAHEL SOUNDS
Alamnou Akrouni
Hypnotic acoustic guitar and self-titled vocal LP. Was named after their village and recorded in the open air.
Discogs rating: 4.57 ★★★★☆

Folk Music of the Sahel Volume 1: Niger — 2014
Various — SUBLIME FREQUENCIES
Wandering griots, Tuareg musicians, raw field recordings and heavy percussion combine in fantastic double LP and photo-book.
Discogs rating: 5.00 ★★★★

Tahoultine — 2011
Mdou Moctar — SAHEL SOUNDS
7" that launched the Tuareg guitarist on the world.
Discogs rating: 4.89 ★★★★

Et Son Orgue — 2013
Mammane Sani — MISSISSIPPI/ SAHEL SOUNDS
Blissed-out late-1970s/early-1980s organ instrumentals.
Discogs rating: 4.72 ★★★★

ETHIOPIA

Éthiopiques 4: Ethio Jazz and Musique Instrumentale, 1969–1974 — 1998
Mulatu Astatqe — BUDA MUSIQUE
Huge-selling Éthiopiques series. Volume 4 reached a worldwide audience after featuring in the film Broken Flowers.
Discogs rating: 4.66 ★★★★

Wede Harer Guzo — 2016
Hailu Mergia and — AWESOME TAPES
the Dahlak Band — FROM AFRICA
A supremely groovy double-LP recording of a live set at the Ghion Hotel nightclub, Addis Ababa, in 1978.
Discogs rating: 4.70 ★★★★

Emahoy Tsegué-Mariam Guèbru — 2017
Emahoy Tsegué-Mariam — MISSISSIPPI
Guèbru
Self-titled solo piano from devout Ethiopian nun.
Discogs rating: 4.76 ★★★★

Assiyo Bellema and Sima! — 2013 & 2016
Various and Tlahoun — MISSISSIPPI
Gèssèssè
Two vinyl compilations drawn from the Éthiopiques series.
Discogs rating: 4.26 ★★★☆
Discogs rating: 4.29 ★★★☆

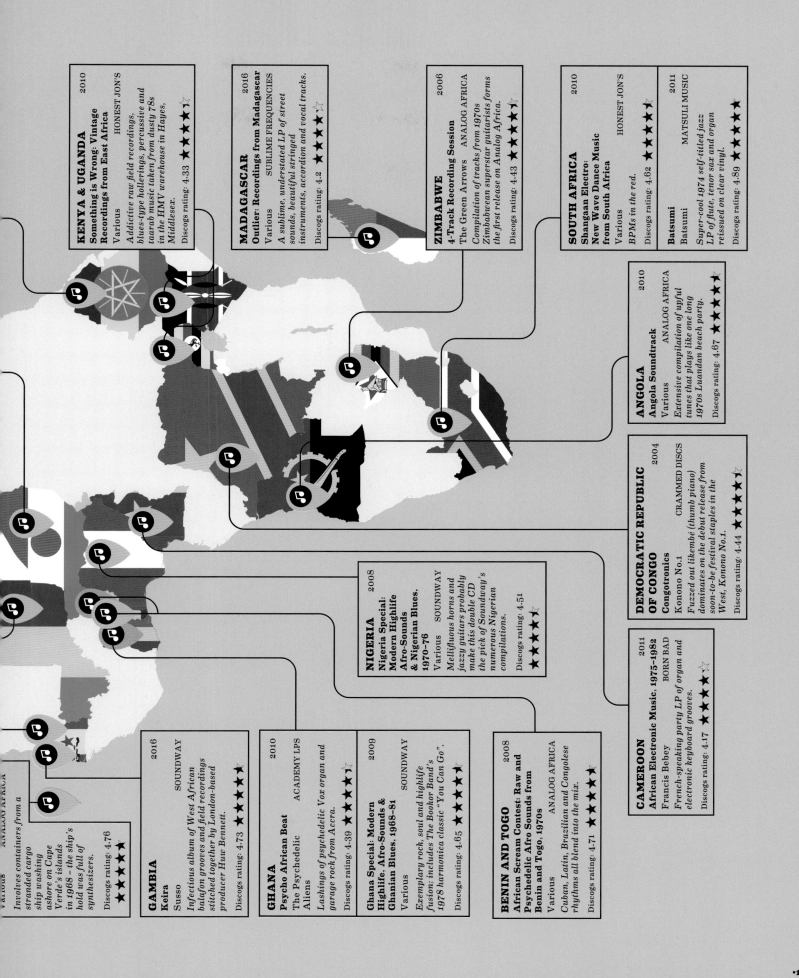

KENYA & UGANDA 2010
Something is Wrong: Vintage Recordings from East Africa
Various HONEST JON'S
Addictive raw field recordings, blues-type hollerings, percussive and taarab music taken from dusty 78s in the HMV warehouse in Hayes, Middlesex.
Discogs rating: 4.33 ★★★☆

MADAGASCAR 2016
Outlier: Recordings from Madagascar
Various SUBLIME FREQUENCIES
A sublime, understated LP of street sounds, beautiful stringed instruments, accordion and vocal tracks.
Discogs rating: 4.2 ★★★☆☆

ZIMBABWE 2006
4-Track Recording Session
The Green Arrows ANALOG AFRICA
Compilation of tracks from 1970s Zimbabwean superstar guitarists forms the first release on Analog Africa.
Discogs rating: 4.43 ★★★★☆

SOUTH AFRICA 2010
Shangaan Electro: New Wave Dance Music from South Africa
Various HONEST JON'S
BPMs in the red.
Discogs rating: 4.62 ★★★★☆

Batsumi 2011
Batsumi MATSULI MUSIC
Super-cool 1974 self-titled jazz LP of flute, tenor sax and organ reissued on clear vinyl.
Discogs rating: 4.89 ★★★★★

ANGOLA 2010
Angola Soundtrack
Various ANALOG AFRICA
Extensive compilation of upful tunes that plays like one long 1970s Luandan beach party.
Discogs rating: 4.67 ★★★★☆

DEMOCRATIC REPUBLIC OF CONGO 2004
Congotronics
Konono No.1 CRAMMED DISCS
Fuzzed out likembe (thumb piano) dominates on the debut release from soon-to-be festival staples in the West, Konono No.1.
Discogs rating: 4.44 ★★★★☆

NIGERIA 2008
Nigeria Special: Modern Highlife, Afro-Sounds & Nigerian Blues, 1970–76
Various SOUNDWAY
Mellifluous horns and jazzy guitars probably make this double CD the pick of Soundway's numerous Nigerian compilations.
Discogs rating: 4.51 ★★★★☆

CAMEROON 2011
African Electronic Music, 1975–1982
Francis Bebey BORN BAD
French-speaking party LP of organ and electronic keyboard grooves.
Discogs rating: 4.17 ★★★☆☆

BENIN AND TOGO 2008
African Scream Contest: Raw and Psychedelic Afro Sounds from Benin and Togo, 1970s
Various ANALOG AFRICA
Cuban, Latin, Brazilian and Congolese rhythms all blend into the mix.
Discogs rating: 4.71 ★★★★☆

GHANA 2009
Ghana Special: Modern Highlife, Afro-Sounds & Ghanian Blues, 1968–81
Various SOUNDWAY
Exemplary rock, soul and highlife fusion; includes The Boohor Band's 1978 harmonica classic "You Can Go".
Discogs rating: 4.65 ★★★★☆

Psycho African Beat 2010
The Psychedelic Aliens ACADEMY LPS
Lashings of psychedelic Vox organ and garage rock from Accra.
Discogs rating: 4.39 ★★★☆☆

GAMBIA 2016
Keira SOUNDWAY
Susso
Infectious album of West African balafon grooves and field recordings stitched together by London-based producer Huw Bennett.
Discogs rating: 4.73 ★★★★

... ANALOG AFRICA
Various
Involves containers from a stranded cargo ship washing ashore on Cape Verde's islands in 1968 – the ship's hold was full of synthesizers.
Discogs rating: 4.76 ★★★★

•125

SOUND MAP OF GERMANY

Typical histories and graphics of rock and pop tend to focus around an Anglo-American axis. Germany, however, has as rich a musical heritage as any nation on earth. Here's a colour-coded genre map of a selection of post-war German music.

KEY

First wave of Kosmiche bands drawing upon ambient, psychedelia, prog and rock.

Second wave of 1970s and 1980s synthesizer and electronic musicians.

Neue Deutsche Welle* new wave, electronic, punk, metal and post-punk noise artists.

Mid-1970s [and later] Berlin in the west.

Techno.

Abstract electronic, ambient soundscapes, minimal techno/dub and reggae, as well as post-classical scores.

Afrobeat in Germany.

BERLIN

Zodiak Free Arts Lab opens in 1968 / Ash Ra Tempel / Kluster / Tangerine Dream

Cluster / Manuel Göttsching / E2–E4

Einstürzende Neubauten / Die Tödliche Doris / Liaisons Dangereuses / The Birthday Party record *Mutiny* and *The Bad Seed EPs* in Hansa Studios

City Slang label sets up in 1990, releasing American records to Europe / Iggy Pop's *The Idiot* and *Lust for Life* / David Bowie's *Low,* and *"Heroes"* / Brian Eno and Tony Visconti in Studio Hansa / Nick Cave and the Bad Seeds and Crime and the City Solution feature on the soundtrack to Wim Wenders's *Wings of Desire*

UFO Club opens in 1988, Tresor opens in 1991, Tresor label also founded in 1991 / Jeff Mills / Underground Resistance and compilations of Detroit techno are among the early releases / Berghain nightclub

Mark Ernsetus and Moritz von Oswald form the Basic Channel label in 1993 and minimal techno,dub-influenced duo,imprint Rhythm and Sound from a base in the Hard Wax record shop / Jan Jelinek / PAN records established, 2008 / Sonic Pieces boutique label established in 2012

HAMBURG

Faust /
Bureau B label

DÜSSELDORF

Kraftwerk / Neu!

La Düsseldorf / Propaganda

D.A.F. (Deutsche
Amerikanische Freundschaft)

Kreidler / Mouse on Mars /
Microstoria / Stefan Betke
aka 'Pole'

COLOGNE

Can, Conny Plank's studio, Godorf

Gas, Wolfgang Voit /
Kompakt record label launched, 1998

FORST

Harmonia

BEVERUNGEN

2012: a promo compilation
in a cardboard sleeve features
several African tracks, the
first output from the
Glitterbeat label

FRANKFURT

Achim Szepanski forms
Mille Plateaux records
in 1993

CHEMINTZ

Raster-Noton label
established, 1996

MUNICH

Amon Düül / Amon Düül 2

Popol Vuh

ÜBERLINGEN

In 2007 Samy Ben Rejeb
releases a collection of
1970s tracks by the Green
Arrows, a guitar band from
Zimbabwe; the first lp on
his new label Analog Africa

Source: "Where 'Krautrock' was bucolic and wistful, forest-bound and buoyed by
warm, instrumental waves of utopian hankering, post-punk German music, later
codified under the banner of Neue Deutsche Welle ('New German Wave'), was, in its
earliest incarnations at least, as brutal as a slab of concrete. " David Stubbs, *Future
Days: Krautrock and the Building of Modern Germany* (2014, Faber)*; Resident Advisor

TWENTY-FOUR HOURS FROM TULSA

Sung by Gene Pitney and written by Burt Bacharach and Hal David, "Twenty Fours Hours from Tulsa" was released in 1963. It tells the story of a man on his way home to his true love who pulls in at a motel and meets a woman. They go to a café, start dancing, then kissing and fall in love. The upshot of which is that Gene won't be coming home now, or ever ... and he was so close.

The question is, where was the motel? Some detective work is required and it starts by knowing where Tulsa is. It's in Oklahoma about 115 miles north-east of Oklahoma City and 265 miles north of Dallas, Texas.

The speed limit in 1963 was set by individual states; it wasn't till the 1974 oil crisis that a national speed limit was imposed. For the purposes of this exercise, let's assume 70mph. With some traffic lights, and driving through towns, let's adjust to an overall average speed of 60mph.

Next, let's examine the 24 hours. We assume that Gene was not going to drive non-stop. In fact, we know he wasn't... because he stopped. A probable breakdown of what the next 24 hours would have held is in the chart below. Thus we can tell how far he was likely to have travelled, and where geographically he would have stopped. Where a city lies in his path a little over 600 miles from Tulsa, we can rule out the lonely and romantic motel stop required for Gene's change of heart.

DENVER

I-70 West: If Gene was on his way home from Colorado, Denver would surely have housed him for the night.

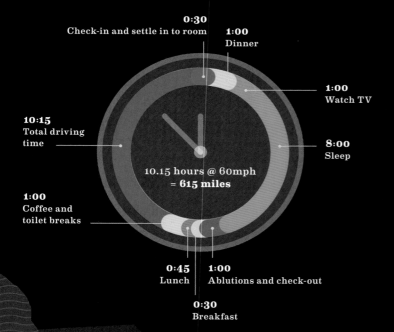

0:30 Check-in and settle in to room

1:00 Dinner

1:00 Watch TV

10:15 Total driving time

10.15 hours @ 60mph = **615 miles**

8:00 Sleep

1:00 Coffee and toilet breaks

0:45 Lunch

1:00 Ablutions and check-out

0:30 Breakfast

ALBUQUERQUE

I-40 West: Albuquerque's location rules out the I-40. Which is a real shame because that's the way to Amarillo.

PECOS

I-20: Coming up from the south-west on the I-20, Gene would have been driving through Pecos and stopped at the beautiful Town & Country Motel. It had a coffee shop too.

STARLITE MOTEL

I-29: Travelling south from South Dakota, Gene could have found himself pulling in to the Starlite Motel on the I-29 for the night.

MINNEAPOLIS

I-35: Minneapolis would have been the obvious place to rest if Gene was on the I-35.

DANIELS' MOTEL

I-39: This road was not in existence in 1963. However, it replaced US Route 51, and 618 miles along US Route 51 Gene would have found the lovely Daniels' Motel – and maybe a beautiful lady.

CHICAGO

I-55: If Gene was travelling along the I-55 (he could also take the I-57), he would most likely bed down in the city of Chicago.

INDIANAPOLIS

I-70 East: The city of Indianapolis lies in the direction of the I-70, 630 miles from Tulsa.

TWIN J MOTEL

I-64: Along the I-64 out of Louisville, Gene would have found himself around Corydon, Indiana, where there was a lovely motel on State Highway 62 called the Twin J Motel.

NASHVILLE

I-40 East: Nashville is almost exactly 615 miles from Tulsa on the I-40.

ATLANTA

I-22: There's no likely motel at the right distance on the I-22 from the direction of Atlanta.

HOUSTON

I-45: Houston and the Gulf of Mexico's coastline are only 500 miles away, which is all too close for Gene.

WHERE GENE IS TRAVELLING FROM

MOST LIKELY   POSSIBLE   IMPOSSIBLE

N

W   E

S

VOYAGER SOUNDTRACK

GEORGIAN S.S.R., chorus, "Tchakrulo"
Collected by Radio Moscow { 2:18 }

PERU, panpipes and drums
Collected by Casa de la Cultura, Lima { 0:52 }

MOZART, The Magic Flute, Queen of the Night aria, no. 14
Edda Moser, soprano. Bavarian State Opera, Munich, Wolfgang Sawallisch, conductor { 2:55 }

AZERBAIJAN S.S.R., bagpipes
Collected by Radio Moscow { 2:30 }

BACH, Brandenburg Concerto No. 2 in F. First Movement
Munich Bach Orchestra, Karl Richter, conductor { 4:40 }

AUSTRALIA, Aborigine songs, "Morning Star" and "Devil Bird"
Recorded by Sandra LeBrun Holmes { 1:26 }

SENEGAL, Percussion
Recorded by Charles Duvelle { 2:08 }

The comparative distance Voyagers 1 and 2 would have travelled listening to each song, if the record was playing on a loop from laun...

VOYAGER 1

VOYAGER 2

"MELANCHOLY BLUES"
Performed by Louis Armstrong & his Hot Seven { 3:05 }

BACH, "Gavotte en rondeaux" from the Partita No. 3 in E major for Violin
Performed by Arthur Grumiaux { 2:55 }

JAVA, Court Gamelan, "Kinds of Flowers"
Recorded by Robert Brown { 4:43 }

JAPAN, Shakuhachi, "Tsuru No Sugomori" ("Crane's Nest")
Performed by Goro Yamaguchi { 4:51 }

ZAIRE, Pygmy girls' initiation song
Recorded by Colin Turnbull { 0:56 }

NEW GUINEA, Men's house song
Recorded by Robert MacLennan { 1:20 }

MEXICO, "El Cascabel"
Performed by Lorenzo Barcelata & the Mariachi México { 3:14 }

"JOHNNY B. GOODE"
Written & performed by Chuck Berry { 2:38 }

VOYAGER GOLDEN RECORD

Launched as long ago as 1977, it could be another 20 to 40,000 years before the *Voyager* spacecrafts burst through the gravitational pull of the sun completely and leave the environs of our solar system forever to break out into "the open sea of interstellar space", as Carl Sagan described it. Once there, there'll be no gas, furious solar winds or burning radiation to erode the craft. The two *Voyagers* will just circumnavigate the centre of the Milky Way galaxy for anywhere between a billion and five billion years, looping along interstellar highways in a sort of ambient drift, hopefully one day to be intercepted by alien lifeforms who also happened to have invented the record player. "In their utter lack of intent to do harm," said Carl Sagan, musing on the possibility that one day the gold discs will be discovered and absorbed by alien beings, "these [records] speak eloquently for us. Perhaps [the aliens] would recognise the tentativeness of our society, the mismatch between our technology and our wisdom . . ."

STRAVINSKY, Rite of Spring, Sacrificial Dance
Columbia Symphony Orchestra, Igor Stravinsky, conductor { 4:35 }

CHINA, ch'in, "Flowing Streams"
Performed by Kuan P'ing-hu { 7:37 }

Sources: NASA, Wikipedia

BACH, The Well-Tempered Clavier, Book 2,
Prelude and Fugue in C, No.1
Glenn Gould, piano { 4:48 }

BEETHOVEN, String Quartet No. 13
in B flat, Opus 130, Cavatina
Performed by Budapest String Quartet { 6:37 }

BEETHOVEN, Fifth Symphony, First Movement
The Philharmonia Orchestra, Otto Klemperer, conductor { 7:20 }

INDIA, raga, "Jaat Kahan Ho"
Sung by Surshri Kesar Bai Kerkar { 3:30 }

BULGARIA, "Izlel je Delyo
Hagdutin"
Sung by Valya Balkanska { 4:59 }

PERU, Wedding song
Recorded by John Cohen { 0:38 }

*VOYAGER I broke through the
termination shock and into the
heliosphere in 2004 – then broke
out of the far edge of the plasma
bubble/heliosphere that protects
our solar system on 25 August
2012 and is now on the brink of
interstellar space, drifting near
the Oort Cloud.*

NAVAJO INDIANS, Night chant
Recorded by Willard Rhodes { 0:57 }

HOLBORNE, Paueans, Galliards,
**Almains and Other Short Aeirs,
"The Fairie Round"**
*Performed by David Munrow & the Early
Music Consort of London { 1:17 }*

SOLOMON ISLANDS, panpipes
*Collected by the Solomon Islands
Broadcasting Service { 1:12 }*

"DARK WAS THE NIGHT"
*Written & performed by Blind Willie Johnson
{ 3:15 }*

*VOYAGER II went through
the termination shock in 2007
and is now close to the edge of
the heliosphere.*

"A golden phonograph record encased in a mirrored golden jacket," is how
Sagan described *The Sounds of Earth* LP – or "Earth's greatest hits" – a copy
of which was attached to the front of both *Voyager I* and *Voyager II*. (It's worth
watching Sagan's short 1980 film on YouTube just to hear him pronounce the
word "recud".) The grooves of the discs contain children speaking greetings in 55
different languages of the world, whale-song, recordings of screaming babies and 116
pictures of humans and the "civilisation" they have created: a lady in a 1970s supermarket eating grapes; a large(ish) gentleman with thinning hair tucking into what looks like a
ham-and-cheese toastie; another woman licking chocolate ice cream. ("Did these humans do
anything other than consume?" an alien in a far-flung galaxy may well wonder at some point in
the distant future. "No wonder their planet immolated.") There's also 90 minutes of recorded music
on the LPs.

The aliens have 5 billion years to find the records, believed Carl Sagan, before "the evolution of the sun
burns the earth to a crisp". For anyone, human or otherwise, keen to hear Kesarbai Kerkar's raga "Jaat
Kahan Ho", it is included on the Mississippi records 2013 compilation, *Kesarbai Kerkar*.

IT'S A LONG WAY TO PERRY COMO

Perry Como, for over 50 years, was one of America's biggest singing and television stars. He was a barber in his hometown of Canonsburg, Pennsylvania until the singing that was his hobby became his life. Surely it's a long way from Como's cross-generational homely appeal to the hip-hop aggression of Eminem's rapping... or maybe not.

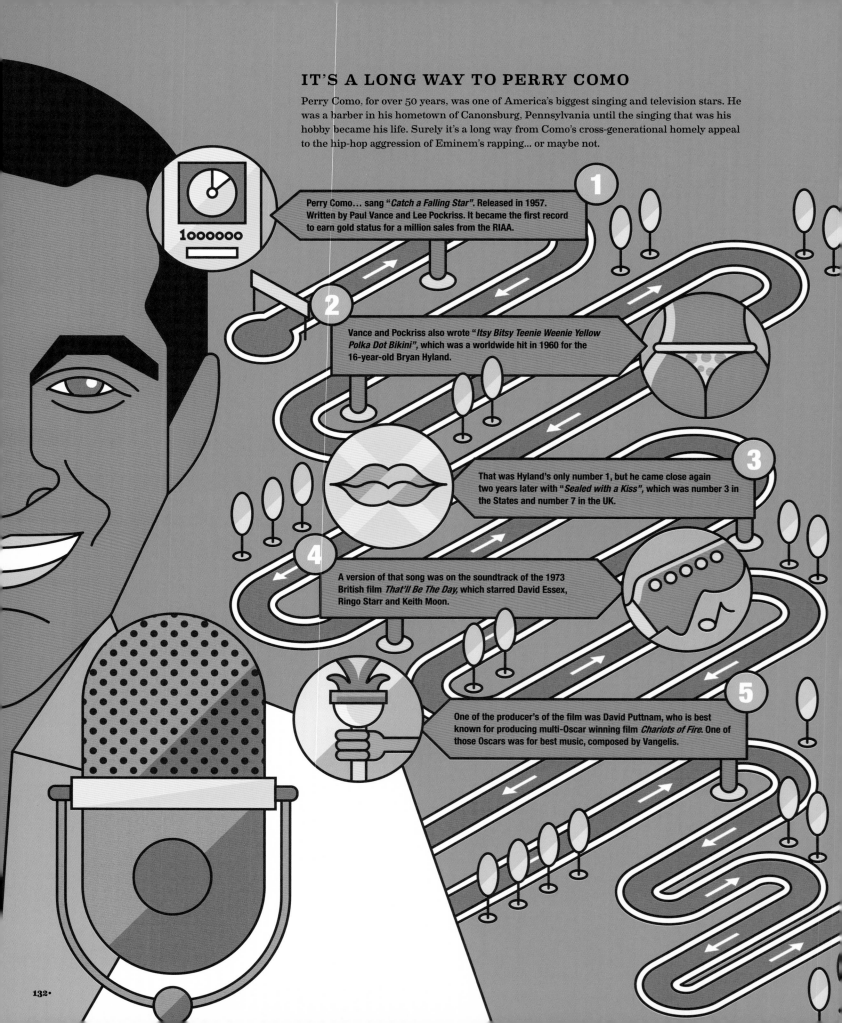

1 Perry Como... sang *"Catch a Falling Star"*. Released in 1957. Written by Paul Vance and Lee Pockriss. It became the first record to earn gold status for a million sales from the RIAA.

2 Vance and Pockriss also wrote *"Itsy Bitsy Teenie Weenie Yellow Polka Dot Bikini"*, which was a worldwide hit in 1960 for the 16-year-old Bryan Hyland.

3 That was Hyland's only number 1, but he came close again two years later with *"Sealed with a Kiss"*, which was number 3 in the States and number 7 in the UK.

4 A version of that song was on the soundtrack of the 1973 British film *That'll Be The Day*, which starred David Essex, Ringo Starr and Keith Moon.

5 One of the producer's of the film was David Puttnam, who is best known for producing multi-Oscar winning film *Chariots of Fire*. One of those Oscars was for best music, composed by Vangelis.

Sources: riaa.com, Wikipedia, imdb.com, theguardian.com

10 Just four years later, in *8 Mile,* Basinger played the mother of… Eminem.

9

Guy Pearce appeared alongside Kim Basinger in *L.A. Confidential,* for which she won an Oscar in 1998.

8 One of Kylie Minogue's other fictional husbands was Jason Donovan. They appeared together in the television soap *Neighbours,* which was also the starting point for Guy Pearce's career.

7 One of the stars of *Blade Runner* was the Dutch actor Rutger Hauer who, in 2000, played Kylie Minogue's husband in the video for her track "*On a Night Like This*".

6 Born in Greece, as Evangelos Odysseas Papathanassiou, Vangelis also wrote the score for the seminal sci-fi film *Blade Runner.*

IT'S ALL IN THE DELIVERY

Sound reaches our ears because of vibrations in the air between us and the source. Our ears have not changed for a very long time, but the sources have evolved at an ever quickening pace. From scratches on a piece of paper to computer code, the journey has been a long one.

KEY

DATE

INVENTION
—
Inventor
×
MEDIUM
First Record / Transmission · Artist

Analogue   Digital   Both

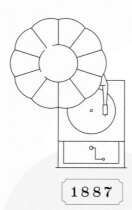

1887

GRAMOPHONE
—
Emile Berliner
×
INITIALLY HARD RUBBER DISCS,
FINALLY VINYL DISCS.
Der Handschuh · Emile Berliner

1896

WIRELESS TELEGRAPHY
—
Guglielmo Marconi
×
HERTZIAN WAVES
Ringing a bell · Guglielmo Marconi

1860

PHONAUTOGRAPH
—
Edouard-Leon Scott de Martinville
×
CARBON ON PAPER
Au Clair de la Lune · Unknown

1877

PHONOGRAPH
—
Thomas Edison
×
TINFOIL ON A CYLINDER
Mary Had a Little Lamb · Thomas Edison

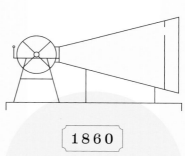

1910

RADIO
—
Lee de Forest
×
HERTZIAN WAVES
Cavalleria Rusticana
·
Enrico Caruso and others

Sources: bbc.co.uk, memory.loc.gov, Wikipedia, history-computer.com, time.com, makeuseof.com, ultimateclassicrock.com, npr.org

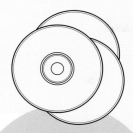

1966

COMPACT DISC
—

James T. Russell

×

PHOTOGRAPHIC FILM

52nd Street · Billy Joel

1963

COMPACT CASSETTE
—

Lou Ottens (Philips)

×

REEL-TO-REEL TAPES BUT
IN CASSETTE FORM

**49 pre-recorded albums, including
3 by Johnny Mathis**

1993

MP3
—

Karlheinze Brandenburg

×

N/A

Tom's Diner · Suzanne Vega

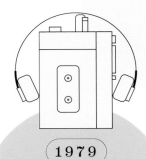

1979

SONY WALKMAN
—

Nobutoshi Kihara

×

VARIOUS

Unknown · Unknown

1928

REEL-TO-REEL
TAPE
—

Fritz Pfleumer

×

CELLULOSE ACETATE
COVERED WITH
IRON OXIDE

Unknown · Unknown

HOW TO PLAY THE THEREMIN

The theremin, a staple of early horror and science-fiction film soundtracks, was developed by Léon Theremin in St Petersburg in the 1920s. It was one of the first electronic instruments, consisting essentially of a wooden box and two metal antennae that serve as oscillators, controlled by hand movements. Robert Moog (see the synthesizer graphics) was also a theremin enthusiast, constructing his own model in 1948 and co-producing with his wife, Shirleigh Moog, Clara Rockmore's album *The Art of the Theremin* as recently as 1977. Rockmore was a world-renowned thereminist and companion of fellow Soviet émigré to the United States, Leon Theremin.

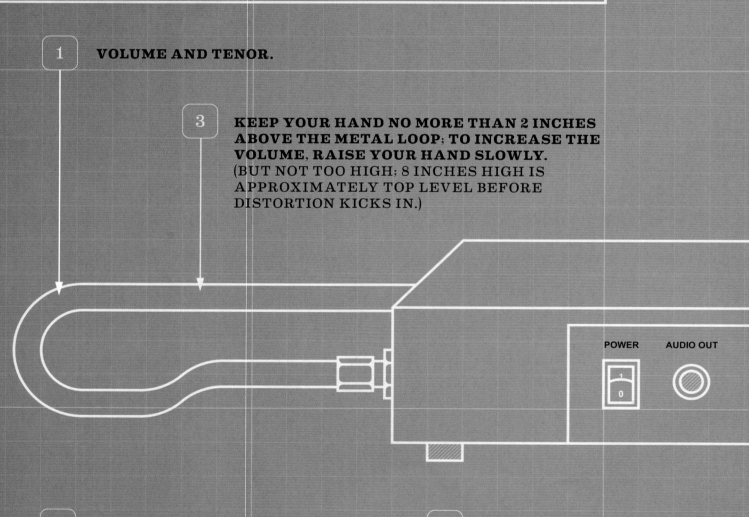

1   **VOLUME AND TENOR.**

3   **KEEP YOUR HAND NO MORE THAN 2 INCHES ABOVE THE METAL LOOP; TO INCREASE THE VOLUME, RAISE YOUR HAND SLOWLY.** (BUT NOT TOO HIGH; 8 INCHES HIGH IS APPROXIMATELY TOP LEVEL BEFORE DISTORTION KICKS IN.)

POWER   AUDIO OUT

5   **CONSULT MANUAL OF CLARA ROCKMORE'S AERIAL FINGERING TECHNIQUE DEVELOPED IN THE 1920S. ESSENTIALLY, FIRST FINGER AND THUMB PRESSED TOGETHER; OTHER FINGERS GRADUALLY OPEN OUT IN STAGES.**

6   **PLAY UP AND DOWN THE SCALE, TRYING TO AVOID MOVING, PUMPING OR DIPPING YOUR LEFT/METAL-LOOP HAND.** (UNLESS YOU'RE LOOKING FOR A STACCATO EFFECT.)

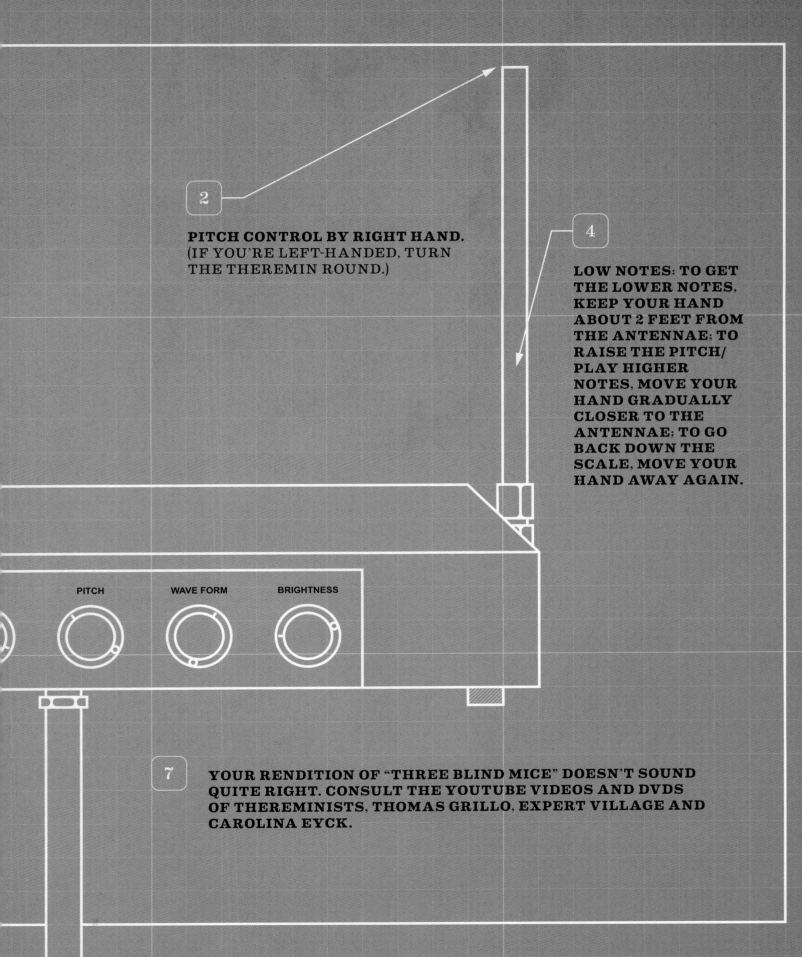

2 PITCH CONTROL BY RIGHT HAND.
(IF YOU'RE LEFT-HANDED, TURN
THE THEREMIN ROUND.)

4 LOW NOTES: TO GET
THE LOWER NOTES,
KEEP YOUR HAND
ABOUT 2 FEET FROM
THE ANTENNAE; TO
RAISE THE PITCH/
PLAY HIGHER
NOTES, MOVE YOUR
HAND GRADUALLY
CLOSER TO THE
ANTENNAE; TO GO
BACK DOWN THE
SCALE, MOVE YOUR
HAND AWAY AGAIN.

PITCH   WAVE FORM   BRIGHTNESS

7 YOUR RENDITION OF "THREE BLIND MICE" DOESN'T SOUND
QUITE RIGHT. CONSULT THE YOUTUBE VIDEOS AND DVDS
OF THEREMINISTS, THOMAS GRILLO, EXPERT VILLAGE AND
CAROLINA EYCK.

TO DIE FOR

Modern-day television soap operas are so called because they were originally sponsored by soap companies and took their melodramatic plots from famous operas. Death, as inevitable as taxes, understandably takes a large place in these stories and comes in a variety of ways...

WHO DIED IN WHICH OPERA

WHO KILLED THEM

Tosca
- Angelotti
- Scarpia
- Cavaradossi
- Tosca

The Ring Cycle
- Fasolt
- Siegmund
- Hunding
- Fafner
- Mime
- Siegfried
- Gunther
- Brünnhilde
- Hagen

Lady Macbeth of the Mtsensk District
- Boris
- Zinovy
- Sonyetka
- Katerina

Dialogues of the Carmelites
- Mother Superior
- Sister Constance's Father
- All of the Nuns

Otello
- Desdemona
- Roderigo
- Otello

Don Giovani
- Don Pedro (Il Commendatore)
- Don Giovani

Aida
- Radamès
- Aida

Carmen
- Carmen

Killers:
- Unknown
- Tosca
- Firing squad
- Fafner
- Wotan
- Rhinemaidens
- Katerina
- Katerina & Sergei
- Katerina
- Overbalances while pushing Sonyetka
- The State
- The State
- Otello
- Don Giovani
- Demons summoned by the ghost of Don Pedro
- Ramfis
- Herself

138·

Sources: Wikipedia, theguardian.com, users.utu.fi, limelightmagazine.com.au

HOW THE DEATH HAPPENED

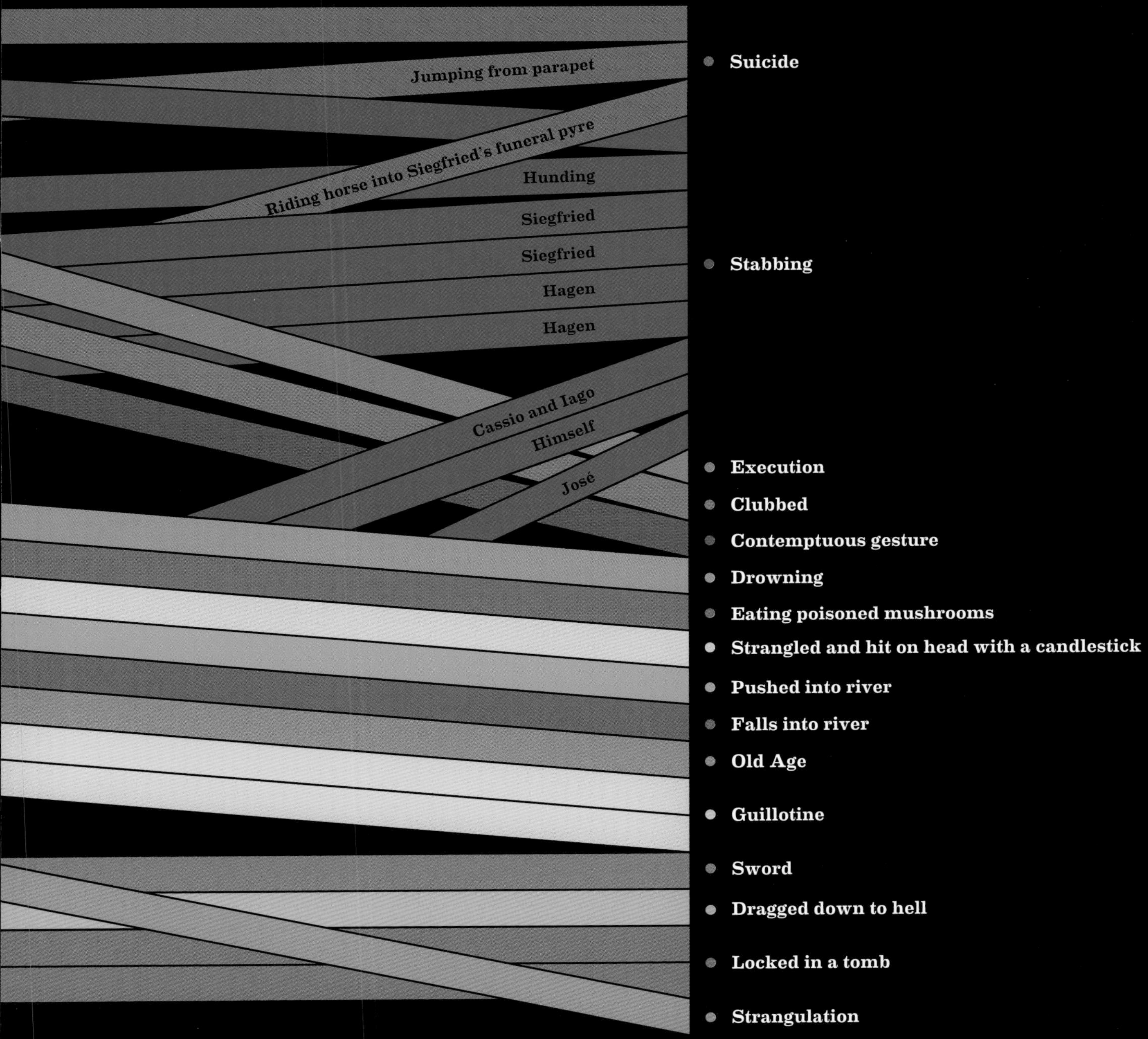

Jumping from parapet

Riding horse into Siegfried's funeral pyre

Hunding

Siegfried

Siegfried

Hagen

Hagen

Cassio and Iago

Himself

José

● Suicide

● Stabbing

● Execution

● Clubbed

● Contemptuous gesture

● Drowning

● Eating poisoned mushrooms

● Strangled and hit on head with a candlestick

● Pushed into river

● Falls into river

● Old Age

● Guillotine

● Sword

● Dragged down to hell

● Locked in a tomb

● Strangulation

WHAT'S IN A NAME

Would U2 be the same band if the lead singer was Paul Hewson? Would Angela Tremble have caused as many men's hearts to flutter as Debbie Harry? And would Henry Deutschendorf have been a major hit on the country circuit? We'll never know because these and many others ditched their birth names before going on stage. Maybe they didn't like their names, maybe they wanted some distance from their families or perhaps a record executive said, "No one's going to buy records sung by Reg Dwight."

Sources: wikipedia, independent.co.uk, imdb.com, mylubbock.us, abcnews.go.com

Original Name **YR** **STAGE NAME**

AGE AT NAME CHANGE

ROCK

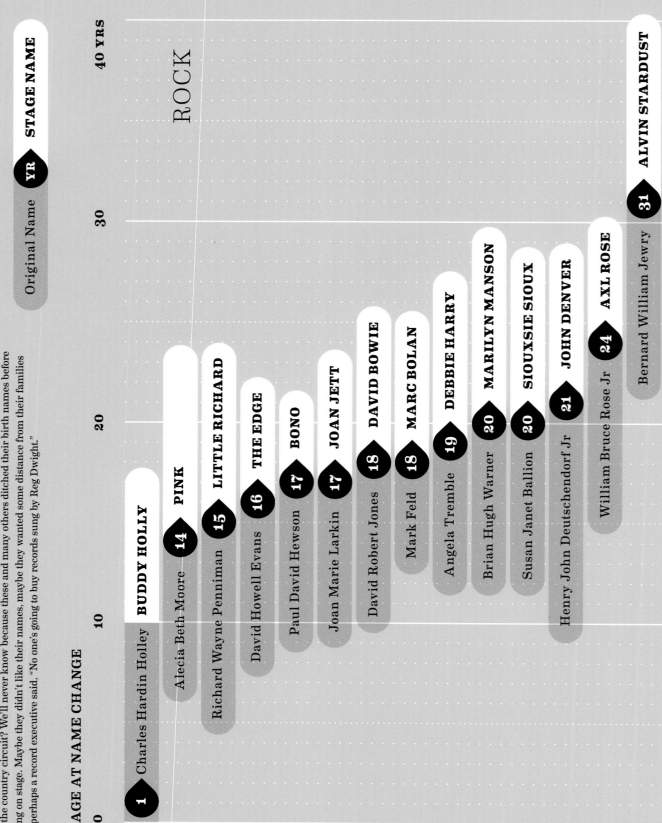

Charles Hardin Holley — 1 — BUDDY HOLLY
Alecia Beth Moore — 14 — PINK
Richard Wayne Penniman — 15 — LITTLE RICHARD
David Howell Evans — 16 — THE EDGE
Paul David Hewson — 17 — BONO
Joan Marie Larkin — 17 — JOAN JETT
David Robert Jones — 18 — DAVID BOWIE
Mark Feld — 18 — MARC BOLAN
Angela Tremble — 19 — DEBBIE HARRY
Brian Hugh Warner — 20 — MARILYN MANSON
Susan Janet Ballion — 20 — SIOUXSIE SIOUX
Henry John Deutschendorf Jr — 21 — JOHN DENVER
William Bruce Rose Jr — 24 — AXL ROSE
Bernard William Jewry — 31 — ALVIN STARDUST

0   10   20   30   40 YRS

POP

STEVIE WONDER — 11
Stevland Hardaway Judkins

CONNIE FRANCIS — 16
Concetta Rosa Maria Franconero

CLIFF RICHARD — 17
Harry Rodger Webb

ALICIA KEYS — 18
Alicia Augello Cook

FRANKIE VALLI — 19
Francesco Stephen Castelluccio

ELTON JOHN — 20
Reginald Kenneth Dwight

LADY GAGA — 20
Stefani Joanne Angelina Germanotta

AL MARTINO — 20
Jasper Cini

SHAKIN' STEVENS — 21
Michael Barratt

KATY PERRY — 23
Katheryn Elizabeth Hudson

PLASTIC BERTRAND — 23
Roger Allen François Jouret

DEAN MARTIN — 23
Dino Paul Crocetti

EMINEM — 14
Marshall Bruce Mathers III

SID VICIOUS — 17
John Simon Ritchie

JOHNNY ROTTEN — 18
John Joseph Lydon

CRYSTAL GAYLE — 19
Brenda Gail Webb

50 CENT — 20
Curtis James Jackson III

OTHER

FATBOY SLIM — 33
Quentin Leo Cook

TAFKAP — 35
Prince (Rogers Nelson)

•141

SUMMER OF LOVE SONGS

The summer of 1967 is often referred to as the Summer of Love. Around 100,000 people descended on the Haight-Ashbury area of San Francisco, which was the epicentre of the (mainly hippie) phenomena. The feeling, though, was repeated in cities all around the world, and certain songs from then will forever evoke memories of that special summer.

   The songs from that time are certainly distinctive, but do the actual lyrics tell us something about that time? Or is it simply the feeling that summer evokes that colour the lyrics in our memories and thoughts? This graphic explores that very issue. The anthem for the Summer of Love was probably Scott Mckenzie's "San Francisco, Be Sure to Wear Flowers in Your Hair", but are the words used just about flowers, love and peace or something else?*

San Francisco, Be Sure to Wear Flowers in Your Hair
Scott McKenzie
125 WORDS
San. Francisco. To. In. A

A Day in the Life
The Beatles
212 WORDS
The. I. And. A. Had

TOP 5 WORDS

Carrie Anne
The Hollies
222 WORDS
Carrie. Anne. Is. Your. Hey

Waterloo Sunset
The Kinks
172 WORDS
I. Waterloo. But. As. Sunset

Pleasant Valley Sunday
The Monkees
149 WORDS
To. Another. Is. Pleasant. Sunday

Gimme Some Lovin'
The Spencer Davis Group
244 WORDS
Gimme. Some. Lovin'. It. You

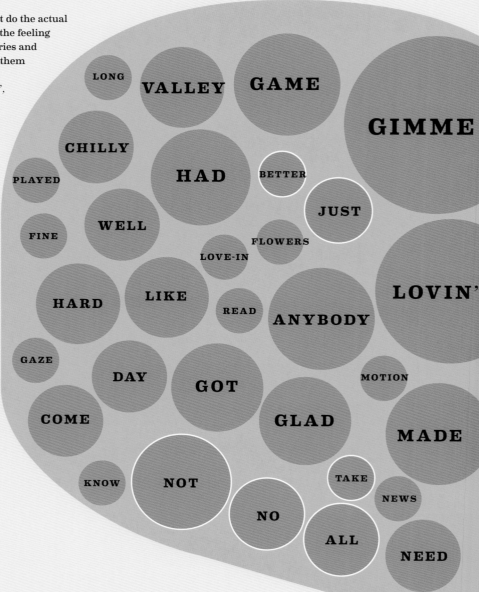

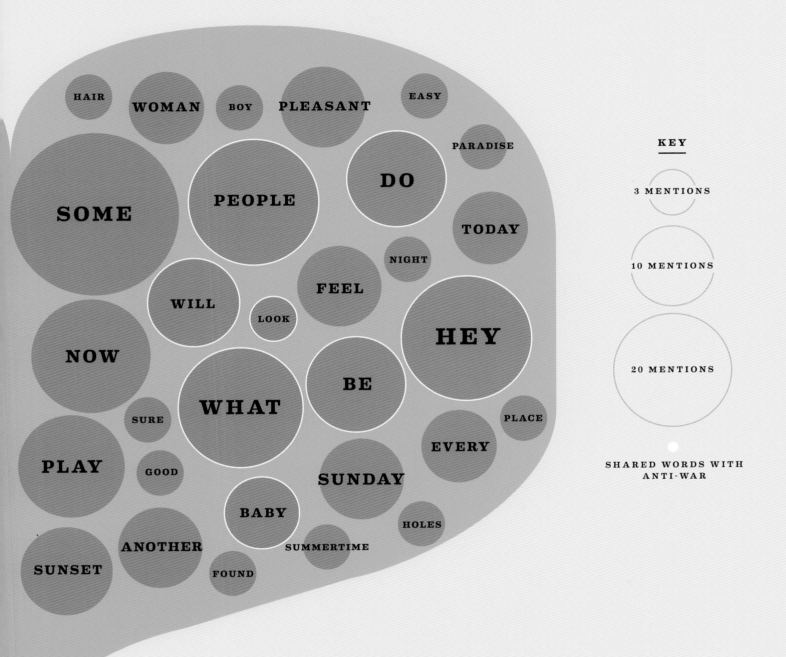

Sources: www.westword.com, allmusic.com
*Various pronouns, conjunctions prepositions etc. have not
been included in the word cloud for obvious reasons.

HAIR
WOMAN
BOY
PLEASANT
EASY

PARADISE

SOME
PEOPLE
DO
TODAY

NIGHT

FEEL

WILL
LOOK

HEY

NOW

BE

WHAT

SURE

PLAY
GOOD
SUNDAY
EVERY
PLACE

BABY

HOLES

ANOTHER
SUMMERTIME

SUNSET
FOUND

KEY

3 MENTIONS

10 MENTIONS

20 MENTIONS

SHARED WORDS WITH
ANTI-WAR

ANTI-WAR SONGS

While 1967 was the apogee of the flower-generation era, the decade as a whole was the high point for protest-song writers. The war in Vietnam spanned the decade and beyond, and the US's involvement had reared a generation who were touched by that conflict, as well as its predecessor in Korea.

The writers of these anti-war songs came from the same generation as the summer-of-lovers and there's obviously a link between promoting love and fighting war. But is it possible to see a difference in these two movements from the words they used and how they used them?*

Give Peace a Chance
John Lennon/ Plastic Ono Band
124 WORDS
Is. And. A. About. All

TOP 5 WORDS

Bring them Home
Pete Seeger
282 WORDS
Bring. Them. Home. I. They

Blowin' in the Wind
Bob Dylan
177 WORDS
The. Many. How. Before. In

The Unknown Soldier
The Doors
146 WORDS
Over. The. All. Hut. Is

Eve of Destruction
Barry McGuire
274 WORDS
The. You. Over. And. Is

For What It's Worth
Buffalo Springfield
208 WORDS
Is. What. Everybody. Down. Going

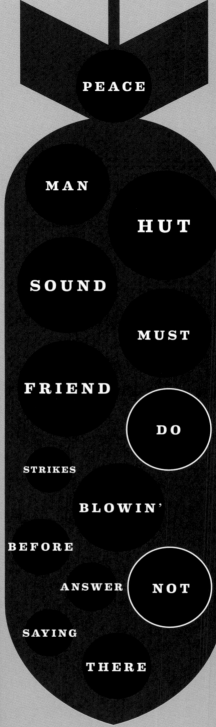

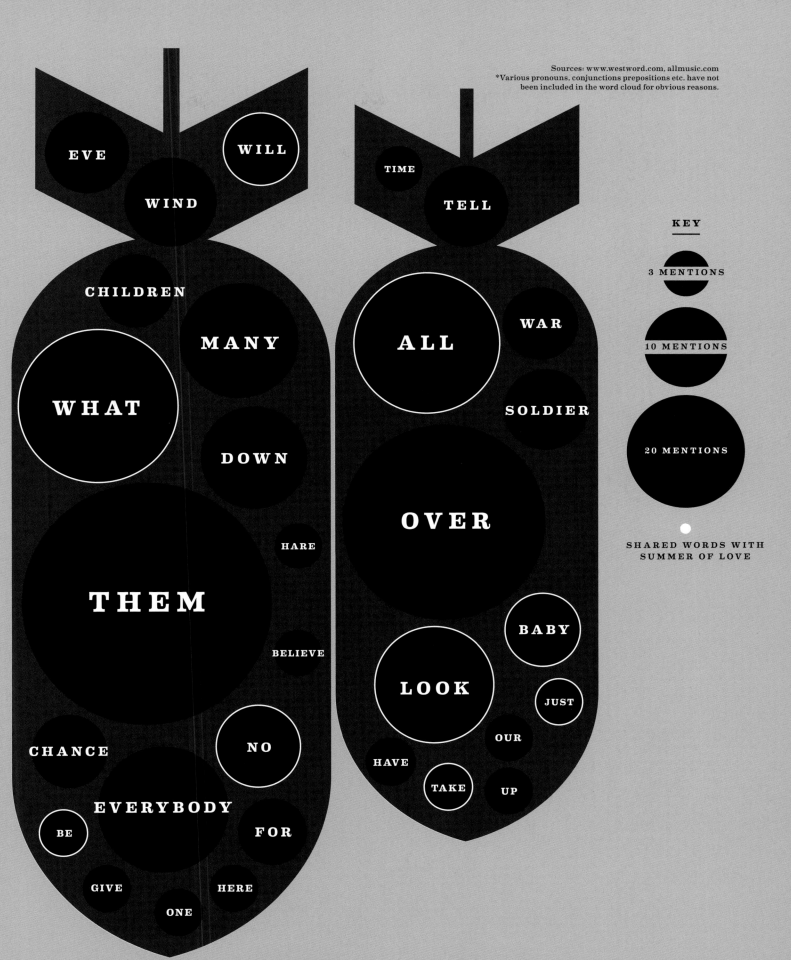

EVE

WILL

WIND

TIME

TELL

CHILDREN

MANY

WHAT

DOWN

THEM

HARE

BELIEVE

ALL

WAR

SOLDIER

OVER

BABY

LOOK

JUST

OUR

HAVE

TAKE

UP

CHANCE

NO

EVERYBODY

BE

FOR

GIVE

HERE

ONE

KEY

3 MENTIONS

10 MENTIONS

20 MENTIONS

SHARED WORDS WITH
SUMMER OF LOVE

UK MUSIC PRESS

There was a time when picking up a music magazine was a weekly ritual: that was before the Internet. The graphic below gives a representative picture of the state of the UK music press over the years. Many magazines haven't made the cut – *Vox* magazine, for instance, set up in 1990, was a quintessential nineties magazine but was closed not too long after healthy circulation figures of 55,000 were published. *Smash Hits* ceased publication in 2006 with a circulation of 120,000, more than the combined present-day circulation of *Classic Rock*, *Metal Hammer* and *Kerrang!* The graphic below gives a representative picture.

At its peak when embracing serious psychedelia

Peaks after embracing Beatlemania

Paper of the jazz age

NEW MUSICAL EXPRESS
Founded 1952

Circulation stays steady through 1960s

1926

1936

1946

MELODY MAKER
Founded 1926

1956

MIXMAG
Founded 1983

1966

RECORD MIRROR
Founded 1954

1976

1986

Sources: theguardian.com, magforum.com, pressgazette.co.uk, *Melody Maker History of Twentieth Century Popular Music* by Nick Johnstone (Bloomsbury, 1999), *The History of the NME: High Times and Low Lives at the World's Most Famous Music Magazine* by Pat Long (Portico, 2012), www.slideshare.net/stanshirokiy/music-magazine-circulation ; BBC, *Rock Criticism from the Beginning*, by Ulf Lindberg, Gestur Guðmundsson, Morten Michelsen and Hans Weisethaunet (Peter Lang, 2005)

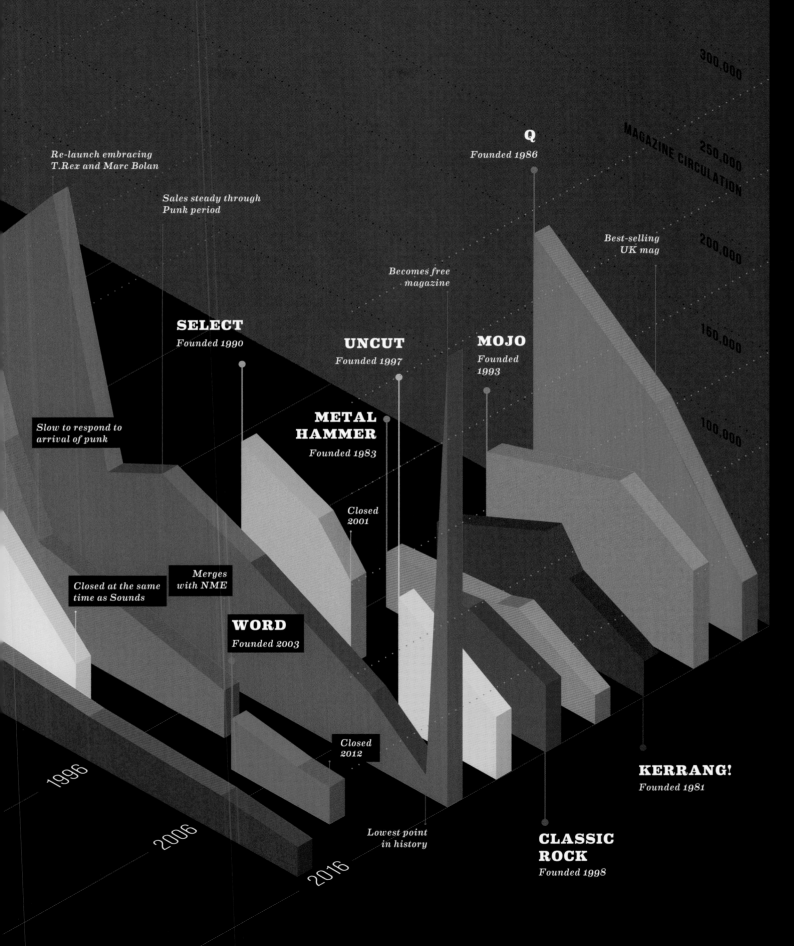

Re-launch embracing
T.Rex and Marc Bolan

Sales steady through
Punk period

Becomes free
magazine

Q
Founded 1986

MAGAZINE CIRCULATION

300,000

250,000

200,000

Best-selling
UK mag

SELECT
Founded 1990

UNCUT
Founded 1997

MOJO
Founded
1993

160,000

100,000

Slow to respond to
arrival of punk

**METAL
HAMMER**

Founded 1983

Closed
2001

Closed at the same
time as Sounds

Merges
with NME

WORD

Founded 2003

Closed
2012

KERRANG!

Founded 1981

Lowest point
in history

**CLASSIC
ROCK**

Founded 1998

1996

2006

2016

HARDCORE MUSIC FAN'S BOOKSHELF (PT.1)

Real musos would have more titles on the Beatles, Bob Dylan, Jimi Hendrix, how to play guitar, and the history of the Fender Stratocaster on their shelves. But here's a library of crucial music titles that would not be out of place in the home of any music nut. There are so many books that the groaning bookshelves graphic runs over two spreads. This page lists high-quality books with over 20,000 sales, along with equally high-quality titles that weren't quite as commercially successful (in grey). Worth noting, though, that the sales figures come from the only reliable UK source, Nielsen BookScan, and they have only been tracking them since 2001; many of the older titles have been given a raw deal here.

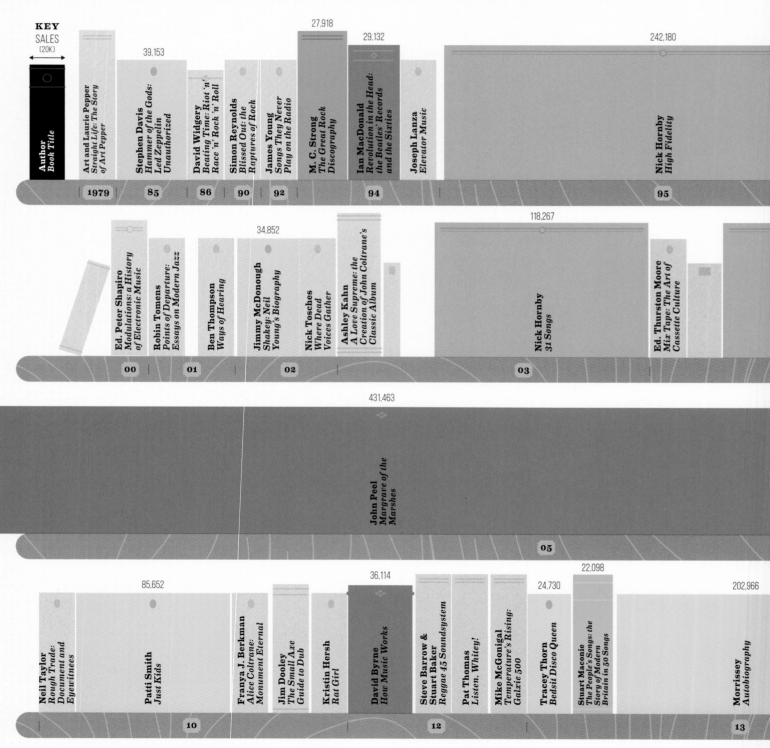

KEY
SALES
(20K)

Author
Book Title

Art and Laurie Pepper *Straight Life: The Story of Art Pepper* — 1979

Stephen Davis *Hammer of the Gods: Led Zeppelin Unauthorized* — 39,153 — 85

David Widgery *Beating Time: Riot 'n' Race 'n' Rock 'n' Roll* — 86

Simon Reynolds *Blissed Out: the Raptures of Rock* — 90

James Young *Songs They Never Play on the Radio* — 92

M. C. Strong *The Great Rock Discography* — 27,918

Ian MacDonald *Revolution in the Head: the Beatles' Records and the Sixties* — 29,132 — 94

Joseph Lanza *Elevator Music*

Nick Hornby *High Fidelity* — 242,180 — 95

Ed. Peter Shapiro *Modulations: a History of Electronic Music* — 00

Robin Tomens *Points of Departure: Essays on Modern Jazz*

Ben Thompson *Ways of Hearing* — 01

Jimmy McDonough *Shakey: Neil Young's Biography* — 34,852

Nick Tosches *Where Dead Voices Gather* — 02

Ashley Kahn *A Love Supreme: the Creation of John Coltrane's Classic Album*

Nick Hornby *31 Songs* — 118,267

Ed. Thurston Moore *Mix Tape: The Art of Cassette Culture* — 03

John Peel *Margrave of the Marshes* — 431,463 — 05

Neil Taylor *Rough Trade: Document and Eyewitnees*

Patti Smith *Just Kids* — 85,652 — 10

Franya J. Berkman *Alice Coltrane: Monument Eternal*

Jim Dooley *The Small Axe Guide to Dub*

Kristin Hersh *Rat Girl*

David Byrne *How Music Works* — 36,114

Steve Barrow & Stuart Baker *Reggae 45 Soundsystem* — 12

Pat Thomas *Listen, Whitey!*

Mike McGonigal *Temperature's Rising: Galxie 500*

Tracey Thorn *Bedsit Disco Queen* — 24,730

Stuart Maconie *The People's Songs: the Story of Modern Britain in 50 Songs* — 22,098

Morrissey *Autobiography* — 202,966 — 13

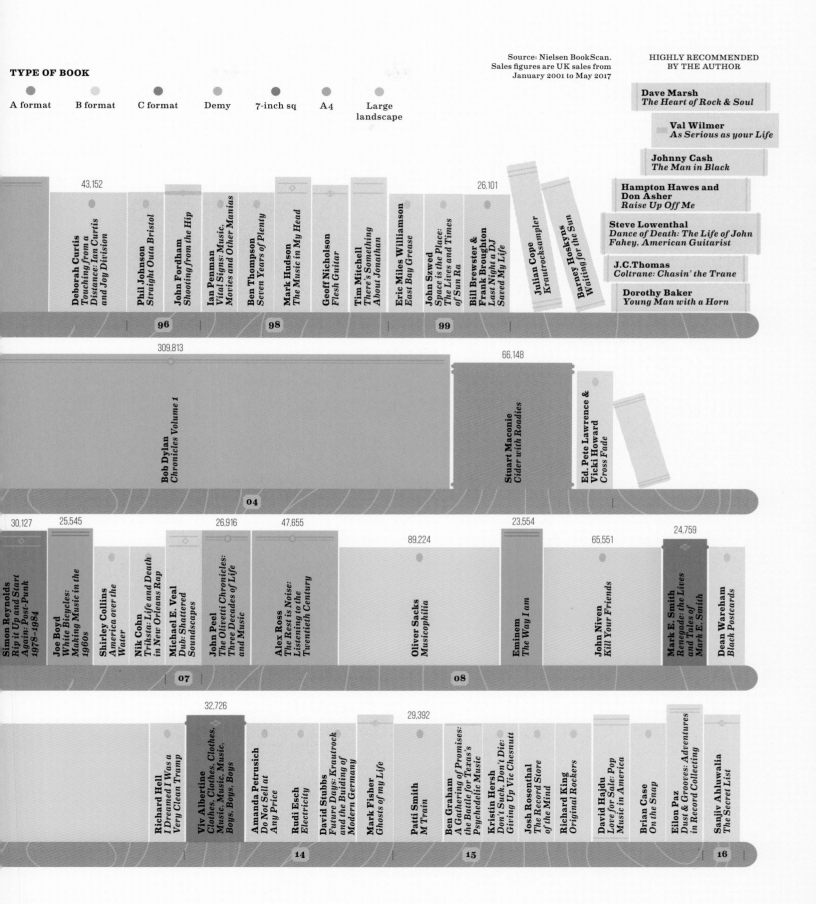

TYPE OF BOOK

- A format
- B format
- C format
- Demy
- 7-inch sq
- A4
- Large landscape

Source: Nielsen BookScan.
Sales figures are UK sales from
January 2001 to May 2017

HIGHLY RECOMMENDED
BY THE AUTHOR

Dave Marsh
The Heart of Rock & Soul

Val Wilmer
As Serious as your Life

Johnny Cash
The Man in Black

**Hampton Hawes and
Don Asher**
Raise Up Off Me

Steve Lowenthal
*Dance of Death: The Life of John
Fahey, American Guitarist*

J.C. Thomas
Coltrane: Chasin' the Trane

Dorothy Baker
Young Man with a Horn

43,152

Deborah Curtis
*Touching from a
Distance: Ian Curtis
and Joy Division*

Phil Johnson
Straight Outa Bristol

John Fordham
Shooting from the Hip

Ian Penman
*Vital Signs: Music,
Movies and Other Manias*

Ben Thompson
Seven Years of Plenty

Mark Hudson
The Music in My Head

Geoff Nicholson
Flesh Guitar

Tim Mitchell
*There's Something
About Jonathan*

Eric Miles Williamson
East Bay Grease

John Szwed
*Space is the Place:
The Lives and Times
of Sun Ra*

**Bill Brewster &
Frank Broughton**
*Last Night a DJ
Saved My Life*

26,101

Julian Cope
Krautrocksampler

Barney Hoskyns
Waiting for the Sun

96   98   99

309,813

Bob Dylan
Chronicles Volume 1

66,148

Stuart Maconie
Cider with Roadies

**Ed. Pete Lawrence &
Vicki Howard**
Cross Fade

04

30,127   25,545   26,916   47,655

Simon Reynolds
*Rip it Up and Start
Again: Post-Punk
1978–1984*

Joe Boyd
*White Bicycles:
Making Music in the
1960s*

Shirley Collins
*America over the
Water*

Nik Cohn
*Triksta: Life and Death
in New Orleans Rap*

Michael E. Veal
*Dub: Shattered
Soundscapes*

John Peel
*The Olivetti Chronicles:
Three Decades of Life
and Music*

Alex Ross
*The Rest is Noise:
Listening to the
Twentieth Century*

89,224

Oliver Sacks
Musicophilia

23,554

Eminem
The Way I am

65,551

John Niven
Kill Your Friends

24,759

Mark E. Smith
*Renegade: the Lives
and Tales of
Mark E. Smith*

Dean Wareham
Black Postcards

07   08

32,726

Richard Hell
*I Dreamed I Was a
Very Clean Tramp*

Viv Albertine
*Clothes, Clothes, Clothes.
Music. Music. Music.
Boys. Boys. Boys.*

Amanda Petrusich
*Do Not Sell at
Any Price*

Rudi Esch
Electricity

David Stubbs
*Future Days: Krautrock
and the Buiding of
Modern Germany*

Mark Fisher
Ghosts of my Life

29,392

Patti Smith
M Train

Ben Graham
*A Gathering of Promises:
the Battle for Texas's
Psychedelic Music*

Kristin Hersh
*Don't Suck. Don't Die:
Giving Up Vic Chesnutt*

Josh Rosenthal
*The Record Store
of the Mind*

Richard King
Original Rockers

David Hajdu
*Love for Sale: Pop
Music in America*

Brian Case
On the Snap

Eilon Paz
*Dust & Grooves: Adventures
in Record Collecting*

Sanjiv Ahluwalia
The Secret List

14   15   16

•149

HARDCORE MUSIC FAN'S BOOKSHELF (PT.2)

The second bookshelf contains a different scale to the first – the width has been scaled down by a factor of 1:10, so where a book of a certain width on the previous graphic had sold 30,000 copies, the same sized book below will only have sold 3,000 copies. Nevertheless, never judge a book by its cover... or its paucity of sales, as the old saying goes. There are many gems here that any music lover should be familiar with.

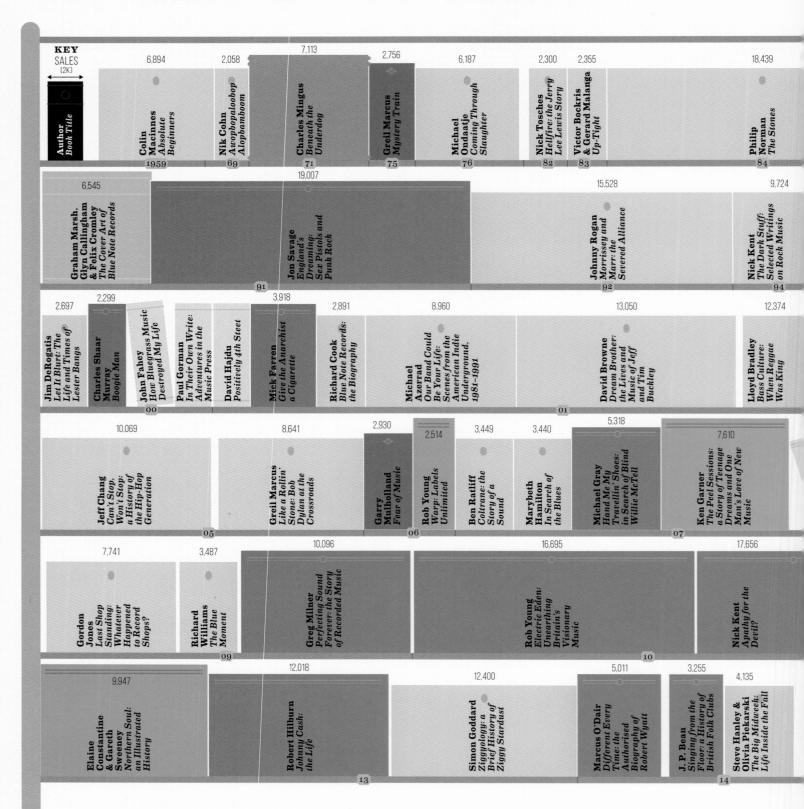

KEY
SALES
(2K)

Author
Book Title

6,894 — **Colin Macinnes** *Absolute Beginners* 1959

2,058 — **Nik Cohn** *Awophopaloobop Alopbamboom* 69

7,113 — **Charles Mingus** *Beneath the Underdog* 71

2,756 — **Greil Marcus** *Mystery Train* 75

6,187 — **Michael Ondaatje** *Coming Through Slaughter* 76

2,300 — **Nick Tosches** *Hellfire: the Jerry Lee Lewis Story* 82

2,355 — **Victor Bockris & Gerard Malanga** *Up-Tight* 83

18,439 — **Philip Norman** *The Stones* 84

6,545 — **Graham Marsh, Glyn Callingham & Felix Cromley** *The Cover Art of Blue Note Records*

19,007 — **Jon Savage** *England's Dreaming: Sex Pistols and Punk Rock* 91

15,528 — **Johnny Rogan** *Morrissey and Marr: the Severed Alliance* 92

9,724 — **Nick Kent** *The Dark Stuff: Selected Writings on Rock Music* 94

2,697 — **Jim DeRogatis** *Let It Blurt: The Life and Times of Lester Bangs*

2,299 — **Charles Shaar Murray** *Boogie Man*

John Fahey *How Bluegrass Music Destroyed My Life* 00

Paul Gorman *In Their Own Write: Adventures in the Music Press*

David Hajdu *Positively 4th Steet*

3,918 — **Mick Farren** *Give the Anarchist a Cigarette*

2,891 — **Richard Cook** *Blue Note Records: the Biography*

8,960 — **Michael Azerrad** *Our Band Could Be Your Life: Scenes from the American Indie Underground, 1981–1991*

13,050 — **David Browne** *Dream Brother: the Lives and Music of Jeff and Tim Buckley* 01

12,374 — **Lloyd Bradley** *Bass Culture: When Reggae Was King*

10,069 — **Jeff Chang** *Can't Stop, Won't Stop, a History of the Hip-Hop Generation* 05

8,641 — **Greil Marcus** *Like a Rollin' Stone: Bob Dylan at the Crossroads*

2,930 — **Garry Mulholland** *Fear of Music* 06

2,514 — **Rob Young** *Warp: Labels Unlimited*

3,449 — **Ben Ratliff** *Coltrane: the Story of a Sound*

3,440 — **Marybeth Hamilton** *In Search of the Blues*

5,318 — **Michael Gray** *Hand Me My Travellin' Shoes: in Search of Blind Willie McTell*

7,610 — **Ken Garner** *The Peel Sessions: a Story of Teenage Dreams and One Man's Love of New Music* 07

7,741 — **Gordon Jones** *Last Shop Standing: Whatever Happened to Record Shops?*

3,487 — **Richard Williams** *The Blue Moment* 09

10,096 — **Greg Milner** *Perfecting Sound Forever: the Story of Recorded Music*

16,695 — **Rob Young** *Electric Eden: Unearthing Britain's Visionary Music* 10

17,656 — **Nick Kent** *Apathy for the Devil?*

9,947 — **Elaine Constantine & Gareth Sweeney** *Northern Soul: an Illustrated History*

12,018 — **Robert Hilburn** *Johnny Cash: the Life* 13

12,400 — **Simon Goddard** *Ziggyology: a Brief History of Ziggy Stardust*

5,011 — **Marcus O'Dair** *Different Every Time: the Authorised Biography of Robert Wyatt*

3,255 — **J. P. Bean** *Singing from the Floor: a History of British Folk Clubs*

4,135 — **Steve Hanley & Olivia Piekarski** *The Big Midweek: Life Inside the Fall* 14

Source: Nielsen BookScan.
Sales figures are UK sales from
January 2001 to May 2017

TYPE OF BOOK

A format · B format · C format · Demy · 7-inch sq · A4 · Large landscape

11,517 — Lester Bangs *Psychotic Reactions and Carburetor Dung*

3,986 — Greil Marcus *Lipstick Traces: a Secret History of the Twentieth Century*

5,144 — Charles Shaar Murray *Crosstown Traffic: Jimi Hendrix and Post-War Pop*

10,616 — Danny Sugerman *Wonderland Avenue: Tales of Glamour and Excess*

8,423 — Geoff Dyer *But Beautiful: a Book About Jazz*

87 · 89 · 91

10,086 — Giles Smith *Lost in Music: a Pop Odyssey*

3,985 — David Toop *Ocean of Sound: Aether Talk, Ambient Sound and Imaginary Worlds*

10,375 — Johnny Green & Garry Barker *A Riot of Our Own: Night and Day with the Clash*

5,619 — Simon Reynolds *Energy Flash: a Journey through Rave Music and Dance Culture*

3,708 — M.C. Strong *The Great Alternative and Indie Discography*

David Cavanagh *My Magpie Eyes are Hungry for the Prize*

4,454 — Colin Harper *Dazzling Stranger: Bert Jansch and the British Folk and Blues Revival*

95 · 97 · 98 · 99 · 00

6,509 — Garry Mulholland *This Is Uncool: the 500 Greatest Singles Since Punk and Disco*

3,010 — David Katz *Solid Foundation: an Oral History of Reggae*

6,311 — Ian MacDonald *The People's Music*

6,559 — Paul Morley *Words and Music: a History of Pop in the Shape of a City*

2,517 — David Toop *Haunted Weather*

13,175 — Mac Montandon *Innocent When You Dream: Tom Waits, the Collected Interviews*

02 · 03 · 04 · 05

4,037 — Michael Bracewell *Re-Make/Re-Model: Art, Pop, Fashion and the Making of Roxy Music*

4,867 — Lavinia Greenlaw *The Importance of Music to Girls*

5,171 — Simon Reynolds *Bring the Noise: 20 Years of Writing About Hip Rock and Hip-Hop*

6,465 — Julian Cope *Japrocksampler: How the Post-War Japanese Blew their Minds on Rock 'n' Roll*

5,713 — David Sheppard *On Some Faraway Beach: the Life and Times of Brian Eno*

3,201 — Travis Elborough *The Long-Player Goodbye*

13,237 — Barney Hoskyns *Lowside of the Road: a Life of Tom Waits*

08 · 09

11,812 — Simon Reynolds *Retromania: Pop Culture's Addiction to its Own Past*

Robert Forster *The Ten Rules of Rock 'n' Roll*

Ed. Rob Young *No Regrets: Writings on Scott Walker*

4,481 — Richard King *How Soon Is Now: The Madmen and Mavericks who made Independent Music 1975–2005*

6,141 — Pat Long *The History of the NME: High Times and Low Lives at the World's Most Famous Music Magazine, 1952—2012*

11,872 — Mike Skinner *The Story of the Streets*

11 · 12

9,216 — David Cavanagh *Good Night and Good Riddance: How Thirty-Five Years of John Peel Helped to Shape Modern Life*

17,535 — Kim Gordon *Girl in a Band*

5,705 — Stephen Witt *How Music Got Free: the Inventor, the Mogul and the Thief*

2,604 — Barney Hoskyns *Small Town Talk*

8,843 — Steve Jones *Lonely Boy, Tales from a Sex Pistol*

2,680 — Hattie Collins & Olivia Rose *This Is Grime*

15 · 16

VINYL RENAISSANCE

There's been a media frenzy over the resurgence of vinyl in recent years. Vinyl is a beautiful thing, but vinyl LP sales still only account for something like 6–7 per cent of all music purchased globally. The following graphics illustrate the fall and rise of vinyl albums bought in the US and UK in recent times. In the UK alone, BPI (British Phonographic Industry) statistics reveal nine years of consecutive growth in vinyl sales from 2007. But the global trend of units of vinyl sold, when placed against sales between 1973 and 1983 (the dawn of the CD), puts the vinyl renaissance into sobering perspective. There were also 45 billion audio streams in 2016 – a 500 per cent increase from 2013.

GLOBAL LP SALES
(figures from IFPI – International Federation of the Phonographic Industry)

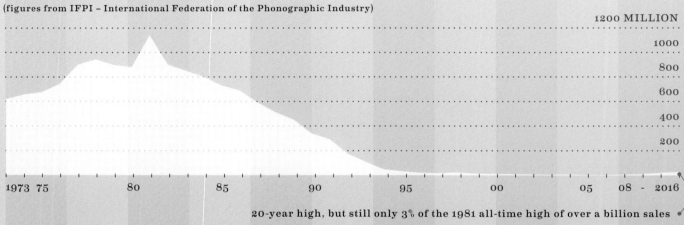

1200 MILLION
1000
800
600
400
200

1973 75   80   85   90   95   00   05   08 - 2016

20-year high, but still only 3% of the 1981 all-time high of over a billion sales

US VINYL LP SALES
(figures from Nielsen Soundscan)

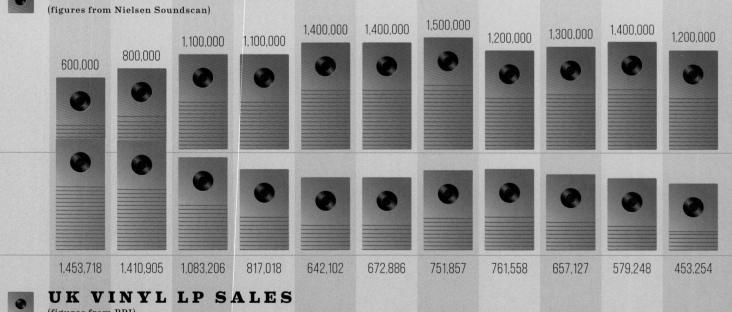

| 600,000 | 800,000 | 1,100,000 | 1,100,000 | 1,400,000 | 1,400,000 | 1,500,000 | 1,200,000 | 1,300,000 | 1,400,000 | 1,200,000 |

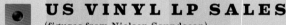

| 1,453,718 | 1,410,905 | 1,083,206 | 817,018 | 642,102 | 672,886 | 751,857 | 761,558 | 657,127 | 579,248 | 453,254 |

UK VINYL LP SALES
(figures from BPI)

| 1994 | 95 | 96 | 97 | 98 | 99 | 00 | 01 | 02 | 03 | 04 |

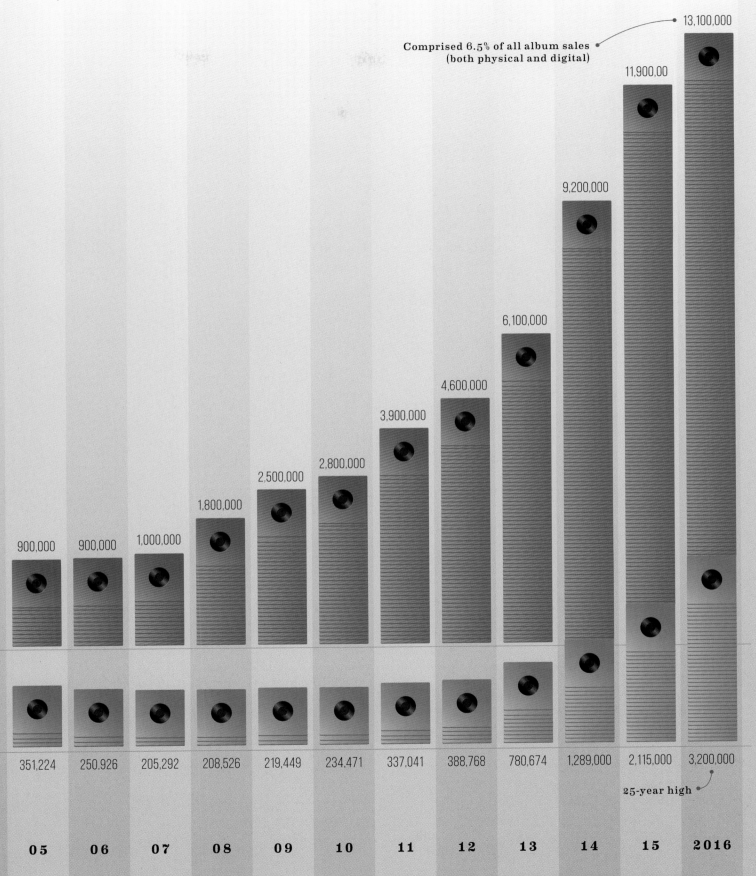

Comprised 6.5% of all album sales
(both physical and digital)

13,100,000

11,900,00

9,200,000

6,100,000

4,600,000

3,900,000

2,800,000

2,500,000

1,800,000

1,000,000

900,000   900,000

05	06	07	08	09	10	11	12	13	14	15	2016
351,224	250,926	205,292	208,526	219,449	234,471	337,041	388,768	780,674	1,289,000	2,115,000	3,200,000

25-year high

Sources: theguardian.com, bpi.co.uk, savethevinyl.org, musicbusinessresearch.wordpress.com

MUSIC WEBSITES (AND OTHERS)
THAT OFFER A DECENT MODERN-DAY ALTERNATIVE
TO THE HEYDAY OF THE MUSIC PRESS

In recent years, the print music press has unfortunately been eroded to such a great extent (see UK Music Press infographic) that many fans have turned elsewhere for their news and reviews. Fortunately, there is a growing online scene where followers of any and every genre can find journalists and communities of like-minded souls to trade thoughts with. From the vast sites like Pitchfork that cater to everyone and everything, to the more eclectic such as the Free Jazz Collective, this graphic should help you start your journey around the online music sphere.

Sources: Facebook Likes as of 14 July 2017

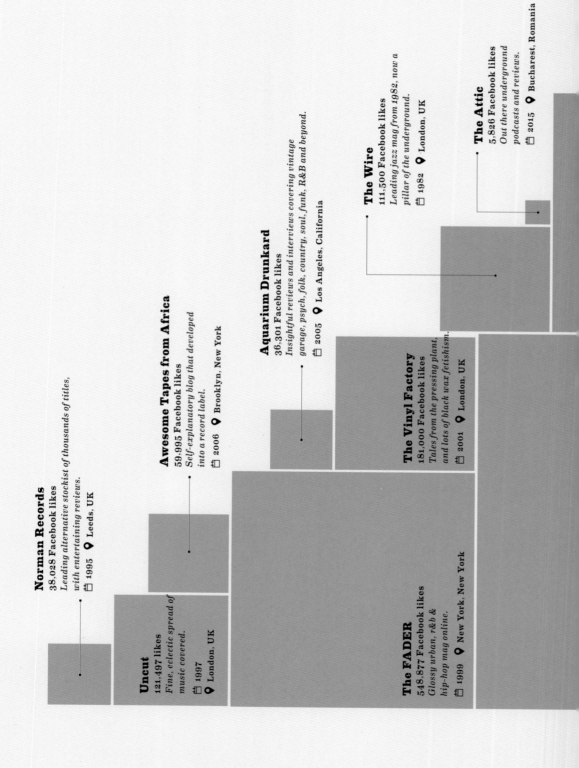

Norman Records
38,028 Facebook likes
Leading alternative stockist of thousands of titles, with entertaining reviews.
🗓 1995 📍 Leeds, UK

Uncut
121,497 likes
Fine, eclectic spread of music covered.
🗓 1997 📍 London, UK

Awesome Tapes from Africa
59,995 Facebook likes
Self-explanatory blog that developed into a record label.
🗓 2006 📍 Brooklyn, New York

Aquarium Drunkard
36,301 Facebook likes
Insightful reviews and interviews covering vintage garage, psych, folk, country, soul, funk, R&B and beyond.
🗓 2005 📍 Los Angeles, California

The FADER
548,877 Facebook likes
Glossy urban, r&b & hip-hop mag online.
🗓 1999 📍 New York, New York

The Vinyl Factory
181,000 Facebook likes
Tales from the pressing plant, and lots of black wax fetishism.
🗓 2001 📍 London, UK

The Wire
111,500 Facebook likes
Leading jazz mag from 1982, now a pillar of the underground.
🗓 1982 📍 London, UK

The Attic
5,826 Facebook likes
Out there underground podcasts and reviews.
🗓 2015 📍 Bucharest, Romania

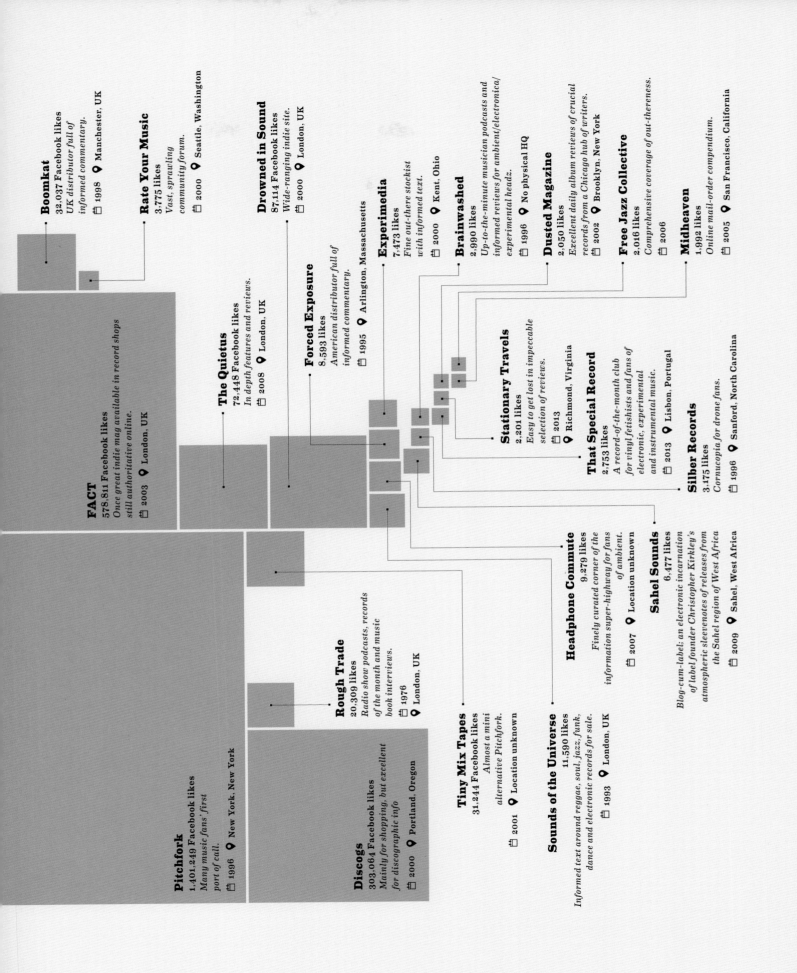

Boomkat
32,037 Facebook likes
UK distributor full of informed commentary.
🗓 1998 📍 Manchester, UK

Rate Your Music
3,775 likes
Vast, sprawling community forum.
🗓 2000 📍 Seattle, Washington

Drowned in Sound
87,114 Facebook likes
Wide-ranging indie site.
🗓 2000 📍 London, UK

Experimedia
7,473 likes
Fine out-there stockist with informed text.
🗓 2000 📍 Kent, Ohio

Brainwashed
2,990 likes
Up-to-the-minute musician podcasts and informed reviews for ambient/electronica/experimental headz.
🗓 1996 📍 No physical HQ

Dusted Magazine
2,050 likes
Excellent daily album reviews of crucial records from a Chicago hub of writers.
🗓 2002 📍 Brooklyn, New York

Free Jazz Collective
2,016 likes
Comprehensive coverage of out-thereness.
🗓 2006

Midheaven
1,992 likes
Online mail-order compendium.
🗓 2005 📍 San Francisco, California

FACT
578,811 Facebook likes
Once great indie mag available in record shops still authoritative online.
🗓 2003 📍 London, UK

The Quietus
72,448 Facebook likes
In depth features and reviews.
🗓 2008 📍 London, UK

Forced Exposure
8,593 Facebook likes
American distributor full of informed commentary.
🗓 1995 📍 Arlington, Massachusetts

Stationary Travels
2,201 likes
Easy to get lost in impeccable selection of reviews.
🗓 2013 📍 Richmond, Virginia

That Special Record
2,753 likes
A record-of-the-month club for vinyl fetishists and fans of electronic, experimental and instrumental music.
🗓 2013 📍 Lisbon, Portugal

Silber Records
3,175 likes
Cornucopia for drone fans.
🗓 1996 📍 Sanford, North Carolina

Pitchfork
1,401,249 Facebook likes
Many music fans' first port of call.
🗓 1996 📍 New York, New York

Discogs
303,064 Facebook likes
Mainly for shopping, but excellent for discographic info
🗓 2000 📍 Portland, Oregon

Rough Trade
20,309 likes
Radio show podcasts, records of the month and music book interviews.
🗓 1976 📍 London, UK

Tiny Mix Tapes
31,244 Facebook likes
Almost a mini alternative Pitchfork.
🗓 2001 📍 Location unknown

Sounds of the Universe
11,590 likes
Informed text around reggae, soul, jazz, funk, dance and electronic records for sale.
🗓 1993 📍 London, UK

Headphone Commute
9,279 likes
Finely curated corner of the information super-highway for fans of ambient.
🗓 2007 📍 Location unknown

Sahel Sounds
6,477 likes
Blog-cum-label; an electronic incarnation of label founder Christopher Kirkley's atmospheric sleevenotes of releases from the Sahel region of West Africa
🗓 2009 📍 Sahel, West Africa

SPEED UP YOUR HOUSE PARTY

OK, we know this looks like a playlist for someone's fiftieth birthday but here's a guide/template to adopt when you want to get the dancefloor moving faster, which features the odd counterintuitive observation (1970s urban classics of the soul and disco variety often have fewer beats per minute than a fair bit of reggae) as well as reinforcing a few home truths. For example, many African beats make for a good catalyst to get on the dance floor. And to make sure the valuable 1960s table lamp is out of the way by the time the drum & bass kicks in. It's also a fact that Ethiopian jazz – jazz, full stop – is virtually impossible to record an accurate figure for. Or at least it threw our Sandberg Sound BPM detector (backed up by a Microsoft/Nokia manual Beat Counter) into a tailspin.*

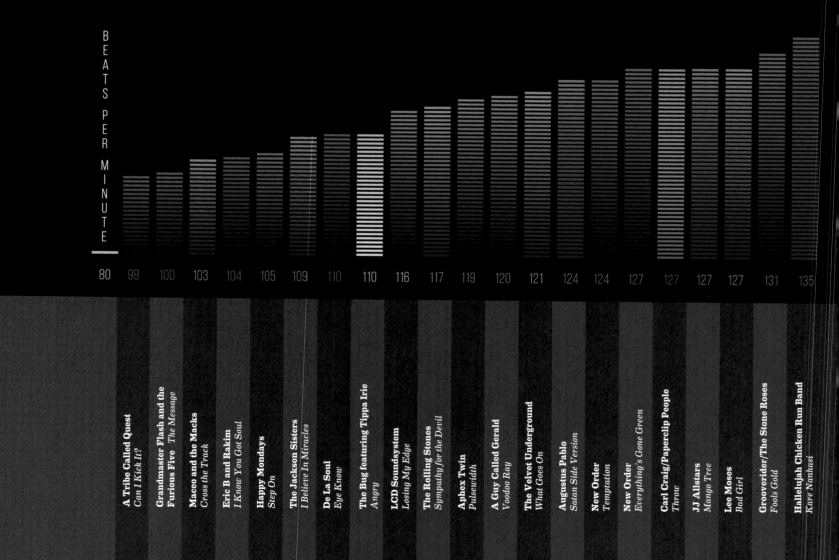

BEATS PER MINUTE

| 80 | 99 | 100 | 103 | 104 | 105 | 109 | 110 | 110 | 116 | 117 | 119 | 120 | 121 | 124 | 124 | 127 | 127 | 127 | 127 | 131 | 135 |

A Tribe Called Quest *Can I Kick It?*

Grandmaster Flash and the Furious Five *The Message*

Maceo and the Macks *Cross the Track*

Eric B and Rakim *I Know You Got Soul*

Happy Mondays *Step On*

The Jackson Sisters *I Believe In Miracles*

De La Soul *Eye Know*

The Bug featuring Tippa Irie *Angry*

LCD Soundsystem *Losing My Edge*

The Rolling Stones *Sympathy for the Devil*

Aphex Twin *Pulsewidth*

A Guy Called Gerald *Voodoo Ray*

The Velvet Underground *What Goes On*

Augustus Pablo *Satan Side Version*

New Order *Temptation*

New Order *Everything's Gone Green*

Carl Craig/Paperclip People *Throw*

JJ Allstars *Mango Tree*

Lee Moses *Bad Girl*

Grooverider/The Stone Roses *Fools Gold*

Hallelujah Chicken Run Band *Kare Nanhasi*

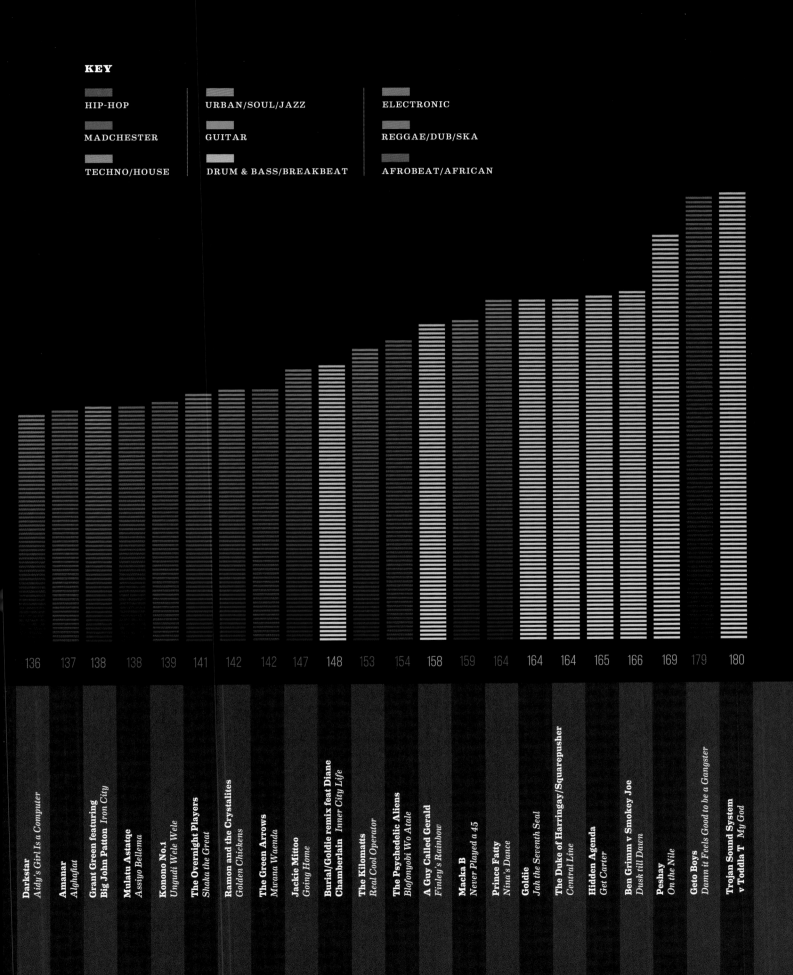

KEY

HIP-HOP

MADCHESTER

TECHNO/HOUSE

URBAN/SOUL/JAZZ

GUITAR

DRUM & BASS/BREAKBEAT

ELECTRONIC

REGGAE/DUB/SKA

AFROBEAT/AFRICAN

| 136 | 137 | 138 | 138 | 139 | 141 | 142 | 142 | 147 | 148 | 153 | 154 | 158 | 159 | 164 | 164 | 164 | 165 | 166 | 169 | 179 | 180 |

Darkstar *Aidy's Girl Is a Computer*

Amanar *Alghafiat*

Grant Green featuring Big John Patton *Iron City*

Mulatu Astatqe *Assiyo Bellema*

Konono No.1 *Ungudi Wele Wele*

The Overnight Players *Shaka the Great*

Ramon and the Crystalites *Golden Chickens*

The Green Arrows *Murana Waenda*

Jackie Mittoo *Going Home*

Burial/Goldie remix feat Diane Chamberlain *Inner City Life*

The Kilomatts *Real Cool Operator*

The Psychedelic Aliens *Blofonyobi Wo Atale*

A Guy Called Gerald *Finley's Rainbow*

Macka B *Never Played a 45*

Prince Fatty *Nina's Dance*

Goldie *Jah the Seventh Seal*

The Duke of Harringay/Squarepusher *Central Line*

Hidden Agenda *Get Carter*

Ben Grimm v Smokey Joe *Dusk till Dawn*

Peshay *On the Nile*

Geto Boys *Damn it Feels Good to be a Gangster*

Trojan Sound System v Toddla T *My God*

BEATING NUMBER ONE

The pace of life has increased dramatically over the past few decades, and it's unsurprising that the beats per minute of the best-selling UK singles per calendar year reflect that. During the first few years of the charts, in the 1950s, the average BPM was a mere 99; "I Believe" by Frankie Laine bottomed out at just 66 BPM. Since then, there has been a steady climb (rapid leaps provided by The Beatles and the fast-paced 1980s) and the 2010s are the first decade that hasn't had a single best-seller timed at under 100 BPM.

Sources: beatsperminuteonline.com, jog.fm, 99; songbpm.com, officialcharts.com

Avg per decade

Beats per Minute

Song Name   Artist

2016
- *One Dance* Drake ft. Wizkid and Kyla
- *Uptown Funk* Mark Ronson ft. Bruno Mars
- *Happy* Pharrell Williams
- *Blurred Lines* Robin Thicke ft. T.I. and Pharrell Williams
- *Somebody That I Used To Know* Gotye ft. Kimbra
- *Someone Like You* Adele
- *Love The Way You Lie* Eminem ft. Rihanna

2010
- *Poker Face* Lady Gaga
- *Hallelujah* Alexandra Burke
- *Bleeding Love* Leona Lewis
- *Crazy* Gnarls Barkley
- *Is This the Way to Amarillo* Tony Christie ft. Peter Kay
- *Do They Know Its Christmas* Band Aid 20
- *Where Is the Love?* The Black Eyed Peas
- *Evergreen* Will Young
- *It Wasn't Me* Shaggy ft. Rikrok
- *Can We Fix It?* Bob the Builder

2000
- *...Baby One More Time* Britney Spears
- *Believe* Cher
- *Candle in the Wind* Elton John
- *Killing Me Softly* Fugees
- *Unchained Melody* Robson & Jerome
- *Love Is All Around* Wet Wet Wet
- *I'd Do Anything for Love (But I Won't Do That)* Meat Loaf
- *I Will Always Love You* Whitney Houston
- *(Everything I Do) I Do It for You* Bryan Adams

1990
Unchained Melody   The Righteous Brothers
Ride On Time   Black Box
Mistletoe and Wine   Cliff Richard
Never Gonna Give You Up   Rick Astley
Don't Leave Me This Way   The Communards
The Power of Love   Jennifer Rush
Do They Know It's Christmas?   Band Aid
Karma Chameleon   Culture Club
Come On Eileen   Dexy's Midnight Runners
Tainted Love   Soft Cell
Don't Stand So Close To Me   The Police

1980
Bright Eyes   Art Garfunkel
Rivers Of Babylon   Boney M.
Mull Of Kintyre   Wings
Save Your Kisses for Me   Brotherhood of Man
Bye Bye Baby   Bay City Rollers
Tiger Feet   Mud
Tie a Yellow Ribbon Round the Ole Oak Tree   Dawn
Amazing Grace   The Royal Scots Dragoon Guards Bands
My Sweet Lord   George Harrison
The Wonder of You   Elvis Presley

1970
Sugar, Sugar   The Archies
Hey Jude   The Beatles
Release Me   Engelbert Humperdinck
Green, Green Grass of Home   Tom Jones
Tears   Ken Dodd
Can't Buy Me Love   The Beatles
She Loves You   The Beatles
I Remember You   Frank Ifield
Wooden Heart   Elvis Presley
It's Now or Never   Elvis Presley

1960
1952–59 Eight Best-Selling Singles

IT'S CHRISTMAS

It seems that every year, Christmas jingles are piped through department stores earlier and earlier, announcing the start of the shopping season. But whether you love them or loathe them, there's no doubting the commercial potential of a Christmas hit. Below are some of the most successful across various mediums, including a bonus alternative Top 10 for those looking for something a little different.

BEST-SELLING UK CHRISTMAS ALBUMS OF THE 21ST CENTURY

- **Michael Bublé**
  Christmas (2011)

- **Rod Stewart**
  Merry Christmas, Baby (2012)

- **Cliff Richard**
  Cliff at Christmas (2003)

- **Jive Bunny and the Mastermixers**
  Ultimate Christmas Party (2003)

- **Elvis Presley**
  Christmas Peace (2008)

- **Mariah Carey**
  Merry Christmas (1994)

- **Andrea Bocelli**
  My Christmas (2009)

- **Aled Jones**
  The Christmas Album (2004)

- **Charlotte Church**
  Dream a Dream (2000)

- **Susan Boyle**
  Home for Christmas (2013)

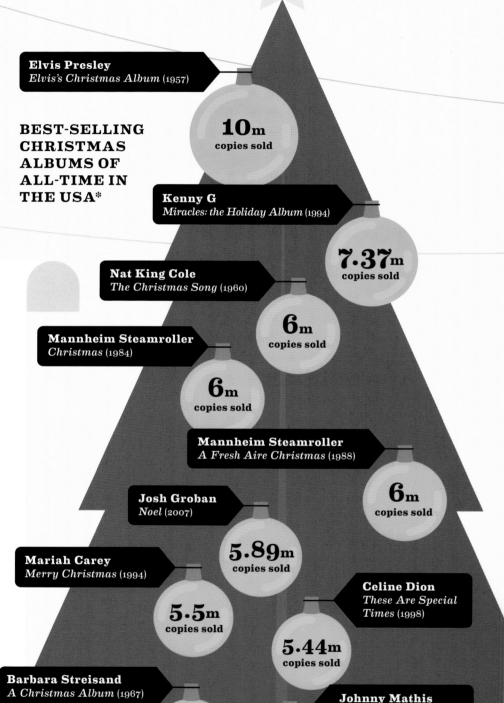

BEST-SELLING CHRISTMAS ALBUMS OF ALL-TIME IN THE USA*

Elvis Presley
Elvis's Christmas Album (1957)
10m copies sold

Kenny G
Miracles: the Holiday Album (1994)
7.37m copies sold

Nat King Cole
The Christmas Song (1960)
6m copies sold

Mannheim Steamroller
Christmas (1984)
6m copies sold

Mannheim Steamroller
A Fresh Aire Christmas (1988)
6m copies sold

Josh Groban
Noel (2007)
5.89m copies sold

Mariah Carey
Merry Christmas (1994)
5.5m copies sold

Celine Dion
These Are Special Times (1998)
5.44m copies sold

Barbara Streisand
A Christmas Album (1967)
5.37m copies sold

Johnny Mathis
Merry Christmas (1958)
5.24m copies sold

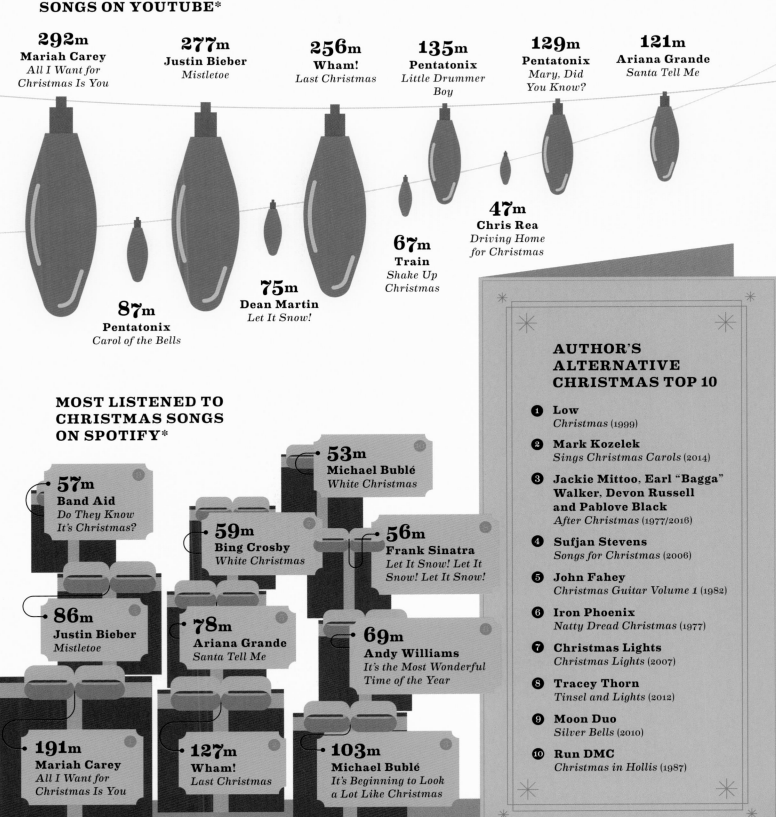

MOST VIEWED CHRISTMAS SONGS ON YOUTUBE*

292m
Mariah Carey
All I Want for Christmas Is You

277m
Justin Bieber
Mistletoe

256m
Wham!
Last Christmas

135m
Pentatonix
Little Drummer Boy

129m
Pentatonix
Mary, Did You Know?

121m
Ariana Grande
Santa Tell Me

87m
Pentatonix
Carol of the Bells

75m
Dean Martin
Let It Snow!

67m
Train
Shake Up Christmas

47m
Chris Rea
Driving Home for Christmas

Sources: billboard.com, officialcharts.com.
*US and UK sales figures accurate as of December 2016.
YouTube views and Spotify listens accurate as of July 2017.

MOST LISTENED TO CHRISTMAS SONGS ON SPOTIFY*

53m
Michael Bublé
White Christmas

57m
Band Aid
Do They Know It's Christmas?

59m
Bing Crosby
White Christmas

56m
Frank Sinatra
Let It Snow! Let It Snow! Let It Snow!

86m
Justin Bieber
Mistletoe

78m
Ariana Grande
Santa Tell Me

69m
Andy Williams
It's the Most Wonderful Time of the Year

191m
Mariah Carey
All I Want for Christmas Is You

127m
Wham!
Last Christmas

103m
Michael Bublé
It's Beginning to Look a Lot Like Christmas

AUTHOR'S ALTERNATIVE CHRISTMAS TOP 10

1. **Low**
   Christmas (1999)
2. **Mark Kozelek**
   Sings Christmas Carols (2014)
3. **Jackie Mittoo, Earl "Bagga" Walker, Devon Russell and Pablove Black**
   After Christmas (1977/2016)
4. **Sufjan Stevens**
   Songs for Christmas (2006)
5. **John Fahey**
   Christmas Guitar Volume 1 (1982)
6. **Iron Phoenix**
   Natty Dread Christmas (1977)
7. **Christmas Lights**
   Christmas Lights (2007)
8. **Tracey Thorn**
   Tinsel and Lights (2012)
9. **Moon Duo**
   Silver Bells (2010)
10. **Run DMC**
    Christmas in Hollis (1987)

THE HIGHEST FORM OF FLATTERY

The earliest tribute bands weren't really tribute bands at all. They were actual bands trying to cash in on an established band's popularity by playing in a similar style, or producing cover versions. Later, they formed because fans genuinely missed the original, or had never had a chance to see them live. Bjorn Again, the ABBA carbon copy, make a grand living out of this. One problem many come up against, though, is the longevity of the original. Why would you watch The Rolling Clones when the original Rolling Stones are still going strong? Although, with the passing years, maybe they should be called the Rolling Crones.

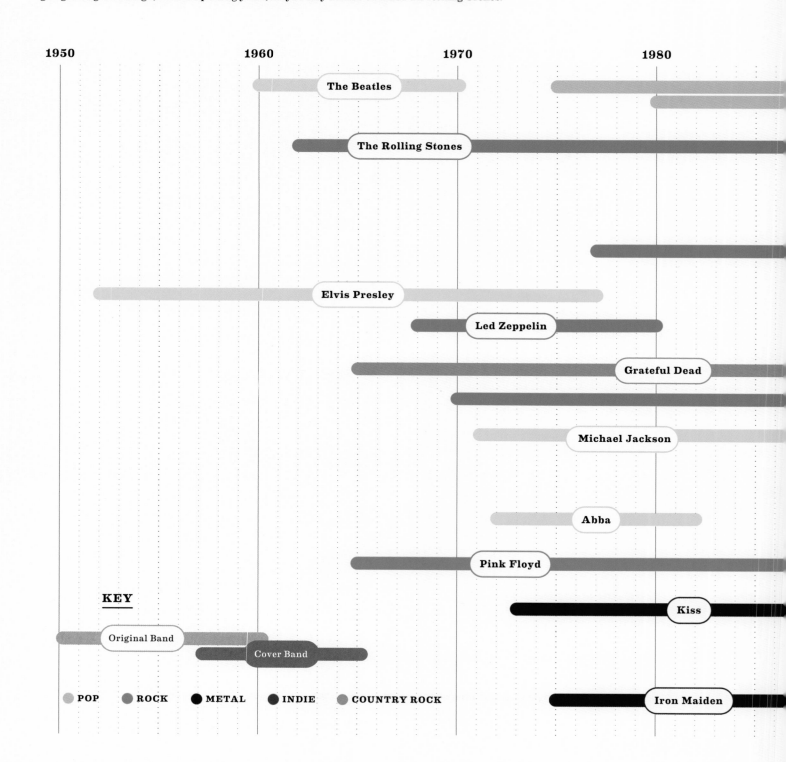

1950   1960   1970   1980

The Beatles

The Rolling Stones

Elvis Presley

Led Zeppelin

Grateful Dead

Michael Jackson

Abba

Pink Floyd

Kiss

KEY

Original Band

Cover Band

● POP   ● ROCK   ● METAL   ● INDIE   ● COUNTRY ROCK

Iron Maiden

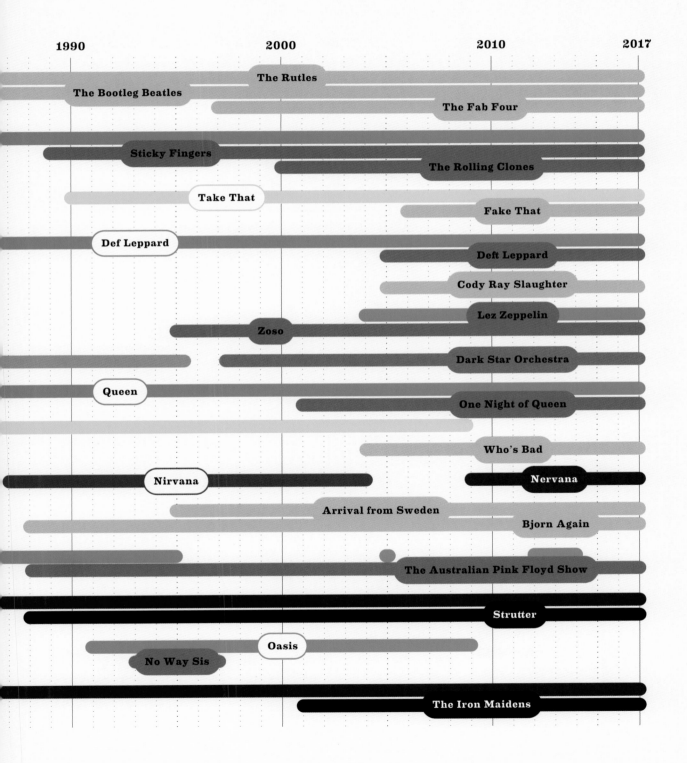

1990 2000 2010 2017

The Rutles

The Bootleg Beatles

The Fab Four

Sticky Fingers

The Rolling Clones

Take That

Fake That

Def Leppard

Deft Leppard

Cody Ray Slaughter

Lez Zeppelin

Zoso

Dark Star Orchestra

Queen

One Night of Queen

Who's Bad

Nirvana

Nervana

Arrival from Sweden

Bjorn Again

The Australian Pink Floyd Show

Strutter

Oasis

No Way Sis

The Iron Maidens

TAPE SPLICING AND LOOPING

Magnetic tape played a revolutionary – and perhaps now, in our digital world, overlooked – role in recorded sound. Here are a few highlights.

1 **Pierre Schaefer** and **Pierre Henry** pioneered tape looping – a short, spliced loop of tape that plays a sample repeatedly – at Studio d'Essai in Paris in the 1940s. Tape looping formed a fundamental part in *musique concrete*, their collage-like manipulating of found sounds which paved the way for modern sampling, hip-hop and today's electronic music. As Jean-Michel Jarre, a former student of Schaeffer's, put it in 2007, "Back in the '40s, Schaeffer invented the sample, the locked groove – in other words, the loop... It was Schaeffer who experimented with distorting sounds, playing them backwards, speeding them up and slowing them down. He was the one who invented the entire way music is made these days."

2 **Terry Riley** is keen on expanding "the sonic horizon" of music, and interested in the grainy textures of tape noise. 1963's looped *Music for the Gift* features the trumpet of Chet Baker.

3 **Pauline Oliverios**: 1966 *Alien Bog* and 1967 *Beautiful Soop* – tape delay pieces inspired by the sound of frogs outside Oliverios's window at the Tape Music Center at Mills College in Oakland, California.

4 In the late summer/early autumn of 1972 **Robert Fripp's** guitar lines are fed into **Brian Eno's** modified Revox A77 twin tape recorder delay system. David Sheppard writes in his biography of Eno, *On Some Faraway Beach*, that the "tapes spooled in and out of each other, allowing the musical signal to bounce from one set of playback heads to the other, building inexorably into loops of shimmering, self-reflecting sound." An effect admirably reproduced in the endlessly repeating mirrored cube/tile effect of the *No Pussyfooting* LP artwork.

5 In 1995 **Philip Jeck**, a Liverpool-based artist best known for his *Vinyl Requiem* played simultaneously on 180 Dansette record players, releases his debut CD *Loopholes*, primarily constructed out of short, looped tape samples.

Sources: *The Wire*, May 2001; fluid-radio.co.uk; factmag.com; David Sheppard, *On Some Faraway Beach: the Life and Times of Brian Eno* (2008, Orion); Terry Riley, Tape Loops YouTube video; Bib Sales Research Department's *Hi-Fi Stereo Hints and Tips booklet*, ed. John Borwick B.Sc., 1973; Amulets' how to make a cassette tape loop in 5 minutesYouTube video; fm3buddhamachine.com

6 In September 2001, in the process of digitizing some old tapes, **William Basinski**, a New York composer, is struck by the melancholy but warm analogue sound of decaying tapes crumbling on each pass through the spindle of the machine. Around the same time, Basinski films some Andy-Warhol-style still footage of the smouldering ruins of the World Trade Centre from the rooftop of his building in Brooklyn. The four-volume *Disintegration Loops* is born; a beautiful, haunting, elegiac set for the early twenty-first century. Basinski continues to take tape loops and set them in graphic scores. He told Pascal Savy of Fluid Radio, "Our memories are made constantly of loops that go around and around – sometimes bad feedback loops continue to plague people and cause them pain and these things need to be resolved. The loops helped me to resolve my own bad feedback loops and let them go. Our world is in a very bad feedback loop now. We need to get rid of it. It's not going to be pretty and eventually things will resolve."

7 Compact loop technology. **Christiaan Virant** and **Zhang Jian** released their first **Buddha Machine** in 2005, a small battery-powered moulded plastic box that allowed the listener to select between 9 ambient loops. Much of this book was put together listening to various loops from the Philip Glass Buddha Machine, released in January 2017 to celebrate the New York composer's 80th birthday.

HOW TO SPLICE ON A REEL-TO-REEL

Obtain a Bib tape-splicer and a yellow Chinagraph pencil, switch off your reel-to-reel tape recorder, then follow these instructions, reproduced from the 1973 edition of the Bib Sales Research Department's *Hi-Fi Stereo Hints and Tips* booklet.

Lift the locking clamps away and upwards from the body of the Splicer. Apply length of recording tape from the left with glossy side upwards across the full length of the Splicer and, whilst holding it in position, lower and lock the left clamp.

Apply the right-hand tape across the Splicer and on top of the first so that the free end passes over and clears the slot. Lower and lock the right clamp.

Place the left forefinger on the tape just to the left of the slot. Draw the edge of the cutter across the slot and remove the surplus tape.

Apply a short length of splicing tape across the two ends of the recording tape which have been cut, pressing it down firmly on the Splicer each side of the tape.

Apply the cutter to the two lateral grooves each side of the recording tape. Remove the surplus splicing tape. Lift the two clamps to remove the jointed tape.

HOW TO MAKE A TAPE LOOP FROM A C90 CASSETTE

Scan the QR code for a 5-minute video, or alternatively go to: www.youtube.com/watch?v=hER3s1NPr_U

GHOSTLY MAP OF LONDON'S RECORD SHOPS

From Honest Jon's in Portobello Road to Sounds of the Universe in Soho and Alan's second-hand emporium in East Finchley, there are still a handful of great record shops in London – the addresses and locations marked on the map below illustrate shops still very much open in the summer of 2017. However, despite a 21st-century south-London renaissance, the ghostly presence of shops of the recent past reveal what vinyl treasures could once be found in the capital.

TYPES OF RECORD SHOP

- Dance
- Jazz
- Soul/Funk
- Second hand
- Global
- Ambient/Electronica/Experimental
- New/Eclectic/Indie
- Reggae/Dub

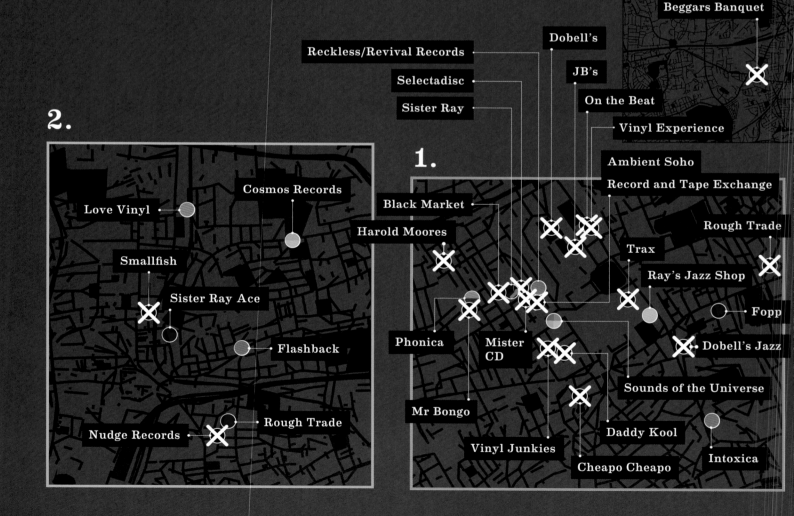

2.

- Love Vinyl
- Cosmos Records
- Smallfish
- Sister Ray Ace
- Flashback
- Nudge Records
- Rough Trade

1.

- Reckless/Revival Records
- Selectadisc
- Sister Ray
- Dobell's
- JB's
- On the Beat
- Vinyl Experience
- Beggars Banquet
- Ambient Soho
- Record and Tape Exchange
- Black Market
- Harold Moores
- Rough Trade
- Trax
- Ray's Jazz Shop
- Fopp
- Phonica
- Mister CD
- Dobell's Jazz
- Mr Bongo
- Sounds of the Universe
- Vinyl Junkies
- Daddy Kool
- Cheapo Cheapo
- Intoxica

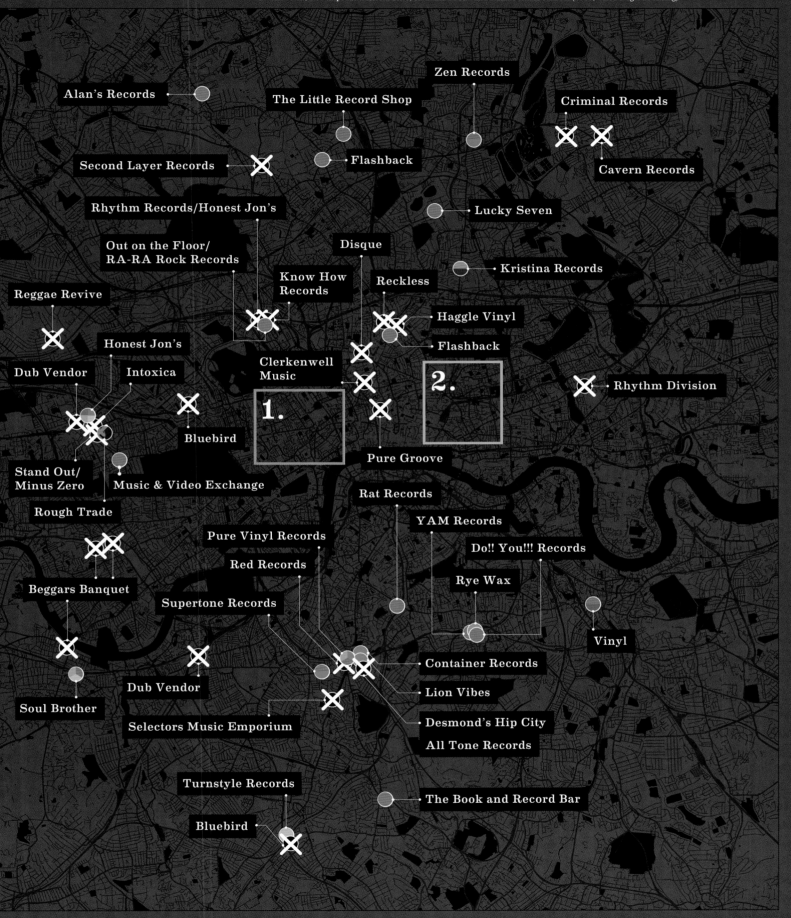

Sources: londonnet.co.uk; guardian.com; Sanjiv Ahluwalia, *The Secret List, London: A Guide to Independent Record Shops* (2016, The Secret List); *Old Rare New, the Independent Record Store*, ed. Emma Pettit and Nadine Kathe Monem (2008, Black Dog Publishing).

Zen Records

Alan's Records

The Little Record Shop

Criminal Records

Flashback

Cavern Records

Second Layer Records

Lucky Seven

Rhythm Records/Honest Jon's

Out on the Floor/
RA-RA Rock Records

Disque

Kristina Records

Know How
Records

Reckless

Reggae Revive

Haggle Vinyl

Clerkenwell
Music

Flashback

Honest Jon's

2.

Rhythm Division

Dub Vendor

Intoxica

1.

Bluebird

Pure Groove

Stand Out/
Minus Zero

Rat Records

Music & Video Exchange

YAM Records

Rough Trade

Do!! You!!! Records

Pure Vinyl Records

Rye Wax

Red Records

Beggars Banquet

Vinyl

Supertone Records

Container Records

Dub Vendor

Lion Vibes

Soul Brother

Desmond's Hip City

Selectors Music Emporium

All Tone Records

Turnstyle Records

The Book and Record Bar

Bluebird

MONEY CAN'T BUY ME LOVE

Of all the subjects covered in music, love has to be at the top of the pile. But working in the business does not necessarily lead to lifelong happiness. The grooves of records run deep with the tears of sadness, which is maybe why the next most popular topic for songs is heartbreak and lost love.

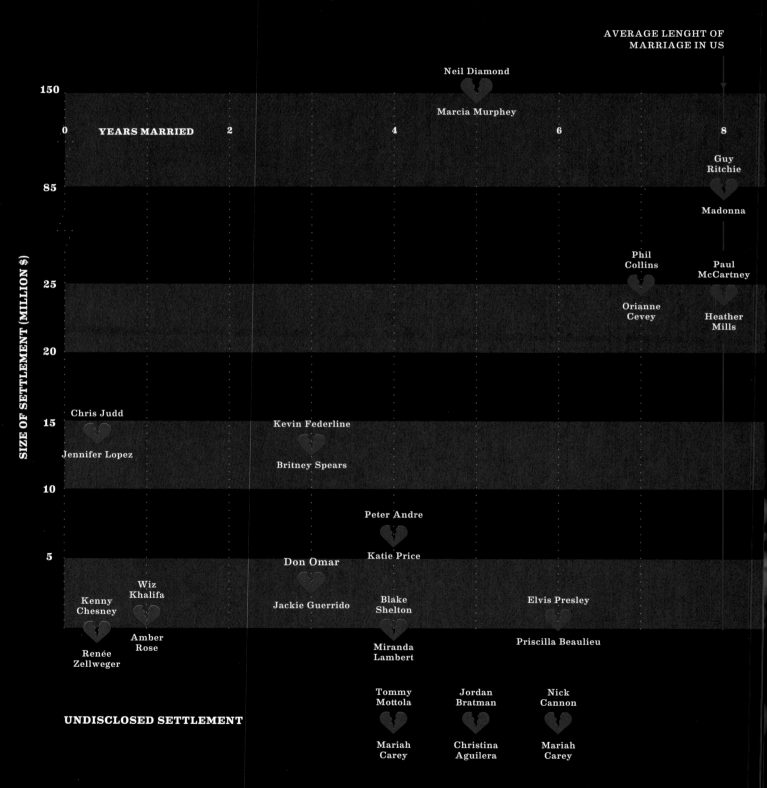

AVERAGE LENGHT OF
MARRIAGE IN US

YEARS MARRIED

0   2   4   6   8

Neil Diamond

Marcia Murphey

Guy Ritchie

Madonna

Phil Collins

Paul McCartney

Orianne Cevey

Heather Mills

SIZE OF SETTLEMENT (MILLION $)

150

85

25

20

Chris Judd

15   Kevin Federline

Jennifer Lopez

Britney Spears

10

Peter Andre

5   Katie Price

Don Omar

Wiz Khalifa

Kenny Chesney   Jackie Guerrido   Blake Shelton   Elvis Presley

Amber Rose   Miranda Lambert   Priscilla Beaulieu

Renée Zellweger

Tommy Mottola   Jordan Bratman   Nick Cannon

UNDISCLOSED SETTLEMENT

Mariah Carey   Christina Aguilera   Mariah Carey

Sources: dailymail.co.uk, marieclaire.com, glamourmagazine.co.uk, newsday.com
hollywoodlife.com, divorcedebbie.com, latina.com, mckinleyirvin.com, correct as of 22/03/17

10   12   14   16   20   24

85

SIZE OF SETTLEMENT (MILLION $)

Gavin Rossdale

25

Gwen Stefani

Lionel
Richie

20

Ronnie Wood

Diane
Alexander

Jo Karslake

Mick Jagger

15

Jerry Hall

Rod Stewart

René
Alizondo

Rachel Hunter   10

Janet
Jackson

5

Martin Isaacs

Mary J Blige

Johnny
Cash

Vivian
Liberto

IT'S A SOCIAL THING

In the days when pop began all that mattered was record sales, chart positions and selling out gigs. These days it's not enough to just make good music – and for people to buy it – you need to have followers, or friends or subscribers. The Internet and the numerous platforms it offers to get close to your favourite artist have changed the way we listen to music and interact with our heroes. What's most important though? Katy Perry may have five times as many twitter followers as Ed Sheeran but he gets twice as many plays per month on Spotify.

KEY

XX

NUMBER OF FOLLOWERS
(MILLIONS)

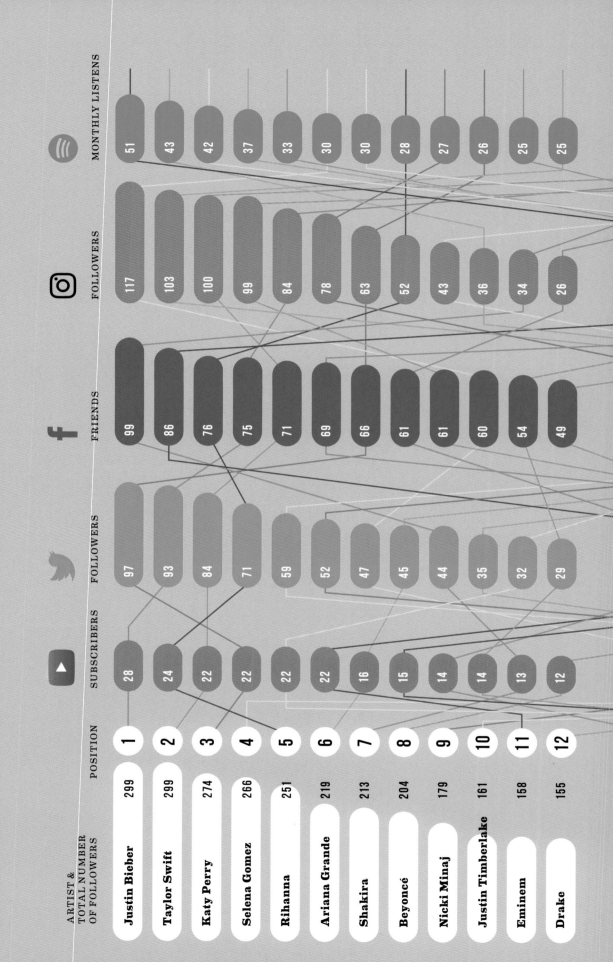

ARTIST & TOTAL NUMBER OF FOLLOWERS		POSITION	▲ SUBSCRIBERS	FOLLOWERS	f FRIENDS	ⓘ FOLLOWERS	⦀ MONTHLY LISTENS
Justin Bieber	299	1	28	97	99	117	51
Taylor Swift	299	2	24	93	86	103	43
Katy Perry	274	3	22	84	76	100	42
Selena Gomez	266	4	22	71	75	99	37
Rihanna	251	5	22	59	71	84	33
Ariana Grande	219	6	22	52	69	78	30
Shakira	213	7	16	47	66	63	30
Beyoncé	204	8	15	45	61	52	28
Nicki Minaj	179	9	14	44	61	43	27
Justin Timberlake	161	10	14	35	60	36	26
Eminem	158	11	13	32	54	34	25
Drake	155	12	12	29	49	26	25

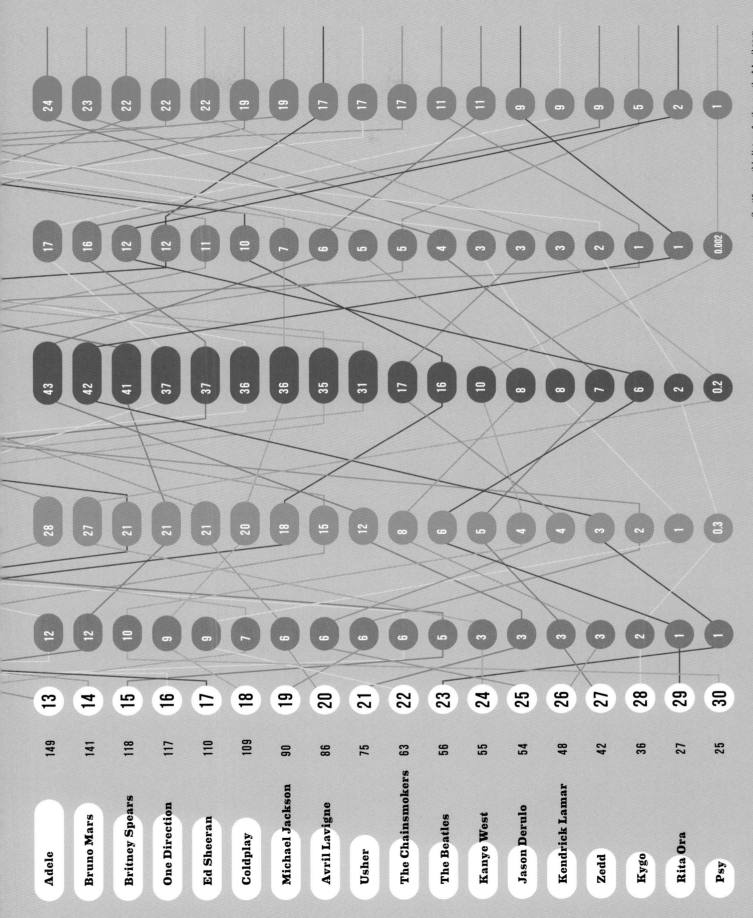

Spotify monthly listens for the month of April 2017.
Social media data correct as of April 2017.

24	17	43	28	12	13	149 Adele
23	16	42	27	12	14	141 Bruno Mars
22	12	41	21	10	15	118 Britney Spears
22	12	37	21	9	16	117 One Direction
22	11	37	21	9	17	110 Ed Sheeran
19	10	36	20	7	18	109 Coldplay
19	7	36	18	6	19	90 Michael Jackson
17	6	35	15	6	20	86 Avril Lavigne
17	5	31	12	6	21	75 Usher
17	5	17	8	6	22	63 The Chainsmokers
11	4	16	6	5	23	56 The Beatles
11	3	10	5	3	24	55 Kanye West
9	3	8	4	3	25	54 Jason Derulo
9	3	8	4	3	26	48 Kendrick Lamar
9	2	7	3	3	27	42 Zedd
5	1	6	2	2	28	36 Kygo
2	1	2	1	1	29	27 Rita Ora
1	0.002	0.2	0.3	1	30	25 Psy

THE MOST SUCCESSFUL LABELS IN HIP HOP

Hip Hop labels have been sorted by their artists' performance on Billboard's "Hot Rap Songs" chart (1989-present). We weight a label's tracks based on its chart rank (#1-#50) and weeks charted.

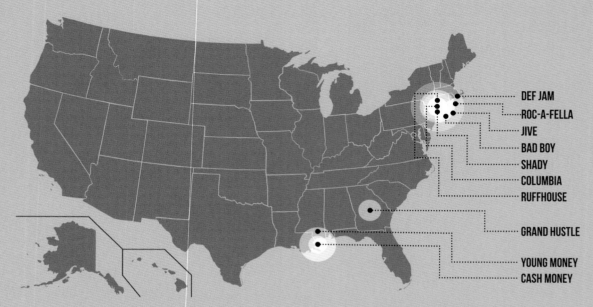

- DEF JAM
- ROC-A-FELLA
- JIVE
- BAD BOY
- SHADY
- COLUMBIA
- RUFFHOUSE

- GRAND HUSTLE

- YOUNG MONEY
- CASH MONEY

DEF JAM

OF CHARTING TRACKS: 152 TRACKS

OF CHARTING ARTISTS: 48 ARTISTS

CUMULATIVE WEEKS ON CHART: 1925 WEEKS

WEEKS ON CHART BY YEAR: 1989—2014

JIVE

OF CHARTING TRACKS: 106 TRACKS

OF CHARTING ARTISTS: 44 ARTISTS

CUMULATIVE WEEKS ON CHART: 1255 WEEKS

WEEKS ON CHART BY YEAR: 1989—2012

RUFFHOUSE

OF CHARTING TRACKS: 41 TRACKS
OF CHARTING ARTISTS: 14 ARTISTS
CUMULATIVE WEEKS ON CHART: 649 WEEKS
WEEKS ON CHART BY YEAR: 1990—2000

COLUMBIA

OF CHARTING TRACKS: 58 TRACKS
OF CHARTING ARTISTS: 24 ARTISTS
CUMULATIVE WEEKS ON CHART: 703 WEEKS
WEEKS ON CHART BY YEAR: 1991—2014

Source: Wikipedia

BAD BOY

OF CHARTING TRACKS: 56 TRACKS

OF CHARTING ARTISTS: 29 ARTISTS

CUMULATIVE WEEKS ON CHART: 1060 WEEKS

WEEKS ON CHART BY YEAR: 1994—2015

YOUNG MONEY

OF CHARTING TRACKS: 83 TRACKS • # OF CHARTING ARTISTS: 9 ARTISTS

CUMULATIVE WEEKS ON CHART: 1322 WEEKS • WEEKS ON CHART BY YEAR: 2009—2015

ROC-A-FELLA

OF CHARTING TRACKS: 86 TRACKS

OF CHARTING ARTISTS: 18 ARTISTS

CUMULATIVE WEEKS ON CHART: 1293 WEEKS

WEEKS ON CHART BY YEAR: 1996—2014

SHADY

OF CHARTING TRACKS: 49 TRACKS

OF CHARTING ARTISTS: 9 ARTISTS

CUMULATIVE WEEKS ON CHART: 735 WEEKS

WEEKS ON CHART BY YEAR: 2000—2014

GRAND HUSTLE

OF CHARTING TRACKS: 46 TRACKS

OF CHARTING ARTISTS: 8 ARTISTS

CUMULATIVE WEEKS ON CHART: 817 WEEKS

WEEKS ON CHART BY YEAR: 2003—2015

CASH MONEY

OF CHARTING TRACKS: 44 TRACKS

OF CHARTING ARTISTS: 14 ARTISTS

CUMULATIVE WEEKS ON CHART: 682 WEEKS

WEEKS ON CHART BY YEAR: 1999—2014

VISIONARY EUROPE

It began in 1956 as a musical competition but over the years it has been many things: from a popularity contest of nations to a way to show deference to a greater power. The musical quality has not always stood up to inspection but for sheer longevity Eurovision has to be applauded. The event is as well known for the countries receiving "null points" as it is for Abba. And yes, Norway are the zero-point champions... but who is the best country overall? Of those who have appeared in at least 20 finals, Russia has the highest average percentage of total points available (but have only won once) with Ireland next and the UK, in spite of recent problems, third. Terry Wogan would have something to say about that.

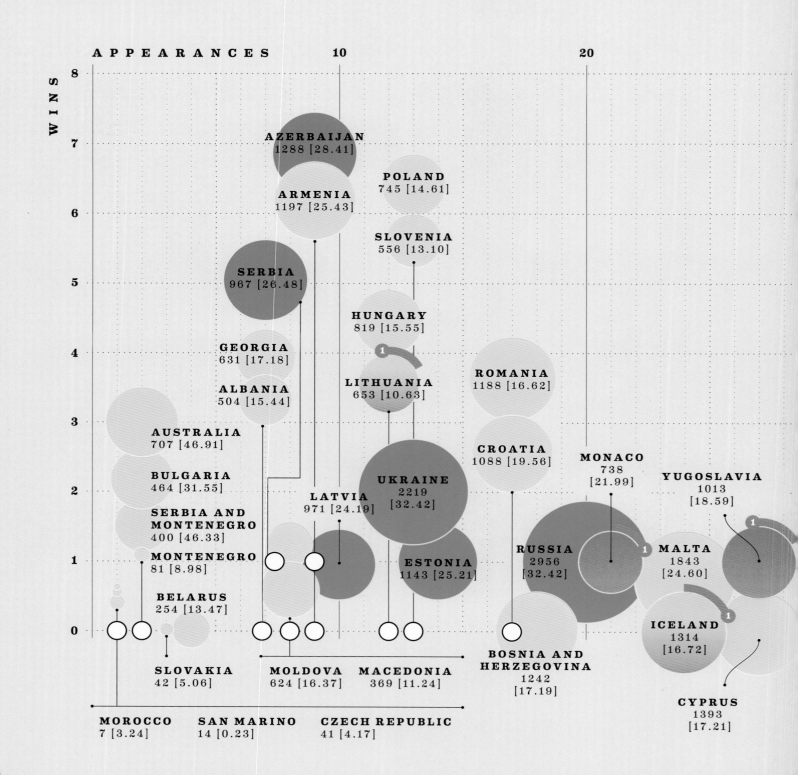

APPEARANCES 10 20

WINS

AZERBAIJAN
1288 [28.41]

POLAND
745 [14.61]

ARMENIA
1197 [25.43]

SLOVENIA
556 [13.10]

SERBIA
967 [26.48]

HUNGARY
819 [15.55]

GEORGIA
631 [17.18]

ROMANIA
1188 [16.62]

LITHUANIA
653 [10.63]

ALBANIA
504 [15.44]

AUSTRALIA
707 [46.91]

CROATIA
1088 [19.56]

MONACO
738
[21.99]

YUGOSLAVIA
1013
[18.59]

BULGARIA
464 [31.55]

UKRAINE
2219
[32.42]

SERBIA AND
MONTENEGRO
400 [46.33]

LATVIA
971 [24.19]

RUSSIA
2956
[32.42]

MALTA
1843
[24.60]

MONTENEGRO
81 [8.98]

ESTONIA
1143 [25.21]

BELARUS
254 [13.47]

ICELAND
1314
[16.72]

SLOVAKIA
42 [5.06]

MOLDOVA
624 [16.37]

MACEDONIA
369 [11.24]

BOSNIA AND
HERZEGOVINA
1242
[17.19]

MOROCCO
7 [3.24]

SAN MARINO
14 [0.23]

CZECH REPUBLIC
41 [4.17]

CYPRUS
1393
[17.21]

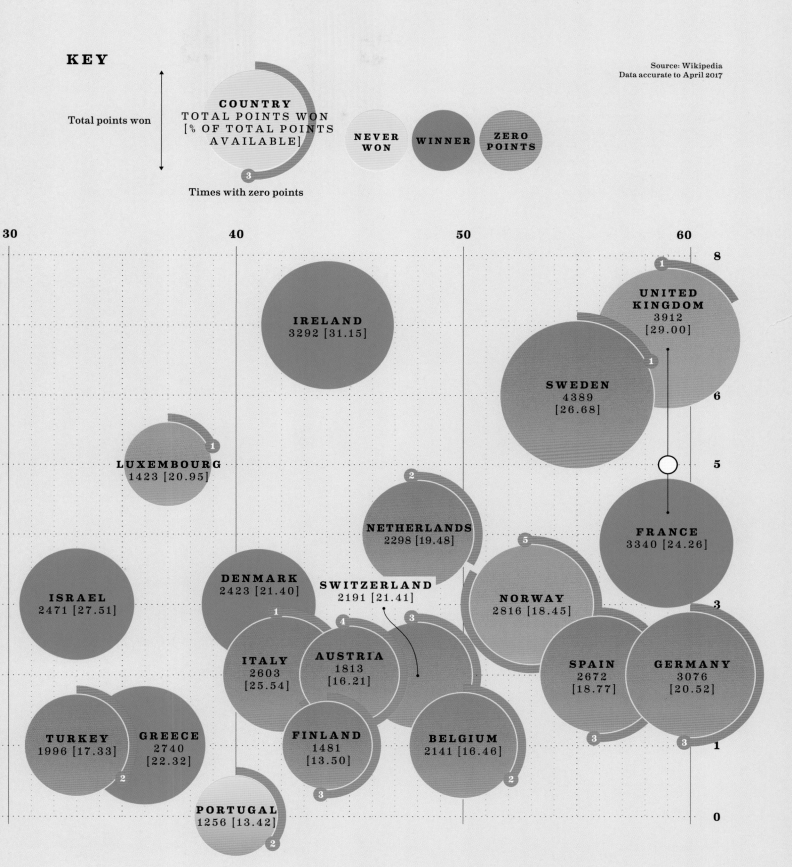

KEY

Total points won

COUNTRY
TOTAL POINTS WON
[% OF TOTAL POINTS
AVAILABLE]

NEVER
WON

WINNER

ZERO
POINTS

3

Times with zero points

Source: Wikipedia
Data accurate to April 2017

30   40   50   60

8

IRELAND
3292 [31.15]

UNITED
KINGDOM
3912
[29.00]

1

SWEDEN
4389
[26.68]

1

6

LUXEMBOURG
1423 [20.95]

1

5

NETHERLANDS
2298 [19.48]

2

FRANCE
3340 [24.26]

ISRAEL
2471 [27.51]

DENMARK
2423 [21.40]

SWITZERLAND
2191 [21.41]

NORWAY
2816 [18.45]

5

3

ITALY
2603
[25.54]

1

AUSTRIA
1813
[16.21]

4

3

SPAIN
2672
[18.77]

GERMANY
3076
[20.52]

TURKEY
1996 [17.33]

GREECE
2740
[22.32]

FINLAND
1481
[13.50]

BELGIUM
2141 [16.46]

3

3

1

2

3

2

PORTUGAL
1256 [13.42]

2

0

•175

ACKNOWLEDGEMENTS

Ian Preece would like to thank Daniel for his calmness and composure on the ball; Charlotte Selby and Russell Knowles at Carlton for putting the squad together; Chris Mitchell for mopping up at the back and filling in many gaps; Robin Thompson for his diligent fact-checking and proofreading; Robin Richards and James Pople for their fine, cool design work (despite me overloading the facts and word-count) and Angela, Edie and Thurston for living through this (plus Thurston also for his grime tips).

Daniel Tatarsky was delighted to form a duet with Ian Preece. Thanks to Charlotte Selby and Russell Knowles at Carlton for assembling the combo and Chris Mitchell for picking up the beat and taking it through to the last verse. Daniel echoes Ian's gratitude to Robin Thompson for his rigorous fact-checking and proofreading; Robin Richards and James Pople for bringing his facts, figures and dates to life in such imaginative and delightful ways. Last but not least thanks to Katie for always singing in the background and Rooney for sleeping through the typing.

CREDITS

INFORMATION CONTENT
Daniel Tatarsky & Ian Preece

PROJECT EDITOR
Chris Mitchell

EDITORIAL
Robin Thompson

ART DIRECTION
Russell Knowles
James Pople

INFOGRAPHICS BY
Robin Richards

ADDITIONAL ILLUSTRATION
Tom Redfern (132-133 Illustration)

PICTURE RESEARCH
Steve Behan

PRODUCTION
Emily Noto